ON
THE PHILOSOPHY OF LANGUAGE

S. Jack Odell
University of Maryland

THOMSON

WADSWORTH

Australia • Canada • Mexico • Singapore • Spain • United Kingdom • United States

Printed in the United States of America
1 2 3 4 5 6 7 09 08 07 06 05

Printer: Thomson West

ISBN 0-534-59581-2

Library of Congress Control Number: 2004116852

For more information about our products, contact us at:
Thomson Learning Academic Resource Center
1-800-423-0563

For permission to use material from this text, contact us by:
Phone: 1-800-730-2214
Fax: 1-800-730-2215
Web: http://www.thomsonrights.com

Thomson Higher Education
10 Davis Drive
Belmont, CA 94002-3098
USA

Asia (including India)
Thomson Learning
5 Shenton Way
#01-01 UIC Building
Singapore 068808

Australia/New Zealand
Thomson Learning Australia
102 Dodds Street
Southbank, Victoria 3006
Australia

Canada
Thomson Nelson
1120 Birchmount Road
Toronto, Ontario M1K 5G4
Canada

UK/Europe/Middle East/
Africa
Thomson Learning
High Holborn House
50–51 Bedford Road
London WC1R 4LR
United Kingdom

Latin America
Thomson Learning
Seneca, 53
Colonia Polanco
11560 Mexico
D.F. Mexico

Spain (including Portugal)
Thomson Paraninfo
Calle Magallanes, 25
28015 Madrid, Spain

Contents

This book is dedicated to Barbara Reed Bradford, my wife and best friend, my two daughters, Lynn Allyson Odell and Erin Odell Bradley, my son-in-law, Lt. Col. John Bradley, MD, and my grandchildren Finn and Fiona Bradley.

Preface

William Alston, one of the most productive contemporary philosophers of language, describes the philosophy of language as "anything philosophers do when they think, qua philosophers, about language."[1] This description, while quite accurate, refers to an extremely inclusive realm of enquiry. In this book I will feature what has been the primary question discussed by philosophers of language during the last hundred years. That question is, "What is word and sentence meaning?"

This work is primarily an introduction to one of the most important perspectives from which to view and understand word and sentence meaning, namely, the referential perspective—the view that meaning is either identical with or only explicable in terms of how words are used to refer to things. It is also an introduction to the various competing perspectives that philosophers have formulated for the express purpose of understanding word and sentence meaning. But it is more than just an explication of the referential approach and its competition; it is, in addition, an attempt to sort out these competing approaches or theories concerning the nature of meaning and referring and an attempt to determine the truth concerning this important philosophical concern.

This book is intended for the student of philosophy, the educated person, and the professional philosopher. It can be used as a textbook for both introductory and advanced courses on these topics: the theory of meaning, philosophy of language, semantic theory, and the foundations of logic. It is meant to challenge introductory students, graduate students, educated and interested people, and professional philosophers to come to grips with, and either defend or refute, the referential theory of meaning.

I will begin at the ground level, presupposing little if any philosophical knowledge, and build upon it, level after level. The goal is for our view of meaning and related topics, various theories, their most subtle and insightful defenders, and the problems of each approach, to be clearly enough understood to enable the reader to enter into the debate, and to thereby enrich his or her personal and intellectual life. Whether I can achieve my multidimensional goal remains to be seen, but some of the books that have had, and continue to have, an influence on me as both a philosopher and a human being are books that have achieved this kind of goal.

The first task to be accomplished in a work of this sort is that of preparing the reader by explaining certain underlying expressions or concepts, including 'word,' 'name,' 'sentence,' 'statement,' 'proposition,' 'sentential meaning,' 'contextual meaning,' 'causal meaning,' and 'conventional meaning.' I will devote the Introduction to this task.

Many logicians and philosophers have been committed to the idea that there is an identity relation of some sort that links referring to meaning. This referential approach has its roots in Greek philosophy. In his monumental work, *Theaetetus*, Plato attributed a version of this approach to Socrates. But, a number of puzzles or paradoxes are generated by this approach. Three of the most influential philosophers of language of the twentieth century, the Gottlieb Frege, Bertrand Russell, and Ludwig Wittgenstein in his *early* work, *Tractatus Logico Philosophicus*, advocated this approach to meaning, and attempted to resolve the paradoxes it involves. In Chapter One, I will explain the referential theory, the paradoxes it generates, and the solutions to these paradoxes that have been advocated by its defenders.

In Chapter Two, I will explain how Wittgenstein reversed his position on the referential theory in his book entitled, *Philosophical Investigations*. In this work, he questioned the basic premise of the referential approach by arguing that referring was just one among many *uses* that language incorporates, and no more important or essential than any of its other uses. According to the later Wittgenstein, the referential theory is, at the core, an ill-conceived theory, and the paradoxes it raises and the questions it poses are pseudo-paradoxes and pseudo-questions. I will also explain, in Chapter Two, how Wittgenstein's emphasis upon linguistic usage to facilitate an understanding of meaning influenced other philosophers. This influence manifests itself both in the criticism of other theories and in formulation of use theories of meaning. And finally, I will explain and critically discusses these use theories of meaning.

In Chapter Three, I will expound and critically examine other theories of meaning rooted in Wittgenstein's *Tractatus*: the verification theory of meaning, the truth conditions theory of meaning, and the inferential theory of meaning. According to the verification theory of meaning, the meaning of a word is reducible to how certain sentences containing that word are verified. According to the truth conditions theory, the meaning of a word is reducible to the relation that exists between certain sentences containing that word and the truth-conditions of those sentences. According to the inferential theory of meaning, the meaning of a word is reducible to the relation that exists between certain sentences containing that word and other sentences that are implied by those containing that word.

In Chapter Four, I will take up a controversy that cuts across the boundaries of the referential/non-referential approaches to meaning. An important distinction exists between a *theory of meaning as reference* and *a theory of referring*. The former equates meaning with reference. The latter attempts to answer the question, "How is it that words designate things?" The theory of meaning as reference and the theory of meaning as truth-conditions both require an answer to this question. The things referred to in the question under consideration could be either objects or truth-conditions. Throughout most of the twentieth century, the dominant theory of referring was the descriptive theory, which says that words designate things by *describing* them. In the sixties, due primarily to the work of Saul Kripke, Hillary Putnam, and Keith Donnellan, this view was seriously challenged, and another theory was proposed to take its place—the causal or historical theory of referring. This theory explains how things are designated by words in terms of a *causal chain* that links the original "dubbing" of a word to its subsequent uses.

In the last forty years, linguistics has had an ever-increasing influence on the philosophy of language. The American philosopher Noam Chomsky is responsible for the development of a syntactic and semantic theory of language that has resulted in what many consider to be a science of linguistics. Chomsky's theory, in the hands of his followers in philosophy, especially Jerry Fodor, in those of computer scientists, linguists, psychologists, and neurologists, is responsible for a subdivision within philosophy that can truly be said to comprise mainstream philosophy today, i.e., *cognitive science*. The Chomsky inspired, Fodor-led, M.I.T. contingent—the primal force in cognitive science—believes that traditional philosophical puzzles concerning meaning, knowing, believing, etc. can be solved by scientific means.

In Chapter Five, I will explain some of the fundamental ideas of cognitive science and why some of Wittgenstein's most influential followers maintain that Wittgenstein's views are both correct and inconsistent with cognitive science. I will then argue that although much that Wittgenstein said in the *Investigations* is inconsistent with the Chomsky/Fodor approach, a restrained reconciliation between Wittgenstein and the cognitive scientists can perhaps be achieved on the basis of a distinction between *causal* and *conventional* meaning.

In the final chapter of this work, Chapter Six, I will argue for an account of meaning that not only distinguishes between a causal theory and a conventional theory, but also distinguishes between (1) literal or sentential meaning—what words or sentences *mean*—and (2) contextual meaning—what a particular person *means by* a specific word or sentence on a particular occasion. This account of meaning is committed to the idea that a philosopher of language or meaning theorist must decide whether she or he is interested in explaining conventional meaning, the traditional task of philosophers, or in explaining the causal mechanisms necessary for human cognition, the task of neurologists and psychologists, computer scientists, philosophers, and linguists. A conventional account of meaning should include an integrated account of both sentential and contextual meaning and not simply relegate the former to semantics and the later to pragmatics, as so many contemporary accounts do. An adequate account of meaning must go beyond resolving the various paradoxes philosophers have generated concerning the concept of meaning. It must also explain (1) how the same expression can have numerous sentential meanings, i.e., be multivocal, (2) how two distinct expressions can have the same sentential meaning, i.e., be synonymous, (3) how an expression can be ambiguous within a sentential context, and (4) how an expression occurring in a sentence in one language can be a translation of a different expression in a different sentence in a different language. The *paraphrastic account* of meaning I offer in Chapter Six does, I am convinced, meet all of these criteria, though I will only explain how it works with respect to (1), (2) and (3). I will refer the reader to an independent work by James Platt that explains how the paraphrastic approach meets criterion (4).

In the *Endnotes* to the text, I refer to the original date of publication wherever I have been able to ascertain it. I commonly, however, use secondary sources, primarily anthologies, and when I do so, although the date within the parentheses is the original date of publication, the page references in my endnotes are always to the secondary source. In my *Bibliography*, I list the publication's original publication date in the first parenthesis, and after indicating the title of the secondary source, I indicate its date of publication within the parentheses concerning location and publisher of the secondary source. When I am unable to determine original publication date, I simply use the date of publication of the secondary source.

Preface

I want to thank Professor Leonard Linsky, who was my mentor and advisor long ago at the University of Illinois. He is responsible for my interest in this topic, and throughout my career I have continued to read and learn from his works on this subject. I will refer to his works a number of times in the course of this book. Any mistakes in interpretation or moments of wrong-headedness are attributable to me alone. I want to thank Mary Christina Wood, who read and commented on my efforts, and who edited the text, for her many helpful comments, and for her impeccable editing. I also wish to thank my former student, Professor Gerard Emershaw with whom I had many discussions about the nature of proper names. His knowledge and insights concerning the relevant literature helped me to better articulate my own views on this subject. In addition, I want to thank my wife, Barbara Bradford, for her support, and helpful editorial suggestions.

---

[1] Alston (1964) xi.

INTRODUCTION

The topic of this work is at the core of what philosophers refer to as the philosophy of language, which is the philosophical study of natural and formal or artificial languages. It involves word and sentence *meaning* and how language is *used*. French, German, Swahili, Latin, English, and Italian are all natural languages. *Natural languages* are systems of communication that are used for everyday purposes, as contrasted with *artificial languages*, such as arithmetic, calculus, geometry, symbolic logic, and programming languages for computers. The philosophy of language includes the theory of meaning, the theory of reference, the theory of truth, semantics, pragmatics, and the philosophy of linguistics.

One of the main questions asked by philosophers of language concerns how various marks and noises take on the property of symbolic representation. How do they become transformed into words and sentences, and hence acquire meaning? How, for example, does the mark 'dog' take on the particular meaning it has in English? Meaning theorists also give accounts of such dimensions of meaning as: multivocality or difference of meaning, synonymy or sameness of meaning (both within a given language and translation between languages) and ambiguity of meaning.

For those who are unfamiliar with philosophical discussions of meaning and referring, many of the basic concepts and distinctions used in these discussions will be new. Much of this introduction will be primarily devoted to familiarizing the uninitiated with the basic vocabulary of the philosophy of language. But it will also include refinements in that basic vocabulary, as well as the introduction of original vocabulary for purposes of clarification.

1

Symbols, Words, and Names

The most fundamental of the relevant expressions involved in discussions of language is the expression 'symbol.' A symbol is a verbal or linguistic representation of something other than itself. When it achieves its end, a symbol can be used to talk and think about what it represents. A symbol can be said to have *personal, restricted* or *conventional* use. A personal use of an expression is when that expression is used as a reminder or marker for an agent's own distinct purposes. This kind of use can be exemplified by a particular person marking an object or thing as a 'thing of interest,' which that person wants to distinguish from other things similar to it. A restricted use of a symbol is when an expression is used by one group of individuals at the exclusion of others. Codes provide the best example of what I mean by a restricted use of a symbol or expression. Conventional use is the kind of use exemplified by the various entries found in dictionaries.

When we communicate with one another we want to be understood, and what we do when we clarify what an expression means, or what we mean by some expression, is to put it into terms with which others are familiar. And we expect others to do likewise for us. In other words, what we do is render unfamiliar expressions in terms of familiar ones, except of course on those occasions' when the referents of our words are present. In those instances, we do what is most efficient, namely, we point to or otherwise indicate the object about which we are talking. Sometimes, we have to do more than this if we really want to be understood. On these occasions a description may better serve to facilitate understanding. If I point to someone and say I don't want to offend her, while referring to her by name, you may be at a loss to understand my fear. But when I describe her as "the Provost of my division", your perplexity vanishes. You understand why I would not want to offend such a powerful person in my place of employment.

When one is giving a lecture, one will often say things that some of the students present do not understand. Those students either look puzzled or raise their hands and indicate that they do not understand what has been said. A *snag* in the process of communicating has occurred. We can and do put such activities back on course by providing an explanation or definition of the word or words causing the puzzlement. If the snag has to do with the name 'Calvin Coolidge,' or a natural kind term like 'armadillo,' the respective snags can be removed by adding 'the 30th president of the United States,' or 'an animal having its head and body encased in an armor of small bony plates in which it can curl up into a ball when attacked.'

2

So far I have only talked about living episodes, where one individual explains the meaning of some expression to another individual. But the students themselves can eliminate these snags by consulting dictionaries, which are compilations of conventional meanings.

Dictionaries can, nonetheless, be misleading, and so we shouldn't be uncritically reliant on them. They give the impression that words have meaning in isolation, when in fact words have meaning only in sentential contexts. The meaning that a word has is a function of the linguistic context in which it appears. Not even proper names can be said to have meaning in isolation. I will say more about this when I explain Bertrand Russell's views.

Dictionaries provide lists of possible meanings. We have to choose among them the one or ones that best enable us to understand sentences about which we are in doubt. The various entries that fall under a given word, what are commonly referred to as various *senses* of that word, comprise a set of synonyms. What one ordinarily does when one consults a dictionary is scan that set of possible meanings looking for words which allow one to make sense of some sentence containing an unknown word or words. There are one-word messages and responses, but they are normally elliptical for some complete thought. We do sometimes attribute meaning to isolated words, but when we do so, what we attribute to them is one of their possible senses. This is mere word association. These kinds of activities are parasitic on the fundamental linguistic activity of communicating.

Ultimately, how we *use* words determines what they mean. There is an intimate connection between what we *mean by* some word, phrase, or sentence and what it can be said to mean. If enough of us use a given word or expression often enough in a non-standard way, that use will eventually become a standard use, and the dictionary will incorporate a new sense. The use of words like 'cool' and 'hot' to express approval illustrates this fact. At any given point in time, there exist new senses for certain recognized words which have not as yet found their way into the dictionary, just as there always exists new words that have not as yet been incorporated into the dictionary. This fact has been recognized in a variety of ways. Language has been said by some to be organic; Wittgenstein likened it to a city with ever-spreading suburbs. Dictionaries are not the final arbiters of whether or not a word has a certain meaning.

Philosophers, particularly logicians, have focused much attention on *singularly referring expressions* (expressions that refer to one and only one thing). The reason for this is that these expressions do not all

3

behave as they should. Consider the sentence 'Jack Odell weighs one hundred and eighty pounds.' The referent of 'Jack Odell' is me and the predicate 'is a person who weighs one hundred and eighty pounds' describes me. We might say that this sentence means that there *is* someone named Jack Odell who weighs one hundred and eighty pounds. But by parity of reason, the sentence 'Apollo does not exist' would mean there *is* someone named Apollo who does not exist (is non-existent). But if he *is* how could he be non-existent? This is paradoxical. It was Bertrand Russell who first used the Apollo example to illustrate one of three puzzles of referring which he maintained that a theory of meaning and referring ought to be able to solve. I will return to this matter in the next chapter.

In addition to words and names, there are also symbols like x, y and z used formally in algebra and logic, and numerals like 6, 13, and 48. In algebra x, y and z are variables used to stand for sums and numbers. In non-algebraic contexts they are used to refer to or stand for a variety of things. Variables are not names. Numerals stand for numbers or quantities, but unlike variables, they might be names. One might claim that '5' names the number five. Five is clearly not a spatial-temporal entity of any sort. But neither is democracy. If we agree that democracy is something, something of an abstract kind, is five also an abstraction? These questions are hard to answer. Nothing prevents us, however, from saying that the numeral '5' may well be a referring expression, even if it is not exactly clear what kind of thing is being referred to.

There are several different kinds of referring expression, and separating and explicating their differences will help us understand why focusing on one kind of case while ignoring the others leads to mistaken views about the nature of things, and about the criteria required for correctly using referring expressions.

Among the designating expressions of a natural language like English there are *individuators,* which are terms used to refer to individuals, such as: 'Sylvia Plath,' 'The Sultan of Swat,' 'the person directly in front of me at the present moment,' 'Brave Arrow,' 'Round Hill, Virginia,' 'Lake Placid, New York,' 'Walt Whitman High School,' 'me,' 'you,' 'this,' and 'that.' Some of these terms are proper names, and some are definite descriptions. Some are personal pronouns, and some are demonstratives. More importantly, some are *descriptive designators,* and some are *non-descriptive designators.* Those which have meaning in the sense of word meaning, and not etymological or associative meaning, are descriptive designators. 'Brave Arrow,' and 'the person directly in front of me at the present moment' are descriptive designators. Their constituents are words. 'Sylvia Plath' is a non-descriptive designator. It has no meaning in the relevant sense. Some proper names, like 'John Brown' have *extraneous meaning*. A john can be a toilet or a prostitute's customer, and 'brown' is a color word.

It is commonplace among logicians, philosophers of language, and linguists to consider many of the kinds of expressions I have classified as individuators to be *indexicals*. Indexicals are context dependent expressions, i.e., their referents are determined by such contextual factors as who talks to whom, when, and where.[1] Most include in their list of indexicals: personal pronouns, demonstratives such as 'this' and 'that,' temporal expressions such as 'now' and 'today,' and locative expressions such as 'here,' and 'there.'[2]

Unlike most philosophers and logicians, I would include in this list *ordinary* proper names as opposed to *logically proper* names. Logically proper names are defined as having *fixed* reference to one and only one thing. Their referents are not contextually determined. But the referents of ordinary proper names do depend upon contextual factors. The referents of names like 'John Brown' and 'Joe Smith' are clearly functions of who talks to whom, when, and where. If I were to say, "John Brown went to Harper's Ferry," to one of my colleagues, I would, under most circumstances mean, and would be taken to mean, that our colleague John Brown had gone to Harper's Ferry. But under other circumstances I might say this and mean, and be understood to mean, that the abolitionist John Brown had gone to Harper's Ferry. I would also include among indexicals various definite descriptions. The referent of expressions like 'the golfer with the highest number of wins on the PGA tour,' 'the person accompanying the woman in the red dress,' 'the present king of France,' and 'the highest ranking member of the U. S. Senate' are also clearly a function of who talks to whom, when and where. I did on several occasions use the first of these descriptions in a sentence at the end of the PGA tour season, to refer to Tiger Woods. This year I might well use it again, but who can say who the referent will be.

In addition to individuators, there are expressions that are primarily used to refer to kinds of things. Not every such expression is governed by the same considerations. General terms like 'red fox,' 'Vizla,' and 'Bic razors' are fundamentally different from general terms like 'game,' 'furniture,' and 'religion.' The former, which I will refer to as *formal abbreviators*, refer to sets of objects, the members of which possess identical characteristics. The latter, which I will refer to, following Wittgenstein, as *family abbreviators*, refer to sets of objects which do not possess identical characteristics, but instead possess overlapping and crisscrossing ones.

The word 'democracy,' like 'justice,' 'truth,' and 'beauty,' is a designator of yet a different kind. Here we quite naturally speak of associated concepts. The word 'concept' has a job to do in our language, but its job description does not include its use as a referent for words like 'dog.' Only philosophers talk about the *concepts* of dog and cat. Such philosophical uses exemplify what Wittgenstein had in mind when he talked about language "being on a holiday." Dogs and cats inhabit the same world we do. They are not abstractions, and so when we want to inform someone regarding what sort of thing they are, we can simply point to one of them, or to cat or dog pictures. Not so for democracy and justice. Dogs and cats are *objects*. Democracy and justice are *abstractions*. I will refer to words like 'democracy,' 'justice,' 'truth,' and 'beauty,' etc., as *conceptors*.

Sentences, Statements, and Propositions
The first problem we encounter when we attempt to say what a sentence is concerns the fact that the term 'sentence' is ambiguous. It can mean either *sentence type* or *sentence token*. Following are two tokens of one type.

(a) Athena is symbolized in the guise of a warrior.

(b) Athena is symbolized in the guise of a warrior.

Sentence types are conventional arrangements of symbols—words and names. *Statements* are uses of sentence types, by specific speakers to assert what is either true or false, as contrasted with questions, commands and greetings.

How about *propositions*? Philosophers, logicians, linguists, and even mathematicians, frequently talk about proposition. But they say conflicting things about what they are. About the only thing agreed to is that they are either true or false. Roughly, what is alleged might be compressed and stated as follows:

Propositions are abstract objects (representations, thoughts, pictures, concatenations of words or concepts, etc.) that stand in some important relation (representational, pictorial, correspondence, etc.) to facts, states of affairs, reality, etc., and exist only in so far as they are embedded within a sentence within a language. They are *thoughts* in the sense in which we can all—

6

Germans, French people, English peoples, Asians, Africans, Americans, etc.—have the same thought.

Gottlob Frege, one of the greatest logicians in the history of logic, sometimes defined a proposition as a thought, but he was careful to distinguish between two senses of 'thought.' There is the thought expressed by "I thought about you last night." My thoughts are not your thoughts nor are yours mine. Now consider the thought of "Galileo thought that the sun was the center of our galaxy." We can both understand the thought that the center of the galaxy is the sun. If you and I both think that the center of our galaxy is the sun, your thinking it and my thinking it are numerically distinct mental events or processes. But we have the *same* thought. This parallels the distinction I drew earlier between sentence types and sentence tokens. Our numerically different thoughts are tokens of the same type. And this would be true if you thought that the center of our universe is the sun, and I thought that the sun is the center of our universe. According to the conventions that govern our language these are just two different ways of saying the same thing.

Some philosophers, like the Wittgenstein of the *Tractatus*, talk about the meaning of propositions. They say things like the meaning of a proposition is a function of the meaning of its constituents, as well as the arrangement of those constituents, i. e. the grammatical or logical form of the proposition. Other philosophers, like the British philosopher P.F. Strawson, talk about the meaning of sentences and define sentence meaning as others define the meaning of propositions. Frege distinguished between the *Sinn* and the *Bedeutung* of a full declarative sentence—a distinction that is often translated as *sense* and *reference*, and sometimes as *meaning* and *reference*. He defined the sense of a full declarative sentence as a proposition, an abstract entity that can be captured by the form: "that p." If I believe that my computer is better than your computer, then I believe "that my computer is better than your computer." Some philosophers, like the American philosopher W. V. O. Quine, reject the idea of such abstract entities and instead talk about sentences as having truth-values. On this view, sentence meanings are functions of the meanings of the expressions (for Quine, conventional responses) that compose them as well as their logical or grammatical form.

Some philosophers, like British philosopher G. E. Moore, use the word proposition in a neutral sense. For them it could mean an abstract entity, a sentence type, a statement, or a meaning of a sentence. But they do claim that, for example, 'Il pleut' expresses the same

7

proposition as 'It is raining,' and either both are true or both are false. On this account of the matter, to *understand* a sentence is to "grasp" the proposition expressed by that sentence. But the notion of a proposition is left unanalyzed. We are left wondering what sort of entity a proposition is.

I personally favor defining propositions as nothing more than the meanings of declarative sentences, and restricting talk of truth or falsity, as opposed to truth-conditions, to talk about statements, in the way that P. F. Strawson does. Strawson recognizes that it is actual uses of sentences that are true or false. Consider the sentence 'The PC I am using is an Hitachi.' If I were to utter this sentence now and make the statement that this PC I am using is a Hitachi, I would be using this sentence to say something that is true. But had I used it earlier today when I was using my office PC, what I would have stated would have been false, because my office computer is a Dell.

What the sentence means is a matter of convention, but its meaning cannot be said to be either true or false. Sentences are not true or false. Neither are their meanings. We can examine a sentence to determine whether its syntax is one we would recognize as well-formed. We can also ask about its meaningfulness and its truth-conditions. We can ask if anyone would ever be likely to use it to make a *statement*. The sentence 'The person directly in front of me has on a blue shirt' is syntactically well formed and is a proper English sentence. If one were to ask if this sentence is true, I would have to reply that the sentence itself is neither true nor false. Sometimes it is used to make true statements and sometimes it is used to make false ones. If I were asked what it means, I would reply by defining any of its constituent words that the questioner did not understand, by explaining what would have to transpire for it to be true, or by providing a paraphrase of its meaning. I would not talk about some abstract entity that is either true or false. The predicates "is true" and "is false" are, as Strawson holds, not predicates of abstract entities nor are they predicates of the meanings of sentences. They are instead predicates of *statements*. They apply only to some particular speaker's use of a particular sentence on some particular occasion. Statements are *alleged states of affairs*. The meaning of a sentence is a matter of convention and is no more mysterious or abstract than that. You do not bump into or otherwise touch, feel, or smell conventions or practices. They are the standard meanings of sentences. They are simply *allegeable states of affairs*.

There is, however, a problem with the idea that a proposition is the standard meaning of a sentence. Consider the following sentence:

I am looking for a lad to work in my yard.

In my neighborhood, this English sentence would be understood as:

> The subject of this sentence is seeking to find a boy to rake leaves, mow and water the lawn, and water the plants.

In Ireland, the same English sentence has a quite different conventional or standard meaning. It would be understood or paraphrased as:

> The subject of the sentence is looking for a person of either sex to work in his or her stable, feeding, grooming, and occasionally exercising horses, and cleaning their stalls.

The truth conditions for these two readings of the same English sentence are different. They allege quite different states of affairs. In order to do justice to these two different conventional meanings that this English sentence has we will have to distinguish between Irish English and American English, or talk about different *cultural contexts* or backgrounds. I will return to this topic after I have further clarified the concept of a statement.

Sentential and Contextual Meaning
The distinction I drew in the preface between *what a sentence means* and *what one means by it on some occasion* becomes relevant when one tries to be more specific about the nature of statements and the difference between them and propositions.

The word 'meaning' is *multivocal*. It has several meanings. The American philosopher William Alston isolated nine, each one of which is distinct from the meaning it has in the phrase 'word meaning.'[3] Word meaning is the kind of meaning that 'meaning' has in the following sentence or *sentential* context:

> I just looked up the meaning of the word 'bachelor' in the dictionary and it means "unmarried male."

It is of paramount importance to distinguish meaning in this sense of the word 'meaning' from what someone *means by* his or her words on some particular occasion, in a particular *speech* context.[4] What I have in mind is what is meant by 'meant' in the following sentence:

> I know that that is what he said, but that's not what he meant.

9

What a sentence means (*sentential meaning*) is what it expresses in isolation from a speech context. It corresponds to the standard use of the sentence. It is a function of what the words mean (semantics) and how they are arranged (syntax). Even though (a) and (b) below are composed of the same words, their words are arranged differently, and it is the different arrangements that account for the difference in meaning between them:

(a) Jane kicked her horse.
(b) Her horse kicked Jane.

What a declarative sentence means is, as previously noted, a proposition or an allegeable state of affairs. What is *meant by* a declarative sentence (*contextual meaning*) can wildly depart from what a particular arrangement of its words mean. A statement is a particular use of a declarative sentence by a particular person on a particular occasion and is either true or false.

Statements are one subset of the class of conventional speech *actions*, what British philosopher J. L. Austin referred to as *illocutions*.[5] In addition to statements, there are warnings, promises, avowals, etc. Often what is meant by a sentence is its standard meaning. Suppose I were to respond to someone who has informed me that she will not accompany me to the movies tonight with: "Why not?" In such a case, I would be using these words with their standard meanings. I would be asking for her reasons for not going to the movies. 'Why not?' has a meaning that is contingent upon context. Its meaning, as opposed to what is meant by it upon some specific occasion, can only be stated with the use of a variable. It means something like "What are your reasons for not doing x?" The x gets understood (philosophers and logicians use the word 'instantiated' when they replace a variable like x with some specific person, place, thing, action, etc.) within the context in which 'Why not?' actually occurs. If you and I have agreed to go to the movies, and I call you at the last minute to inform you that I am not going to attend the movies with you, you will likely respond with: "Why not?" In this case, the x is understood to be tied to (or instantiated by) "attending the movies." But if I inform you that neither of us will be able to go to the movies, and you respond with the question under consideration, any number of events could be the explanation for why we will be unable to carry out our plans: the electricity in the area of the theater has been knocked out by the storm; you are my brother and our father has had a heart attack; my car, which is our only means of transportation, has been stolen, etc. Another way to put this point is to claim that although 'Why not?' is conventionally understood to be elliptical for 'Why not x?', what it means does not vary. Its meaning is fixed, but it must be understood to contain an *uninstantiated* variable.

But there are few limits on what someone *might* mean by what they say on a specific occasion. When a customer says to a bartender, "Why not?" in response to his asking him if he wants another drink,, the customer is not seeking a reason for not having another drink. He is, in fact, using what is formally a question as a command. In such a case it is appropriate to speak of what is *meant by* the speaker as a *paraphrase*. If you don't understand what was meant by the "Why not?" of the bartender case, it would be quite natural for me to use the sentence 'Yes, give me another drink' as an explanation of what the customer meant, which is, saying-in-other-words what the customer meant. In this particular *speech* context, what the words *mean* is of little or no use in figuring out what the customer meant. In this case the customer is certainly not asking the bartender to provide him with reasons not to have another martini, even though this interpretation is dictated by what the words actually mean. The grammatical form as well as the meaning of 'Why not?' has changed. It is no longer a question, but is instead a request.

We need to draw a distinction between a *standard* meaning and a *non-standard* one to explain this difference between the movies case and the bartender case. In the movies case 'Why not?' has its standard meaning, but in the bartender case it has a non-standard meaning. The standard meaning of an utterance will be a function of what its words mean. A non-standard meaning of an utterance will not simply be a function of what its words mean. It will instead also be a function of accepted usage. Most of us understand perfectly that although we are departing from what the words mean in 'Why not?', we can use it, in keeping with a current practice, to order a drink. We also know that it is often used to order other things as well, or even to affirm that we will do something. One person says to another person, would you promise not to lie to me anymore, and the other person says "Why not?"

A critic might well object at this point by asking, "What about sentences that express tautologies or necessary truths?" A *tautology* or a necessary truth is a claim that could not be false. To deny a tautology would amount to contradicting oneself. An example of a tautology would be 'Triangles have three sides.' And what about sentences that express commonly accepted facts: 'Mars is a planet,' 'George W. Bush is the present president of the United States,' etc.? Since I have sided with Strawson and argued that it is only statements or uses of particular sentences and not their meanings that are true or false, how can I explain the fact that if you asked most people whether any of these sentences is true of false, they would reply that they are true? This response to our questions is tied to the fact that ordinary speakers do not make all the distinctions they would be willing to make if these distinctions were pointed out to them.

The rules governing ordinary or everyday discourse allow us to ignore or blur important distinctions where ignoring them does not have serious consequences. But when one is doing philosophy, one often has to look more carefully at what motivates a response to determine if it can be ignored in favor of an account which would have conceptual or theoretical advantages. Most people would, I think, upon reflection give up the idea that it is sentences that are true or false in favor of the idea that it is what sentences mean or the propositions that they express that are true or false. Most would agree that sentences are only vehicles for our thoughts, beliefs, hopes, etc. If, however, we take seriously the natural response to our inquiry about the sentences 'Triangles have three sides' and 'Mars is a planet,' and assume that it is their meanings (propositions) that are true or false, and not statements, how are we to respond to questions like, "Is the proposition expressed by the sentence, 'The person directly in front of me at this time has on a purple shirt' true or false?" Obviously, we would have to reject this question as senseless. But if a speaker were to use that sentence on an occasion where there is actually in front of the speaker a person wearing a purple shirt, we would certainly concede that *what s(he) said* was false. So are we to conclude that both propositions and statements have truth-values? We could. But for the sake of a unified account why not say that in the case of tautologies or sentences concerning indisputable facts, any one who uses them with their standard meanings intact would be *stating* something true?

It is, however, quite important that we understand that it is only specifiable *uses* of sentences that have truth-values. It is *statements* that have truth-values. A sentence like, 'The king of France is wise' can be used in a variety of ways. It can be used to *warn* someone in the king's court that the king has his eye on him, that he had better be careful. It can be used *to poke fun at* the king if it is said with a hint of sarcasm. It can even be used to praise another person for her/his actions if the setting or *speech context* is right. Suppose for some reason two lovers have decided that whenever they are particularly pleased with one another's wit, sagacity, appearance or demeanor they will say aloud, "The king of France is wise."

12

A *cultural* context is a society or nation like the United States or Ireland. It is like a *function* in logic. It has a range and its range is as extensive as the language spoken throughout the United States, or Ireland, or as limited as a particular dialect spoken only in the hills of Kentucky. A *speech* context is considerably more limited. It is limited to an actual concrete situation in which a particular sentence or string of words is used by a particular person to say something.

Contextual meaning is, as its name implies, a function of the total context of the utterance, which involves, among other things, body language, intonation contour, and background conditions. Interest in this kind of meaning has increased in contemporary philosophy. In the early part of the last century, interest centered around sentential meaning. Russell more than anybody, but also Frege to a lesser extent, focused upon it and ignored contextual meaning. This made Russell's views vulnerable to P. F. Strawson's attack—an attack which I will explicate fully in Chapter Two.

Various Theories of Meaning

While recognizing that there has been a "bewildering diversity of approaches, conceptions, and theories" concerning meaning, William Alston in his excellent trailblazing work, *The Philosophy of Language*, claims that most of them "can be grouped into three types": the *referential*, the *ideational* and the *behavioral*.[6] The first type identifies meaning with referring. The meaning of an expression is the thing to which it refers. The ideational type identifies meaning with mental entities, concepts, ideas, or thoughts. On this view a word means the concept or idea to which it refers or with which it is associated. The behavioral theorist identifies meaning with the stimuli and responses words evoke. I want to add three further categories: *tripartite, causal,* and *conventional* theories. The tripartite theory recognizes that although the referential theory is essentially right as far as it goes, it nevertheless falls short. It incorporates a third entity into the mix, namely, what the speaker *intends* to refer to. According to this theory, the referent of a word is determined by the speaker's intention.

Wittgenstein, in his early work, *Tractatus Logico Philosophicus*, advocated the *tripartite* version of the referential theory, and I will explain this theory and his reasons in favor of it in Chapter One. In his later work, *Philosophical Investigations*, he argued against it. His critique of it contrasts talk about the meaning of expressions with talk about the uses of expressions. He cautions us to "ask not for the meaning of an expression but instead ask for its use." This idea has led various other philosophers to identify meaning with use, and to pursue a use theory of meaning.

From the perspective of history, the most widely held theory of meaning is the referential theory, although the ideational theory has had lots of defenders. The ideational approach is really just a variation of the referential theory. Instead of taking the referents of words to be objects in the world, it takes them to be ideas or sensations. The referential approach has its roots in Greco Roman philosophy. In his monumental work, *Theaetetus*, Plato attributed a version of it to Socrates. Saint Augustine also advocated and defended a version of it in his *Confessions*. In modern philosophy, David Hume presented an *ideational* version of it in his *Inquiries*. It continued to be widely held, without generating a serious or systematic critique, into the twentieth century, where it enjoyed its most productive period, especially in the work of Frege, Russell, and the Wittgenstein of the *Tractatus*. Paradoxically, it was the third figure in this trio who, in his later work, *Philosophical Investigations*, was largely responsible for the formidable critique it suffered in the last half of the twentieth century.

The development of the referential theory in the twentieth century is largely tied to the idea that natural languages are inadequate vehicles for the expression of philosophical and scientific truth. The most serious charge brought against them was that they were, in the words of Bertrand Russell, "frightfully vague." Frege and Russell led the charge against the usefulness of natural language. Both of them offered formal systems which they viewed as being "ideal" for the tasks of philosophy and science. Russell's efforts to develop such a language led to the production of *Principia Mathematica*, which he wrote in collaboration with Alfred North Whitehead, and to the doctrine of logical atomism, which he and Wittgenstein developed in separate works. It was Wittgenstein's efforts to defend the referential approach to meaning in the *Tractatus* that eventually led to his rejection of it in his later work. We will look carefully both at Russell's effort to develop an ideal language in his work, "The Philosophy of Logical Atomism," and Wittgenstein's version of logical atomism in his earlier work. Understanding the work of the early Wittgenstein will help us to better understand his later critique and the emergence of the use theory of meaning.

The title of this book would seem to imply that meaning and referring are two different things. But as the previous paragraph makes clear, many philosophers would disagree with this idea. Some maintain that they are identical. Just consider the question, "To whom were you referring when you said that you thought one of the most recent presidents of the United States might well be one of our country's greatest presidents?" One might well answer this question by saying, "I meant William Jefferson Clinton." But one might have just as properly said "I was referring to William Jefferson Clinton." One might claim that these two responses are just different ways of saying the *same* thing. Bertrand Russell, who influenced many other philosophers, embraced the view that meaning is identical with reference. I will be focusing a good deal of attention on Russell's views in Chapter one, where I will also examine Frege's views and those of the early Wittgenstein.

Endnotes

---

[1] Allwood, Anderson, Dahl, (1979) p. 121.

[2] See the entries under the term 'indexical' in both the *Oxford Dictionary of Philosophy,* and *The Cambridge Dictionary of Philosophy.*

[3] Alston (1964) pp. 10-11.

[4] It was the British philosopher Paul Grice who is responsible for this distinction. See Grice (1961).

[5] I will return to this topic in the chapter on meaning and use.

[6] Alston (1964) pp. 11-12.

1
Meaning as Referring

Many logicians and philosophers, including two of the most important logicians of the twentieth century, Gottlob Frege and Bertrand Russell, are among those who have been committed to the idea that there is an identity relation that links referring to meaning. Both Russell and Frege were, however, puzzled by the implications of this alleged identity. Simply put, their puzzlement can be explained by focusing on two different questions. First, if meaning is reference, if what a word or name means is what it refers to, what are we referring to when we use names like 'Santa Claus,' 'Pecos Bill,' 'the present king of France,' 'the locomotive-sized object on my lap,' 'the whole number between 4 and 5,' or 'the round square'? Neither Santa Claus nor Pecos Bill exists. They are creatures of myth and folklore. And it is empirically impossible for anything the size of a locomotive to be on my lap. There is no whole number between 4 and 5, and the round square is a logically contradictory notion. Second, if meaning is reference, what are the referents of the so-called logical words like 'negation,' 'not,' 'if . . . then,' 'either or,' 'provided that,' 'if and only if,' 'and,' etc.? I will begin by focusing on the first question and postpone the latter question until I take up Wittgenstein's views.

For the referential theorist, two distinct approaches are possible regarding the first question. One can maintain that 'Pecos Bill,' 'the round square,' etc., name or refer to nothing, which would seem to entail that they are meaningless. But if these names are meaningless, how come 'The round square is an impossible object,' and 'Pecos Bill rode a large blue bull everywhere,' are not meaningless. Surely, if their subject terms were meaningless the sentences themselves would have

16

to be meaningless. Not only are they meaningful, but most non-philosophers would say or agree that if someone were to assert them, she would be saying something true about the round square, and something false about Pecos Bill. The other possible approach to this dilemma would be to claim that the names or words in question do have referents, but their referents are not physically existent objects. They are instead objects of thought. Both Frege and Russell take the first approach, and attempt to reconcile the facts that although it is true that 'Pecos Bill' and 'the round square' lack reference, the sentences concerning these non-existent objects do make sense. The German philosopher and psychologist Alexius Meinong takes the second approach and tries to establish that, although Pecos Bill and the round square are objects without being, in the ordinary sense of the word 'being,' they do share with all objects of thought a distinct though different kind of being. They can *be* thought or talked about.

Frege

Frege, with the publication in 1879 of a short treatise on logic and language, the *Begriffsschrift*, which translates *Concept Script,*, determined the course that philosophy followed throughout much of the twentieth century.[1] This remarkable book of less than a hundred pages attempted to reduce mathematics to logic, introduced a new formal language—predicate or functional logic or calculus, that is still taught in most logic courses throughout the world today—and emphasized the importance of the analytic approach to logic. In order to develop the predicate calculus he had to find the means for formalizing such terms as 'some,' 'all,' 'everything,' 'there exists some thing x,' 'nothing,' 'no person,' etc. He accomplished this by introducing the concept of, and a notation for, quantification. This enabled him to explain how ordinary language masked an essential distinction between predicates and terms of quantification. For example, natural languages are misleading regarding the words 'existence' and 'nothing.' We say things like "Trent Lott has a racist past" and "The majority leader of the senate exists." As far as ordinary grammar is concerned, both sentences are of subject/predicate form. The predicate of the first is 'has a racist past.' The predicate of the second is 'exists.' It is one thing to say that Lott has the properties or characteristics of a person with a bigot's past. It is another to say that the majority leader of the senate has the property of existence. On Frege's analysis, the former like all one place predicates has the logical *form*, $\phi\alpha$ (where 'ϕ' is some property and 'α' is the name of some person), but the latter's logical form is quite different. Frege's interpretation of it would be: "there exists an x such that x is

17

the majority leader of the senate." Its logical form is '∃x (φx),' (where '∃x' means "there exists at least one thing such that" and 'φx' means x has the property φ). If we instantiate the form of the former by letting 'R' stand for the predicate "has a racist past," and let 't' abbreviate and stand for the name 'Trent Lott,' the result is Rt. The result of instantiating the latter by letting 'L' stand for "is the majority leader of the senate would be ∃x (Lx).

As regards the word 'nothing,' we say such things as "Fiona is in the room" and "Nothing is in the room." Here the grammar of ordinary language indicates that the subject of the former is *Fiona* and that of the latter is *nothing*. Both appear to be of the form, φα. But given that the former means that a person, place, or thing (namely, Fiona) is in the room, while the latter means that there is no person, place, or thing in the room, they cannot both have the same form. If they did, the latter would have to mean that there is in the room a nothing, which is unintelligible. The true form of the latter is ~∃x (φx), where ~∃x means "it is not the case that there exists an x such that." The latter is thus understood to mean that there does not exist any x that is in the room. The former when instantiated by allowing 'f' to stand for the name 'Fiona,' and 'R' to stand for the predicate "is in the room" becomes Rf; the latter is ~∃x (Rx). So the forms are, when instantiated, revealed to be quite different. In this way Frege eliminates certain confusions inherent in ordinary language.

Frege also took important steps toward the formulation of a theory of meaning with consequences for any theory of meaning. He *modeled* his approach to meaning on the naming paradigm. Names like 'Norman Bates,' 'Venus,' 'the Morning Star,' 'Walter Johnson High School,' and 'Sedalia, Missouri' can all be said to be signs or symbols, and their function can be said to stand for or refer to persons, places, or things, all of which Frege considered to be *objects*.

In the *Begriffsschrift*, Frege distinguished between a *sign*, for example 'the morning star,' and its *reference*, the planetary body. He considered the latter to be the meaning of the former. But when he applied this idea to the concept of identity, which was of considerable importance to him as a mathematician and logician, he was forced to conclude that identity was a relation that obtained between signs (names) for things. In his later work "Ueber Sinn und Bedeutung" he justifies the conclusion of the earlier work thus:

The reasons that speak in its favor are the following: "a = a" and "a = b" are sentences of obviously different cognitive significance: "a = a" is valid *a priori*, and, according to Kant, is to be called analytic; whereas, sentences of the "a = b" often contain very valuable extensions of our knowledge and cannot always be justified in an *a priori* manner. The discovery that it is not a different and novel sun which rises every morning, but that it is the very same, certainly was one of the most consequential ones in astronomy. . . . What one wishes to express with "a = b" seems to be that the signs or names 'a' and 'b' name the same thing; and in that case we would be dealing with those signs: a relation between them would be asserted. But this relation could hold only inasmuch as they name or designate something. The relation, as it were, is mediated through the connection of each sign with the same nominatum. This connection, however, is arbitrary. You cannot forbid the use of an arbitrarily produced process or object as a sign for something else. Hence, a sentence like "a = b" would no longer refer to a matter of fact but to our manner of designation; no genuine knowledge would be expressed by it.[2]

In essence, if identity were a relation between objects then there would be no difference between saying something of the form 'a is identical with a' and saying something of the form 'a is identical with b.' But that would mean that the meaning of 'Venus is identical with Venus,' would not differ in meaning from 'Venus is identical with the evening star.' But, of course, they do differ in meaning. The thought or proposition conveyed by the first example is trivially true, but the second example conveys an extremely important astronomical discovery. His *retraction* of the view that identity is a relation between signs, which occurs at the end of the above quote, is a bit more complicated. What he is getting at can be made clear by recognizing that a foreigner could know that speakers of English used the signs in question to refer to the same thing and not have any idea what was meant by 'Venus is the morning star.' He could understand our conventions of usage, or manner of designation, and thus know that English speakers use 'Venus' to refer to the same thing that they refer to as 'the morning star.' But if he does not know what the two expressions mean, he will not apprehend what information is conveyed by 'Venus is the morning star.' For these reasons he recognized the need for a third entity to account for the difference between 'a = a' and 'a = b.'

In addition to the sign or name and its referent (*Bedeutung*), he added the concept of *Sinn* or sense, which he defines as "mode of presentation." He explicates the concept of *Sinn* by asking the reader to imagine three lines a̱, ḇ, and c̱ connecting the vertices of a triangle with the midpoints of the opposite sides. Since the point of intersection of a̱ and ḇ and the point of intersection of ḇ and c̱ are the same point, he asks us to recognize that though the referent is the *same* for both expressions, there are *two different presentations* of it. He further illustrates what he means by having us consider the expressions 'the morning star' and 'the evening star.' They refer to the same planet, Venus, but the mode of presentation is different for each. We are presented in the one case by "the first bright star in the morning." In the other case, our attention is focused on Venus via "the first bright star in the evening." In a footnote to "Ueber Sinn und Bedeutung," Frege makes the following point about the senses of everyday proper names:

> In the case of genuinely proper names like 'Aristotle' opinions as regards their sense may diverge. As such may, e.g., be suggested: Plato's disciple and the teacher of Alexander the Great. Whoever accepts this sense will interpret the meaning of the statement "Aristotle was born is Stagira" differently from one who interpreted the sense of 'Aristotle' as the Stagirite teacher of Alexander the Great. As long as the nominatum[3] remains the same, these fluctuations in sense are tolerable. But they should be avoided in the system of a demonstrative science and should not appear in a perfect language.[4]

The implication here is that senses are descriptions. This idea is the basis of the *descriptive theory of referring*. As I mentioned in the preface, it was the dominant theory of referring in the philosophy of language until Saul Krike, Hillary Putnam, and Keith Donnellan challenged it in the sixties, and proposed in its place the *causal or historical theory of referring*. Both theories have their defenders and detractors. Because of its importance I will devote all of Chapter Four to this controversy. Although Russell is a descriptive theorist, his analysis allows us, as we shall see shortly, to eliminate descriptions in favor of propositional functions (a concept introduced by Frege).

One of Frege's major contributions to our topic is the distinction between *two* senses of meaning. There is the meaning of "I meant the person in the red shirt when I said that someone in the room is too tiresome to be believed." And there is the meaning exemplified by, "What does the expression 'democracy' mean?" The referent, or

Bedeutung, is what is meant in the first case. The *Sinn*, or sense, is what is meant in the second case. Frege describes his position as follows:

> A proper name (word, sign, combination, expression) expresses its sense, and designates or signifies its nominatum. We let a *sign express* its sense and *designate* its reference.[5]

Frege acknowledges that signs or names are not always used to refer to their referents. They do so only when they are used in the *customary manner*. Often we wish to speak about the words themselves, however, as we do when we quote someone, for example, Frege said "Signs express their senses and designate their nominata." Here we are quoting Frege's words.[6] In such cases of *direct* quotation the words one uses *do not refer* to their customary referents. They refer to the words the quoted person actually used.[7] In *indirect* discourse,, instead of directly quoting someone, we convey what he *meant* to say. If, for example, I were to say that Frege said that linguistic symbols conveyed their meanings and referred to objects, I would be attempting to convey his meaning and not his actual words. This kind of discourse is usually characterized by use of a *that-clause*. According to Frege, names or signs, when used in indirect discourse, have *indirect* referents as opposed to their *customary ones*. In ordinary discourse, signs or names have or express their *customary senses*. But in indirect discourse, their customary senses become their referents. For Frege, the referent of a sign (name) is a function of sentential context. A sign's referent depends upon the kind of sentence in which it occurs. Sometimes a sign refers to its customary referent, sometimes to itself, and sometimes to its indirect referent, which is its customary sense. Consider the following sentences containing the name 'General Grant.'

    (a) General Grant was President Lincoln's favorite general.

    (b) Stonewall Jackson said, "General Grant is a drunk."

    (c) Stonewall Jackson thought that General Grant was a drunk.

According to Frege, if I said (a), I would be referring to Grant. But if I said (b), I would be referring to the words that Stonewall Jackson used to make his statement. But if I said (c), I would be referring to his idea (*Sinn*) of Grant. In (a) the referent (*Bedeutung*) of 'General grant' would be the man Grant. In (b) it would be Jackson's words. In (c) it would be Jackson's conception (*Sinn*) of Grant. In (a) the meaning or sense (Sinn) of the expression 'General Grant' would be a description, such as *the North's best general*, and it is the referent (Bedeutung) in (c).

Frege extends the naming model to whole declarative sentences. Accordingly, he treats full declarative sentences as names. Their senses (*Sinn*) are the thoughts they express. But by thought he means not some individual's thought, which for him would be to make the mistake of the empiricists, who treated thoughts as mental entities. What he means by a thought is something that *every person can appreciate*, something with objective status. It is what we refer to when we say things like, "Consider the thought conveyed by the words 'God is everywhere.'" What he has in mind is what is *commonly* expressed by a sentence, namely, its meaning, or what some philosophers refer to as a proposition. On this account of the matter, 'Der Himmel ist blau,' 'The sky is blue,' and 'Blue is the color of the sky,' all convey the same thought, or express the same proposition.

Given that a full declarative sentence is a name, which for Frege expresses a sense or proposition, what, one might wonder, is its referent or the object it names? We understand how Grant can be the referent of 'General Grant,' but what would the sentence 'General Grant was President Lincoln's favorite general' refer to? Frege's answer to this question is one of his most controversial doctrines. He claims that full declarative sentences name either the True or the False. They name truth-values. He says:

> By the truth-value of a sentence I mean the circumstance of its being true or false. There are no other truth-values. For brevity's sake I shall call the one the True and the other the False. Every declarative sentence, in which what matters are the nominata of the words, is therefore to be considered as a proper name; and its nominatum, if there is any, is either the True or the False.[8]

Although for Frege every name has a sense, not every name has a nominatum or referent. Consider what he says about the sentence, 'Odysseus deeply asleep was disembarked at Ithaca.' According to Frege, since it is likely that Odysseus never existed, it is likely that although the name in question has a sense, it does not have a referent. And because a full declarative sentence does not have a referent if one of its referential elements or names lacks a referent, the sentence in question lacks a referent, and is thus neither true nor false[9]

If, however, we consider the references of full declarative sentences to be either the True or the False, and accept Leibniz's principle, the principle of substitutivity, which Frege did, we will encounter a serious problem regarding such sentences as, 'Copernicus believed that the planetary orbits are circles.'[10] The principle of substitutivity, POS, when instantiated to names can be stated thus:

> Whenever a name 'a' is used to refer to the same object as the name 'b,' 'a' can be substituted for 'b' in any sentential context . . . b . . . without changing the truth-value of . . . b . . . , and the same is true for 'b.'

Consider now the sentence within the sentence 'Copernicus believed that the planetary orbits are circles,' namely, 'the planetary orbits are circles.' Since the planetary orbits are in fact ellipses and not circles, it is false. Given POS, it follows that if we substitute for the name 'The planetary orbits are circles,' any name having the same referent, the truth-value of 'Copernicus believed that the planetary orbits are circles,' will not be altered. But the implication of this contention is absurd. Since the referent of 'The planetary orbits are circles' would be the False, it would have to follow that Copernicus believed every false proposition.[11] It is obviously false, however, that Copernicus believed that Saddam Hussein is the king of Siam.

There are two ways to avoid this conclusion. One can either deny the validity of POS or deny that the referent of 'The planetary orbits are circles' in the sentence about Copernicus is somehow not the False. Frege's distinction between customary and indirect reference, allows him to solve this puzzle by the latter means. (This puzzle is, as we shall see when we consider Russell's views concerning meaning and referring, one of the three puzzles of referring that Russell claimed a satisfactory theory of referring must be able to solve)

As we learned previously, Frege holds that sometimes the referent of a sign or name is its customary sense. This will often be the case when a sign or name is *embedded* within a larger sentence context, governed by what philosophers refer to as *verbs of propositional attitude*, such as, believing, knowing, wishing, willing, choosing, etc. This view of the matter allows Frege to claim that the referent of an expression, in this case a full declarative sentence—'The planetary orbits are circles'—is, when embedded within a verb of propositional attitude, not the False, but instead its indirect referent or customary sense, namely, the proposition that the planetary orbits are circles. Since the proposition expressed by the sentence 'The Planetary orbits are circles' is different from the proposition expressed by the sentence 'Saddam Hussein is the king of Siam' the former cannot be substituted

23

for the latter, and thus it does not follow that because Copernicus believed the former, he must have believed the latter.

In summary, in order to understand the nature of identity, Frege had to add an element to his original analysis of symbolic representation. Originally he thought that all he needed were signs and their referents. He added the idea of a sense. He argues that all names have a sense, though not all have referents. He considers all declarative sentences to be names. They too all have sense, but not all have referents. Their senses are propositions, and their referents are truth-values. But when they are embedded within verbs of propositional attitude their customary senses become their referents.

Russell

Russell's interest in language, like Frege's, was motivated by a desire to eliminate what he considered to be the inherent ambiguity of natural languages. Russell and his student/colleague Wittgenstein are the originators of the metaphysical theory known as logical atomism. This theory incorporates a doctrine about the nature of language, and one about the relation of language to reality. Russell wrote the "Introduction" to Wittgenstein's *Tractatus*, and in it he lays out what he takes to be their shared perspective on the nature of language and its relation to reality. He claims that Wittgenstein "was concerned with the conditions which would have to be fulfilled by a logically perfect language." He also claims that "the question Wittgenstein is trying to answer is 'What relation must one fact (such as a sentence) have to another in order to be capable of being a symbol for that other?'" According to Russell, Wittgenstein is also "concerned with the conditions for accurate Symbolism, i.e. for Symbolism in which a sentence means something quite definite." But, according to Russell, practically speaking, "language is always more or less vague."[12] On the basis of these observations, Russell concludes:

logic has two problems to deal with in regard to Symbolism: (1) the conditions for sense rather than nonsense in combinations of symbols; (2) the conditions for uniqueness of meaning or reference in symbols or combinations of symbols. A logically perfect language has rules of syntax which prevent nonsense, and has single symbols which always have a definite and unique meaning. Mr Wittgenstein is concerned with the conditions for a logically perfect language—not that any language is logically perfect, or that we believe ourselves capable, here and now, of constructing a logically perfect language, but that the whole function of language is to have meaning, and it only fulfils this function in proportion as it approaches to the ideal language which we postulate.[13]

This description of Wittgenstein's concerns is certainly true of Russell's own concerns. (But as we shall see when we examine Wittgenstein's views later on in the present chapter, it misrepresents Wittgenstein.) There are at least two observations he makes about Wittgenstein that do represent the views of both: "the essential business of language is to assert or deny facts," and "the first requisite of an ideal language would be that there should be one name for every simple, and never the same name for two different simples."[14]

In Russell's "The Philosophy of Logical Atomism," he condemns our common everyday beliefs and the assertions we make based upon them as "fearfully vague." The task of philosophy, as he conceives it, is to replace these vague and imprecise everyday beliefs with beliefs which are inherently clear and precise, by developing a formal language entirely free of the vagueness inherent in natural languages. Russell is convinced that he and the mathematician/philosopher Alfred North Whitehead, in their joint effort to develop a formal language from which all of mathematics could be derived, *Principia Mathematica*, had provided the rudiments of just such a language. All that remains to be accomplished, as far as he is concerned, is to delineate and describe principles upon the basis of which one could generate the *vocabulary* for this language. In his work on Logical Atomism, he attempts to do just that. Logical Atomism was the result of a joint endeavor by Russell and the early Wittgenstein. And although there are significant differences in the kind of account each gave, they shared a common understanding as regards how this should be done, and what kinds of problems it is meant to address and resolve.

The followers of Hegel, some of whom were Russell's teachers, considered reality to be one single thing. They thought that tables, chairs, books, people, planets, etc., were just momentary aspects of the one reality. Russell rejects this idea. At the outset of "The Philosophy of Logical Atomism," Russell explains that his approach is "atomistic," in as much as the world consists of many separate things, and does not, as the Hegelians thought, consist merely in phases and unreal divisions of a single reality. He explains that the atoms are "logical" rather than physical. They are revealed by logical and not chemical analysis. There are two kinds of atoms: (1) particulars—"little paths of color, sounds, momentary things" and (2) predicates or relations. He holds that logical analysis is the only way for us to learn the truth about the world.

25

In order to arrive at a language free from the vagueness which characterizes natural languages, we must, according to Russell, provide terms with strictly fixed and determinate meaning. Before proceeding to specify exactly what characteristics these terms will have to possess, Russell explains what he means by a *fact*. Facts are what they are no matter what we may think about them. They are independent of our beliefs about them. They are required to provide content to our beliefs. They are expressed by our claims about the world. They render what we say to be either true or false. They are expressed by whole sentences. Facts are expressed "when we say that a certain thing has a certain property, or that it has a certain relation to another thing; but the thing which has the property or the relation is not what I call a 'fact'."[15]

There are, according to Russell, two kinds of facts: particular facts and general facts. A specific sense-datum's being white is his example of a particular fact. All humans being mortal is his example of a general fact. He cautions us against supposing that one could "describe the world completely by means of particular facts alone."[16] He offers a proof that one cannot so describe the world. He asks us to suppose that we have listed all the particular facts in the universe. Would we then, he asks, have a complete list of all existent facts? No, says Russell. Our list would not be complete because it leaves out the fact that it is complete. In order to complete the list we would have to add the general fact that all particular facts are contained on our list.

Russell proceeds by distinguishing between those things which are logically complex, and those things which are logically simple. He needs this distinction for the reduction of the complex to the simple. Our common sense assumption that most of the objects to which we attach proper names, for example, Socrates, Rumania, Twelfth Night and Piccadilly, are actually complex objects, is, he asserts, mistaken. We wrongly assume that such objects as these are "complex systems bound together in some kind of unity, that sort of a unity that leads us to the bestowal of a simple appellation." For Russell, such complex objects as these do not actually exist. He claims that they are simply "logical fictions."[17]

Take the statement "Piccadilly is a pleasant street." Is there any single constituent in the fact that this statement describes which can be said to correspond to the name 'Piccadilly'? The answer to this question is, according to Russell, that there is no single constituent of this fact, simple or complex, which could be referred to by this expression. Although 'Piccadilly,' "on the face of it, is the name for a certain portion of the earth's surface," to define 'Piccadilly' one would, we are told, "have to define it as a series of classes of material entities."

In other words, if I asked you to tell me to what does the name 'Piccadilly' refer, you would probably say that in addition to some portion of the earth's surface, it refers to the pavement, the lampposts, and some specifiable set of buildings, presently occupied by a specifiable number of shops, theaters, etc. And if I wanted you to be more specific, you could provide me with a full description of each of these things. Such a description or list would constitute, according to Russell, a class of things, which means that Piccadilly is a class of objects. But the lampposts, streets, etc. are transitory—what is there today is not precisely what was there a year ago. Lampposts get destroyed and are replaced by others. Businesses fail or lose their leases, and are replaced by others. This is why Russell says that when we are talking about Piccadilly, we are talking about a *series* of classes—classes the members of which are in flux.

For Russell, abstractions like classes do not refer to objects, and so they are unreal—logical fictions. If I asked you how many hounds the Potomac Hunt owns, you would count them. If I asked you how many different hound colors you observed as you counted the hounds, you would, if you were a hound aficionado, say there are two classes, lemon and whites, and tricolors. There are no black and tans. If I asked you to point to or pet one of the tricolors, it would be easy for you to do so, but if I asked you to point to or pet the class—that *thing* that is the class—of tricolors, you would be at a loss. Classes do not exist the way that dogs do. Classes are abstractions. You can pen up all the tricolors, but you cannot pen up or otherwise confine a class.

Russell treats human beings the same way he treats Piccadilly. For him, Socrates is nothing more than the series of his experiences, and as such, a logical fiction. But as Kurt Gödel points out, what Russell means by the term 'exits' is not what we usually mean by it. What Russell means when he says that these things do not exist is, according to Gödel, "only that we have no direct perception of them."[18]

In "On Denoting," which he wrote earlier than "The Philosophy of Logical Atomism," Russell distinguishes between *proper names* like 'Scott,' which refer to existent things, and *incomplete symbols* like 'Apollo,' which are incomplete because they do not refer to existent things (see below, p. 36, for a more detailed account of the concept of an incomplete symbol). The meanings of proper names are the existent things to which they refer. But in "The Philosophy of Logical Atomism" he distinguishes *logically* proper names and incomplete symbols, and relegates all ordinary proper names to the realm of the incomplete symbol. Only logically proper names can have unambiguous meaning. They are said to refer to *simple objects*, or particulars, objects whose existent nature is so simple as to preclude ambiguity. Having isolated what he means by a logically proper name, he contrasts this with a fact. For Russell, facts are *genuinely* complex objects. About facts, he says:

> Facts are . . . plainly something you have to take account of if you are going to give a complete account of the world. You cannot do that by merely enumerating the particular things that are in it: you must also mention the relations of these things, and their properties, and so forth, all of which are facts, so that facts certainly belong to an account of the objective world, and facts do seem much more clearly complex and much more not capable of being explained away than things like Socrates and Rumania.[19]

Socrates is, as we learned previously, just a series of classes, a logical fiction. The same is true of Rumania. That is how they can be explained away.

Russell continues his analysis by defining the word 'proposition' which he defines as being composed of symbols, symbols which "we must understand in order to understand the proposition." Excluding the logical components of propositions ('and,' 'or,' 'not, 'if . . . then,' 'if and only if,' etc.), Russell defines "the meanings of the symbols" composing propositions as "the components of facts."[20] By defining propositions in this way, he is defining them as most philosophers would define sentences, specifically sentence *types*, not sentence *tokens*. The proposition or sentence type 'This is white' has as its meaning the fact that it describes. The meaning of 'this' is the thing that is white, and the meaning of 'white' is the whiteness of the thing referred to by 'this.'

Russell then postulates a hierarchy of facts starting with the simplest and building up to the more complex. The simplest sort of facts are, according to Russell, "those which consist in the possession of a quality by some particular thing," as, for example, what is referred to by the proposition 'This is white.' The next simplest would be referred to by such sentences or propositions as 'This is to the left of that,' followed by such facts as those referred to by such sentences as 'A gives B to C.' Such facts are referred to as 'monadic,' 'dyadic,' 'triadic,' 'tetradic,' etc., depending upon whether the relation involves one, two, three, four, etc., number of terms. This whole hierarchy is said by Russell to "constitute" what he calls *atomic facts*—the simplest sort of fact. The sentences describing these facts are defined as *atomic propositions*. And every atomic fact is said to involve one *component*,

28

namely a monadic, dyadic, triadic, etc., relation, and the *terms* of the relation, which are particulars. In atomic propositions, the symbols expressing the relations are said to be *predicates*, and the symbols expressing or standing for particulars are *logically proper names*.[21]

Molecular propositions are composed of atomic propositions. Molecular propositions, such as, 'This is white and that is red,' 'This is red or it is purple,' 'If this is white, it is colored,' etc., are said to be *truth-functional*. To say that they are truth-functional is to say that their truth-values are functions of the truth-values of their constituent parts. If it is true that this is white, and it is true that that is red, then it follows that it is true both that this is white *and* that is red.[22]

Russell criticizes natural languages because they do not embody a distinction between various levels of language, a shortcoming that results in puzzles about the classes of classes that do not contain themselves as members. This defect Russell remedies by the incorporation of the *theory of types* into his version of a perfected (ideal) language. No analysis of Russell's ideal language views, and particularly his logical atomism, would be complete without coverage of this theory. It is not an easy theory to explain. Even Whitehead expressed frustration regarding it, and many different opinions exist among logicians and mathematicians regarding its nature. I will do my best to explain it without distorting Russell's intentions.

In *Principia*, Russell and Whitehead attempted to reduce mathematics to logic by reducing numbers to classes. Understood in this way, it would seem that a class could be understood *extensionally* as simply the conjunction of a collection of objects. Such reductionism is, however, hampered by the paradoxes which are engendered by the concept of classes. What about those classes of objects which have infinite numbers as members? What would a conjunction of such a class look like? Would it not have to be an infinite conjunction? And what are those objects which make up the null class, which are classes that have no members, such as the class of all humans who are over twenty feet tall? Worse than this, however, is that what follows from the fact that from any class of objects n one can make 2^n selections, is that even in the case where n is infinite, 2^n is greater than n. So if we assume that n is the total number of things, and include within it the total number of things that can be composed from it, we arrive at the self-contradictory result that the total number of things that exist is greater than their totality.

To provide a better understanding of this paradox, Russell asks us to consider a class with just three members, a, b, and c. The first selection we are asked to make is the selection of no terms, then of *a* alone, followed by *b* alone, and then *c* alone. Then we are asked to select *bc, cab, ab,* and *abc.* We now have 8 selections, which can be determined ahead of such inductive procedures via the formula 2^n, where *n* is the number of terms. If there are two terms then the formula would yield 4 selections. He concludes "that the total number of things in the world is not so great as the number of classes that can be made up out of those things." And, we can construct on these grounds "a perfectly precise arithmetical proof that there are *fewer* things in heaven or earth than are dreamt of in *our* philosophy."[23]

Such considerations led Russell to give up the idea that classes could be analyzed extensionally, and to treat them instead *intensionally, i.e.* as classes of objects satisfying or instantiating propositional functions. The class of humans is just that collection of objects which yields true values for the function "x is human." Russell can now eliminate classes by reducing statements about classes to statements about corresponding propositional functions.

But this kind of reductionism generates serious difficulties of its own. There is a serious problem concerning classes which are, and those which are not, members of themselves. In the case of ordinary classes, like the class of dogs, one would likely say that this is a class which is not a member of itself, i.e. classes are not dogs. Consider, however, the class composed of all such classes, namely, those classes which do not contain themselves as members. Now let us ask about *this* class as we did about the class of dogs: does it contain itself as a member? Paradoxically, if we suppose that it *does,* it follows that as such it is one of those classes that *does not* contain itself as a member. If, on the other hand, we assume that it *does not* contain itself as a member, then it *is* one of those classes that does not contain itself as a member. In either case, we contradict ourselves.[24]

Another paradox which Russell considers is the paradox of Epimenides, the Cretan who claimed that all Cretans are liars. Russell recasts it as a question: if a man makes the statement 'I am lying,' is he lying or not? If he is lying, then that is what he says he is doing, so he is telling the truth and not lying. But if he is telling the truth, then he is lying, and so not telling the truth.[25]

To overcome such paradoxes as these, Russell devised the theory of types. He originally introduced it in a 1908 article entitled "Mathematical Logic as Based on the Theory of Types." He refined it in *Principia Mathematica,* and explicated it further in "The Philosophy of Logical Atomism." In *Principia,* he explicates the notion of a propositional function by saying that it is "something which contains a

30

variable x, and expresses a *proposition* as soon as a value is assigned to x." He also claims that a propositional function "is what ambiguously denotes some one of a certain totality, namely the values of the function." From which it follows, according to Russell, that "this totality cannot contain any members which involve the function, since, if it did, it would contain members involving the totality, which, by the vicious-circle principle, no totality can do."[26] In short, no function F(x), can be instantiated by itself, as in 'F(Fx).' The function "is human," can be instantiated by Socrates with the result "Socrates is human." Instantiating this function by itself, however, would result in "is human is human," which is, senseless.

This contention of Russell's, that a propositional function cannot contain itself as a member, the essence of the so-called "simple theory of types,"[27] provides an immediate solution to the paradox about the class of classes which are not members of themselves. What follows if one adopts the simple theory of types is that the question whether it is true or false that such a class does contain itself as a member is itself revealed to be meaningless. The question would be as senseless as asking if a full marble bag contains itself.

The person claiming that he is lying will have to say what type of liar he is. If he claims "I am asserting a false proposition of the first type", then he will be, according to Russell, asserting a proposition of the second type. So, since he is not asserting a proposition of the first type, he remains a liar, and there is no contradiction. "Similarly," according to Russell, "if he said he was asserting a false proposition of the 30,000th type, that would be a statement of the 30,001st type, so he would still be a liar."[28]

The theory of types is, as Reichenbach recognized, the bedrock principle underlying the object language/metalanguage distinction, a distinction we will discuss later when we examine the verification theory of meaning. Although Tarski is often credited with introducing this distinction,[29] it was, according to Reichenbach, simply "an extension of the theory of types to a theory of levels of language." As proof of this claim, Reichenbach quotes from Russell's introduction to Wittgenstein's *Tractatus*:[30]

> every language has, as Mr. Wittgenstein says, a structure concerning which, *in the language*, nothing can be said, but there may be another language dealing with the structure of the first language, and having itself a new structure, and that to this hierarchy of languages there may be no limit.[31]

31

What the object language/metalanguage distinction involves can best be understood by focusing upon the difference between talking about objects, on the one hand, and talking about talk itself, on the other. My dog Suzy is a German shepherd. What I stated, call it S, with the previous sentence is a fact *about* my dog. Suppose now I state that my statement about Suzy is true. With this last statement, call it MS, I am saying something *about* my previous statement S, and not about my dog Suzy. As in the case of the theory of types, the recognition of metalanguages forces one to acknowledge the existence of a hierarchy of metalanguages. I can, for example, say that MS is true, call this statement MS1, and this would be a statement about MS. This last statement, MS1, is a statement about a statement, MS, about a statement, S, about a dog. To state that MS1 is true, call it MS2, is to make a statement about a statement, MS1, about a statement, MS, about a statement, S, about Suzy, and so on.

No one offers a better and more concise exegesis of Russell's program than does the British philosopher J. O. Urmson. He claims that Russell

> considered that a logic from which the whole of mathematics with all of its complexities can be derived must be an adequate skeleton . . . of a language capable of expressing all that can be accurately said at all. . . . he came to think that the world would have the structure of this logic, whose grammar was so perfect, unlike that of the misleading natural languages. As the logic had individual variables in its vocabulary, so the world would contain a variety of particulars, the names of which would be constants, to replace, as extra-logical vocabulary, these variables; as the logic required only extensional, truth-functional, connectives between its elementary propositions, so the world would consist of independent, extensionally connected facts; as the techniques of logic could define and thus make theoretically superfluous the more complex and abstruse concepts of mathematics, so, by the application of the same techniques the less concrete items of the furniture of heaven and earth, . . . could be defined and eliminated.[32]

Although Russell has had considerable influence upon how philosophers view the topic of referring, his interest in the topic was initially stimulated by Meinong, with whom he came to disagree quite strongly.[33] Two of Russell's most important and influential works on the subject of referring and the puzzles inherent in the doctrine that meaning is reference are his 1903 book *Introduction to Mathematical*

Philosophy and his 1905 essay "On Denoting." In the former he claims that a name "is a simple symbol, directly designating an individual which is its meaning, and having this meaning in its own right, independently of the meaning of all other words." This is inconsistent with Frege's view.

Unlike Frege, Russell does not distinguish between two senses of meaning, meaning as sense and meaning as referent. As Russell puts it in "On Denoting," the difference between them is that Frege "distinguishes, in a denoting phrase, two elements, which we may call the *meaning* and the *denotation*," while in the theory, "which I advocate, there is no *meaning*, and only sometimes a *denotation*."[34] Russell argues against Frege's theory that names have both a sense and a reference by focusing upon those cases where "denotation seems to be lacking." According to Russell:

> If we say "the King of England is bald," that is, it would seem, not a statement about the complex *meaning* "the King of England," but about the actual man denoted by the meaning. But now consider "the King of France is bald". By parity of form, this also ought to be about the denotation of the phrase "the King of France". But this phrase, though it has a *meaning* provided "the King of England" has a meaning, certainly has no denotation, at least in any obvious sense. Hence one would suppose that "The King of France is bald" ought to be nonsense; but it is not nonsense, since it is plainly false.[35]

Russell's point is that since Frege requires there to be both a sense and a reference for denoting phases, his view must be mistaken because there are numerous cases where reference is lacking. The denoting phrase 'the king of France' is a case in point, and any sentences in which it is a component would, according to Russell, have to be false, and not nonsense as one would expect it to be on Frege's account.

Russell's criticism of Frege is unconvincing. It presupposes that every proposition is either true or false. It also seems to presuppose that for Frege every denoting expression has *both* a Sinn (sense) and a Bedeutung (denotation or referent). Frege clearly acknowledges, however, that some denoting expressions are *without* denotation. The example he uses to make this point is 'Odysseus' in 'Odysseus deeply asleep was disembarked at Ithaca.' Frege denies that the proposition expressed by the sentence about Odysseus is "plainly false." For him the proposition is neither true nor false. The same goes for the proposition about the present king of France. For Russell, every

33

proposition is either true or false. For Frege, some are true, some are false, and some are neither true nor false. Nowhere does Russell provide a convincing argument that he is right and Frege is wrong. Had he better understood what Frege was saying, he might have insulated his view from the attack Strawson would launch against it nearly fifty years after "On Denoting" was published. I will say more about this in the next chapter.

But why, one very well may ask, does Russell hold that denoting phrases have no meaning but only sometimes have a denotation? The answer is that for Russell such expressions as 'the King of England' and 'the King of France' are not actually denoting expressions. They are instead, for him, *incomplete symbols*, which means, as we previously determined, that they have no meaning in themselves. They do, however, contribute to the meaning of sentences in which they occur. Such expressions as the two in question, as well as all expressions of the form 'the x is P,' which are interpreted to entail that "there is one and only one thing x that is P," are referred to as *definite descriptions*. Names that have no denotations, like 'Odysseus,' are *disguised* definite descriptions, and should be replaced by the descriptions they abbreviate. We will soon turn to more details concerning this doctrine, but let it suffice for now to recognize that by 1918 the views of Frege and Russell can apparently be reconciled regarding the function of descriptions. Frege claimed that the sense of a name like 'Moses' is some commonly shared description or mode of presentation. Eventually, Russell will consider all ordinary proper names to be definite descriptions masquerading as proper names.[36] The descriptions hiding under the mask of proper names are commonly shared ones, such as 'the sun God' for 'Apollo.' I will return to this idea shortly.

In "On Denoting," Russell poses three paradoxes or puzzles regarding the thesis that meaning is simply referring. These puzzles, he alleges, are the result of inadequacies inherent in natural language. He claims, moreover, that these paradoxes provide a test for the adequacy of any philosophical theory of referring. He claims that such paradoxes serve the same purpose for logic that experiments do for science—they are tests. A theory of referring is, according to Russell, tested by its ability to resolve these paradoxes. He claims that his theory of descriptions meets the challenge by offering solutions to all three.[37]

The first of these puzzles can be stated in the form of an argument, the first premise of which is the *principle of substitutivity*:

(P1) If terms 'a' and 'b' refer to the same thing, then one of them can always be replaced by the other in any sentential context without change of truth-value.

The second premise of the argument is an alleged historical fact about the curiosity of King George IV concerning Sir Walter Scott, who was not widely known to have authored *Waverley*:

(P2) George IV wished to know whether Scott was the author of *Waverly*.

Premise three alleges a fact about English usage:

(P3) The expressions 'Scott' and 'the author of *Waverly*' refer to the same person.

On the basis of these three premises one can validly infer the following:

(C) George IV wished to know whether Scott was Scott.

But, (C) is not what George IV wanted to know. The conclusion is false. This fact seems to undermine the very concept of "validity." To say that an argument is *valid* is to say that it has a valid form. To say that it has a valid form is to say that when its premises are true, its conclusion *must* be true. So, asks Russell, "Why is the conclusion false?"

The second puzzle is linked to the *law of the excluded middle*, which asserts that either p or not p is true (contradictory propositions cannot both have the same truth-value). Although this is a time-honored and venerable principle of logic, Russell argues that there appear to be exceptions to it in ordinary language. Russell makes his point by having us focus on the following pair of sentences:

The present king of France is bald.
The present king of France is not bald.

Which one is true? According to Russell, since there is at present no king of France, it follows that nothing is both the king of France and bald (or tall, slender, intelligent, or anything else, for that matter). To claim otherwise, as one does when one claims that he is bald, is to claim what is false. But what about the claim that he is not bald? According to the law of the excluded middle, it has to be true. But, by the same reasoning previously used to show that it is false that he is bald, it follows that it is also false that he is not bald. Since there is no present king of France, there cannot be anything which is both the present king of France and non-bald.

The third paradox has to do with the inconsistency involved in denying the existence of anything (such denials are referred to as *negative existential assertions*.) Consider the following example:

(a) Apollo does not exist.

According to Russell, if one were to state the following three sentences, one would apparently be making true statements:

(1) (a) expresses a true proposition.[38]
(2) (a) is about Apollo.
(3) (a) is *logically equivalent*[39] to sentence (b).[40]

(b) There is no such thing as Apollo.

But, as Russell realizes, although they may all appear to be true, they cannot all be consistently asserted, because if (1) and (3) are true, then (b) is true, and there is no such thing as Apollo, so (2) would have to false. On the other hand, if (2) is true, then (b) is false, and if (3) is true as well, then (1) would also have to be false. If, however, (2) and (1) are both true, then (3) will have to be false, since it would follow that (a) and (b) have different truth-values.[41]

Having stated these three different puzzles or paradoxes of referring, Russell offers solutions to them which are derived from his *theory of descriptions*. The insight that motivates this theory is Russell's recognition that we are seduced by ordinary language into treating all denoting expressions equally. We regard them all as names, and as such we interpret each one of them to refer to a specific object, the object that is the meaning of the name. In a "logically proper" language, an ideal language, we would never be tempted to do that. In such a language, all names would be logically proper names, which, as we saw earlier, for Russell always refer to particulars.

According to Russell, denoting phrases, like 'the present king of England,' 'the present king of France,' 'some men,' 'all men,' and 'the center of mass of the solar system at the first instant of the twentieth century,' unlike proper names, "never have any meaning in themselves." Russell calls them *incomplete symbols*. In *Principia Mathematica*, he defines the expression 'incomplete symbol' as "a

36

symbol which is not supposed to have a meaning in isolation, but is only defined in certain contexts." He goes on to say:

> Whenever the grammatical subject of a proposition can be supposed not to exist without rendering the proposition meaningless, it is plain that the grammatical subject is not a proper name, i.e. not a name directly representing some object. Thus in all such cases, the proposition must be capable of being so analyzed that what was the grammatical subject shall have disappeared.[42]

In "On Denoting," Russell uses the following example as an illustration in the application of his theory of descriptions:

> The father of Charles II was executed.

Its analysis must, according to Russell, capture the uniqueness of the expression 'the.' We do sometimes refer to someone as the son of so and so when so and so has several sons. But in its strict use 'the' involves uniqueness. Russell's analysis of the above example is as follows:

> 'It is not always false of x that x begat Charles II and that x was executed and that "if x begat Charles II, y is identical with x" is always true of y.'

This analysis can be simplified as:

> There exists one and only one x who begat Charles II,
> and that x was executed.

The analysis eliminates the definite description or denoting phrase 'the father of Charles II' and thus eliminates the illusion that the phrase in question is a name, the meaning of which is the object to which it refers. In order to fully appreciate the effectiveness of the theory of descriptions we must test its ability to solve the three puzzles of referring discussed above.[43]

Consider the puzzle concerning George IV. If we apply the pattern of analysis provided by the theory of descriptions, our second premise is recognized to be ambiguous because it can be analyzed as either (A) or (B):

> (A) One and only one thing wrote Waverly, and George IV wished

37

to know if that thing was Scott.

(B) George IV wished to know if one and only one thing wrote Waverly, and if that thing was Scott.

To interpret it as (A) is, according to Russell, to accord to the descriptive phase in question a *primary occurrence*, whereas to interpret it as (B) is to accord to it a *secondary occurrence*. To accord a primary occurrence to a descriptive phrase is to interpret it to have what logicians call "existential import," which is to regard it as committing one to the existence of its alleged referent. To accord a secondary occurrence to a descriptive phase does not involve existential import.[44] (This distinction has significant bearing on Russell's resolution to the puzzle concerning the present king of France, but it has no significance here.) Either interpretation of the second premise enables us to appreciate how Russell's theory solves our puzzle regarding George IV. Examination of both interpretations reveals that the troublesome expression 'the author of Waverly' has been eliminated, and thus it cannot be substituted for by 'Scott.'

What Russell wants us to understand is that the puzzle only exists because natural languages are misleading. Logical analysis allows us to remove these confusions. What looks like a name, 'the author of *Waverly*,' turns out not to be one. The source of confusion lies in the syntax of ordinary language, which treats all substantives the same. They are all treated as designators or names. A proper syntax of the sort provided by Russell's logic distinguishes between true designators and incomplete symbols. In such a logic or "ideal" language, puzzles like the one about George IV cannot arise.

The syntactic rules of ordinary or natural language recognize no formal distinction between 'Walter Scott was a Scotsman' and 'The author of Waverly was a Scotsman.' Both are expressions of the subject-predicate format. The rules of syntax for Russell's logic recognize that they are quite different in logical form. While the former is of the genuine subject-predicate form, and says that some predicate applies to the object referred to by the name in question, the latter is a disguised existential assertion which really says:

There exits one and only one x such that x both authored Waverly and is a Scotsman.

The second puzzle, the present king of France puzzle, is also solved by applying the theory of descriptions. But here the distinction between a primary and a secondary occurrence of a descriptive phrase becomes all-important. According to Russell, the sentence 'The present king of France is bald,' when analyzed in the manner recommended by the theory of descriptions, accords a primary occurrence to the descriptive phrase 'the present king of France.' Its analysis is:

(Spo) There exists one and only one x such that x is at present king of France and bald.

Its denial, 'The present king of France is not bald,' is, however, ambiguous and subject to the following two analyses depending upon whether or not the descriptive phase 'the present king of France' is accorded a *primary* or a *secondary* occurrence. If it is accorded a primary occurrence, it is analyzed as:

not (Spo) There exists one and only one x such that x is at present king of France and non-bald.

Since there is at present no king of France to be either bald or non-bald, (Spo) and not (Spo) are, according to Russell, both false.[45] And although the law of the excluded middle appears to be invalidated, we need not worry. For, according to Russell, when we accord a secondary occurrence to the descriptive phase 'the present king of France' we get:

not (Sso) It is not the case that there exists an x such that x is both at present the king of France and bald.

Interpreted in this way, the denial of 'The present king of France is bald,' is true. According to Russell, this interpretation is the true contradictory of 'The present king of France is bald.' So, the law of the excluded middle is preserved, and our paradox is resolved.

The third puzzle, the one concerning negative existential assertions, does not appear at first glance to be one that lends itself to solution by means of the theory of descriptions. The sentence in question, 'Apollo does not exist,' does not contain any definite descriptions. Again we are deceived by appearances. As far as ordinary language is concerned, the sentence in question is of subject-predicate form and does not differ in any important respect from 'Finn is a non-adult.' From the perspective of ordinary language, the subject of predication in this case is my grandson, and the predicate is "is a non-adult." Since Finn is only four years old, the predicate "non-adult" can be attributed to him. Similarly, since Apollo, a mythological God, did

39

not actually exist, the predicate "non-existence" can be attributed to him. But how can a non-existent thing *be* anything?

The resolution of the third puzzle lies in the perfected language of *Principia Mathematica*. This logically perfected language incorporates the idea that existence is not a predicate or a property. Like Frege's, Russell's analysis treats existence as a property or attribute of propositional functions. To say that a propositional function exists is to say that it is instantiated. The predicate 'is human' becomes a propositional function when it is predicated of a variable, as in 'x is human.' Socrates instantiates this propositional function in 'Socrates is human.' The name 'Socrates' is not a logically proper name,[46] but at the time Russell wrote "On Denoting" it, like 'Scott,' was treated as a complete symbol, and not as a description masquerading as a name. 'Apollo' was, however treated as a masquerader.

The description that is hidden under the mask of ordinary language for 'Apollo' can be revealed, according to Russell, by consulting a classical dictionary. It is 'the sun-god.' Substituting this description for 'Apollo' in (a) produces:

(a) The sun-god does not exist.

In other words, this solution of Russell's for the puzzle concerning Apollo, involves understanding that (a) is not about a non-existent entity, but rather is actually a denial that anything instantiates the propositional function 'is a sun-god.' Russell is now in a position to resolve our dilemma concerning the impossibility of the following to all be true:

(1) (a) expresses a true proposition.
(2) (a) is about Apollo.
(3) (a) is *logically equivalent* to sentence (b).

(b) There is no such thing as Apollo.

His resolution of the puzzle consists in maintaining that although (1) and (3) are true, (2) must be false. (a) is not about Apollo, but is, instead, about the non-instantiation of the propositional function in question. Russell's solution, though certainly brilliant, is not the only solution that has been proposed by philosophers.

I will now summarize what I take to be the most important similarities and differences in the views of Frege and Russell. For Frege, the meaning or sense (Sinn) of an ordinary proper name is a definite description. Although Russell's views regarding ordinary proper names changed between 1903, when he wrote "On Denoting," and 1918, when he wrote "The Philosophy of Logical Atomism," they were not significantly different from those of Frege by 1918. By then, he considered *all* ordinary proper names to be disguised descriptions. Their terminology is different, however, and it should not be ignored. Frege simply explains the *sense* (meaning) of a proper name in terms of a description, while Russell, who refuses to distinguish between the sense of a proper name and its referent, regards descriptions, not as senses, but as proper substitutions for proper names. Nevertheless, the similarity in their views may well be sufficient to class them together as descriptive theorists regarding referring, as so many contemporary philosophers do, especially those who oppose the descriptive theory in favor of the causal or historical theory. I will take this topic up again in Chapter Four.

Although the views of Frege and Russell can be reconciled regarding ordinary proper names, they do not agree regarding the status and nature of propositions. For Russell, sentences expressing propositions are not names, and they do not name truth-values. For Frege, they are names, and they do sometimes refer to truth–values, though at other times they are truth-valueless, i.e. they do not refer to the True or the False. For Russell, there are no truth-valueless propositions. They are always either true or false.

Now it is time to look at a quite different version of the reference theory of meaning. Alexius Meinong, as I previously noted, not only initially stimulated Russell's interest in the topic of referring, but also takes a quite different approach concerning non-existent entities than the one taken by both Russell and Frege. Frege and Russell attempt to reconcile the fact that although it is true that a name like 'Pecos Bill' lacks reference, the sentences concerning such non-existent objects do make sense. Meinong tries to establish that although Pecos Bill is an object without being, in the ordinary sense of the word 'being,' he does share with all objects of thought a distinct though different kind of being. As we shall see, Meinong's views regarding non-existent objects enable him to offer a very different solution to Russell's third puzzle concerning Apollo.

Meinong

Meinong's views are difficult to understand, which is evidenced by the fact that so many first-rate philosophers have misinterpreted him. Russell[47] and William Alston,[48] are among those who have misinterpreted him. It is as important to understand what he is not saying as it is to understand what he is saying. For this reason, I shall explicate his views in both of these ways.

According to Meinong, there is more than one kind of *being*. He distinguishes between *existence* and *subsistence*. Horses, men, dogs, cats, tables, atoms, planets, etc., are existent things, whereas, abstractions, like numbers, relations, propositions, classes, etc., are subsistent things. He claims, moreover, that these categories are *mutually exclusive*. He does not, however, claim that non-existent things, like Pecos Bill and Apollo, are subsistent things—a view many of his critics have attributed to him. Alston makes this mistake in the following passage:

> Meinong, who started with the assumption that every meaningful expression in a sentence (at least any meaningful expression that has the function of referring to something) must have a referent; otherwise, there would be nothing for it to mean. Hence, when we have an obviously meaningful expression that refers to nothing in the real world, for example, 'the Fountain of Youth,' in the sentence, 'De Soto was searching for the Fountain of Youth,' we must suppose that it refers to a "subsistent" entity, which does not exist but has some other mode of being. This doctrine . . . is based upon a confused assimilation of meaning and reference. . . . [49]

Alston's mistake is of the variety designated by Oxford philosopher Gilbert Ryle to be a *category mistake*. [50] A category mistake is placing an entity in the wrong category. Physical things, such as tables, planets, dogs, etc., make up one category. Abstractions, such as democracy, justice, etc., comprise another. The first category excludes the second and vise versa. An example that involves a number of category mistakes is one suggested by the linguist Noam Chomsky, 'Colorless green ideas sleep furiously.' Colorless things are not the kind of thing that can be said to be green. Ideas are not the kind of thing that can be said to be green. Ideas are not the kind of thing that can be said to sleep. And finally, sleeping is not the kind of thing that can be said to be done furiously. As far as Meinong is concerned, fountains are the kind of thing that can either exist or not exist. They are not the kind of thing that can either subsist or non-subsist. To claim that a non-existent fountain, like the Fountain of Youth, is subsistent is like claiming that ideas can be green. It does not, on Meinong's account of the matter, make sense.

Meinong does, however, say things that help to explain why philosophers like Alston and Russell misinterpret him. He talks about the being and non-being of various kinds of things, and alleges that when one asserts, for example, that there are marble fountains, it follows not only that there are marble fountains, but also that there is another kind of *object*, which is *the being* of marble fountains that is *the object of the assertion* in question. It is this kind of being that explains why the assertion in question is true. He refers to such an object as an *Objective* (Objektiv). Objects like fountains, persons, etc., are objects in the usual sense of the term. But as Linsky has pointed out, "though all mental acts are directed towards objects, the objects of cognitive acts (knowing, believing, supposing) are objects of a special kind called objectives."[51] According to the American philosopher Roderick Chisholm, "Other philosophers have used the term 'proposition' pretty much as Meinong uses 'Objective'."[52] Linsky explicates this idea further as follows:

> What we see is an object in 'the strict sense', for example, a cat. But we 'judge' or 'assume' not a cat but, for example, *that the cat is on the mat*, or as Meinong sometimes puts it, we 'judge' *the being of the cat on the mat*. There is, then, besides objects in the strict sense, a special class of objects like *the being of the cat on the mat* or the *non-being of the cat on the mat* which are objects of cognitive acts. If what is judged is true, then the objective of the judgment subsists. The cat and the mat exist, but the objective *the being of the cat on the mat (that the cat is on the mat)* does not exist it subsists.[53]

Given this account of the matter, it is easy to see what Chisholm meant when he claimed that Meinong uses 'Objective' to mean what philosophers commonly mean by a proposition. As I pointed out in the introduction, on one interpretation of the word 'proposition,' all propositions are said to be either true or false. Philosophers commonly talk about *the proposition that* so and so is true or false. According to this interpretation of Meinong, the sentence 'the cat is on the mat' is said to convey the proposition (Objective) *that the cat is on the mat*. And, that proposition is true or not depending upon the situation of the cat. But what about false propositions? What are we to say about them?

Are false propositions for Meinong subsisting things as well? If I were to judge that I presently have a five dollar bill in my right hand trouser pocket, I would, according to the use of the expression 'proposition' now under consideration, be asserting that there is in that pocket a five-dollar bill. That would be tantamount to saying what is false. According to Meinong, since I would be asserting the being of a

43

five-dollar bill in my pocket, what I would be asserting is *non-subsistent*. Apparently then, when the object of my judgment is non-subsisting, I judge falsely, as I would, indeed, if I judged that I have a five-dollar bill in my trouser pocket, for it is empty. All propositions are, as we have seen, said to be either true or false. For Meinong all Objectives are either subsistent or non-subsistent.

According to Meinong, we can be said to judge truly of non-subsisting or non-existing *objects*. He claims that various predicates are appropriately applicable to such objects. He formulates this idea by claiming that the *Sosein* (so-being) of an object is independent of its *Sein* (being), which is an important step in Meinong's solution to Russell's third puzzle. That Apollo is a male god is true independent of the fact that he is non-existent. But we must also understand his concept of *aussersein* in order to fully understand his solution. Literally, 'aussersein' means "being outside of being." What he means by this is, according to Linsky,

> best viewed as simply recognizing in a rather 'pretentious' way such things as that the subject term of a subject predicate proposition may very well denote something that does not exist, e.g., Santa Claus. That some propositions about Santa Claus are true and some false is obvious. For example, 'Santa Claus lives at the South Pole' is false. Still, it is a proposition about Santa Claus. Meinong's doctrine of *aussersein* seems to me best interpreted as a recognition of such facts as these: That Santa Claus is denoted by the subject term of the above proposition, that Santa Claus is not Paul Bunyan though neither Santa Claus, nor Paul Bunyan exists. The doctrine of the independence of *Sein* from *Sosein* recognizes the fact that some propositions about Santa Claus and Paul Bunyan are true and some false, though neither Santa Claus nor Paul Bunyan exists.[54]

In other words, such objects as Santa Claus, Paul Bunyan, and Apollo, as pure objects, have a *kind of being* beyond existing and subsisting, which they share with all objects of thought and talk. *Aussersein* is the kind of being that anything has which can *be* thought or talked about.[55] The Meinongian solution to Russell's puzzle concerning Apollo would be to deny that 'Apollo does not exist' is logically equivalent to 'There is no such thing as Apollo,' which is to deny that statement (3), in Russell's formulation of the puzzle, is true. However, as Linsky also points out, Meinong believes that although existence is opposed to non-existence and subsistence is opposed to non-subsistence, *aussersein* "is opposed to nothing. No object can fail to have it."[56] Linsky argues:

> For suppose that there was some variety of non-being opposed to this kind of being, as there is something of the same type of existence and subsistence that is opposed to them. Then for us to judge that an object had this kind of non-being, we would have to ascribe a fourth kind of being to the object.[57]

If this fourth kind of being is also opposed to a fourth kind of non-being, this would force us to acknowledge a fifth kind of being, and so on for an infinite hierarchy of kinds of being. And thus, as Linsky points out, the way Meinong avoids the infinite regress is to suppose that there is a kind of being that is unopposed. Moreover, unless we suppose that this third kind of being is unopposed, the puzzle about negative existentials, the puzzle about Apollo, can be regenerated in terms of a fourth kind of being. We simply pose the puzzle by revising (1), which is, 'Apollo does not exist.' It becomes 'Apollo does not *aussersein*.' This formulation would force us to talk about Apollo's *non-aussersein* status, and we would be right back where we started. We would be assigning a fourth kind of being to Apollo. This is not the end of the matter, however, and the reason it does not end here is because we do not have what I shall refer to as a *descriptive* account of *aussersein*.

It is one thing to say that something is required to accomplish x. It is another thing to explain what that thing is. Clearly Apollo, Santa Claus, and Paul Bunyan can *be* thought or talked about. Perhaps, if we explicate or define *aussersein* as kinds of things that can be thought or talked about, we can see how the kind of being they have as objects of thinking or talking must be unopposed.

Suppose one wishes to deny this claim. How would one do it? By offering an example of a *non-aussersein* object? But how is that possible? Any example offered would have to be thought of and talked about, and that means that it has *aussersein*. This argument would seem to be sufficient to derail further objections to Meinong's account. Unfortunately, there is one further issue.

Meinong says: "Not only is the much heralded gold mountain, but the round square is surely round as it is square" and "In order to know that there is no round square, I must make a judgment *about* the round square."[58] In other words, both the golden mountain and the round square possess *aussersein*. I can agree with him about the gold mountain. I have no trouble imagining or talking about golden

45

mountains, Greek Gods, Santa Claus, Pecos Bill and various and sundry other imaginary entities of myth, fiction and folklore. Unfortunately, a contradictory object like a round square exceeds my imaginary powers. Can the answer to this difficulty be resolved by dropping the idea of being able to *imagine* or think about such an object, and simply restricting the definition of an *aussersein* object to that which can be *talked about*? Or, perhaps, we should put this idea in terms of linguistic entities, names like 'the round square,' and claim simply that they can be the subject terms of subject/predicate propositions, as when I said above that I could not conceive of a round square. I could, however, put the string of letters 'Giszzz' in the same predicate format. But it is not a name, although it could be. One could use this string to name a child, a horse, the next concert tour of The Rolling Stones, or even the round square. But in those cases, I would be using 'Giszzz' to name something. Otherwise, it would not be a name. And so it would seem that even though I cannot conceive of a round square, because it is contradictory, it does not follow that the subject of a meaningful subject/predicate proposition has to make sense. To say that a round square is a logical impossibility, or that it cannot be conceived, or that it is a contradictory object is to assert what is true, a subsistent proposition. But what exactly are we asserting when we assert this?

Russell would claim, as he did regarding Apollo, that nothing exists that instantiates the propositional function, "x is both round and square," or nothing is both round and square. One could, however, make a stronger claim by utilizing a more recent development in logic, *modal logic*. In modal logic, we distinguish between "it is possible that," and "it is necessary that."[59] An ordinary language rendition, as opposed to a symbolic rendition of the proposition about the round square, would be stated in modal logic as: "It is not possible that any x is both round and square," or "Nothing could possibly be both round and square at the same time," or "It is not possible to instantiate the propositional function of being at the same time both round and square." The meaning of 'square' is inconsistent with the meaning of 'round.' To be round precludes being square. I can imagine, think, conger up, or picture a round object. I can do likewise for a square object. What I cannot imagine, think, conger up, or picture is an object that is both round and square.

Russell's first order predicate calculus interpretation of what is meant by the claim that round squares do not exist, which is that nothing instantiates the conjunctive predicate function of being both round and square, has a distinct advantage over Meinong's view because it assigns *no* kind of being to round squares. The modal interpretation does an even better job of saying what one wants or means to say about round squares.

Nevertheless, while I think that Russell's views are superior to Meinong's views regarding contradictory objects, there remains something about Meinong's views that is, some would argue, superior to Russell's views. As far as fictional, mythological, folkloric, etc., objects are concerned, I can not only talk about them, I can conceive of them. There are such things, and they are non-real things. So while it is true that nothing instantiates the conjunctive predicate of being a fat little man dressed in red, who lives at the North Pole, utilizes a sled pulled by twelve tiny reindeer to deliver presents to all the children in the world within a twelve hour period, I can imagine such a creature. He is a non-existent man. And, in addition, it is *true* both that some creatures of mythology are centaurs, and that some creatures of mythology are not centaurs. But according to Russell, both claims are *false* because both imply that creatures of mythology exist. Like Linsky, I think that this aspect of Meinong's view needs to be somehow retained. So I would like to be able to retain the predicate logic that Russell helped pioneer, and at the same time maintain the idea that we can say true things about fictional, mythological, and folkloric beings. Linsky provides us with the means for doing so.

According to Linsky, all we have to do is retain the predicate logic, and add an *operator* that ranges over non-real things. When an assertion is embedded within the scope of this operator, its implications are different from those it would have when it is not so embedded. Statements, claims, propositions, etc. about real or existing things, even subsisting ones, would continue to be analyzed as they have been by Russell. But claims regarding non-actual things (the set of which would, of course, need to be further specified) would be analyzed differently. Consider the following sentence pair:

(a) Some dogs are vicious animals.
(b) Some dogs are not vicious animals.

Both are *true*, and would be analyzed by Russell as follows:

(a') At least one x is both a dog and a vicious thing.
(b') At least one x is both a dog and a non-vicious thing.

In Russell's logic, we would symbolize the predicates in question 'is a dog' and 'is a vicious thing,' respectively, as 'Dx,' and 'Vx,' and negation or 'not' as '~' and then symbolize (a') and (b') as follows:

(a'') $\exists x \, (Dx \cdot Vx)$

(b'') $\exists x \, (Dx \cdot \sim Vx)$.

Now consider this different sentence pair:

(c) Some creatures of mythology are centaurs.
(d) Some creatures of mythology are not centaurs.

If we analyze this pair as we did the former, we would get:

(c') At least one x is both a creature of mythology and a centaur.
(d') At least one x is both a creature of mythology and a non-centaur

Since neither creatures of mythology nor centaurs exist, both (c') and (d') are *false*. Since (c') and (d') are said by Russell to be formally equivalent to (a') and (b'), he would formalize (c') and (d') as:

(c'') $\exists x \, (Mx \cdot Cx)$

(d'') $\exists x \, (Mx \cdot \sim Cx)$.

On Linsky's analysis, however, (c') and (d') are both *true*. But we must first introduce symbols for each of the following: 'x exists in fiction,' 'x exists in mythology,' 'x exists in the comic strips,' 'x exists in the movies and plays,' etc., or we must allow all non-actual kinds of being to be subsumed under one operator, such as A, which is defined as "in the non-actual world." (c) and (d) would now be analyzed as:

(c''') in the non-actual world there exists at least one x which is both a creature of mythology and a centaur.

(d''') in the non-actual world there exists at least one x which is both a creature of mythology and a non-centaur.

Both are true, and their respective symbolic representations would be:

(c'''') $A \, \exists x \, (Mx \cdot Cx)$
(d'''') $A \, \exists x \, (Mx \cdot \sim Cx)$

But what advantage is gained by adopting Linsky's emendation to Russell's version of predicate logic? If you were asked if it is true that in mythology some of its creatures are centaurs and others are non-centaurs, what would be your reply? You would, I venture, say yes, which means that (c) and (d) are both true. But according to Russell they are both false. Linsky's solution does justice to our ordinary concepts of truth and falsity. On his analysis both are true. I will return to this issue again in the next chapter, when I explain how the Wittgenstein of the *Investigations* would resolve the controversy that Strawson's attack on Russell's theory of descriptions engenders.

Both Frege and Russell consider the referential puzzles to be evidence that ordinary or natural languages, while sufficient for everyday discourse, are inadequate for the tasks of philosophers, logicians, and scientists. Ordinary language does not: (1) provide the means for distinguishing quantification from predication the way Frege's perfected language does, (2) recognize the distinction between actual proper names and disguised ones, and (3) enable us to recognize the various different logical forms inherent in language (as does Russell's theory of descriptions). Ordinary language generates puzzles as regards concepts like "identity," "existence," "something," "nothing," "negative existentials," "classes that do not contain themselves as members," and leaves unresolved the consequences of embedding various identities within verbs of propositional attitude.

Many philosophers have adopted the same conclusions that Frege and Russell draw. They hold that the task of the philosopher/logician is to construct a perfected or ideal language. The expression of precise and unambiguous beliefs or propositions requires a language that,, unlike ordinary language, is constructed from the outset for this purpose.

Meinong's views concerning the status of proper names and general terms are *compatible* with the idea that natural languages, though in need of explicit acknowledgement that there are various kinds of being, are quite adequate for unambiguous communication. At the very least, as we have seen, they support natural language usage. The predicates 'is true' and 'is false' are given a role consistent with their ordinary or natural language usage. We are able to imagine an endless number of non-existent entities, and we are able to talk about them without confusion.

Wittgenstein was strongly influenced by Frege and Russell, but he also strongly disagreed with *each* of them. As I pointed out earlier on in this section, I disagree with Russell's claim, in his introduction to the

Tractatus Logico-Philosophicus, that Wittgenstein was in search of a logically perfect language. Instead, as will be clarified in the next section of this chapter, I believe that Wittgenstein was trying to find the *essence* of natural language.

Wittgenstein of the Tractatus Logico-Philosophicus

As far as the Wittgenstein of the *Tractatus* was concerned, there is only one language, since all languages are subject to the same basic logical considerations. He does not talk about ordinary or colloquial English or German, but instead talks about ordinary or colloquial language. And he claims, "All propositions of our colloquial language are actually, just as they are, logically completely in order" (*Tractatus* 5.5563). This is not to say, however, that Wittgenstein thought that ordinary language is, in all of its manifestations, perfectly in order. On the surface, it is fraught with various ambiguities. He says that even 'is' can mislead. It sometimes serves to indicate the possession of a property or characteristic, as in 'He is tall.' At other times it indicates a relation of identity or equality, as in 'Cicero is Tully.' At other times it is used to express existence, as in 'God is (exists)' (T 3.323). This ambiguity leads to fundamental confusions in philosophy (T 3.324). He claims that the only way to avoid such confusions is to employ an unambiguous symbolism, which is one that "obeys the rules of logical grammar—of logical syntax." And although he recognizes that the logical symbolism of both Russell and Frege attempts to exclude such confusions, it does not succeed in eliminating *all* of them (T 3.325).

For Wittgenstein, the logic of ordinary language is hidden beneath the surface. It must be mined. The logical structure of all languages is the same. He claims that "definitions are rules for the translation of one language into another," and that "every correct symbolism must be translatable into every other according to such rules." And he says, "that it is *this* which all have in common." (T 3.343) Ordinary language, he instructs us, "is a part of the human organism and is not less complicated than it." And, for this reason, "from it, it is humanly impossible to gather immediately the logic of language." Ordinary language, he tells us, "disguises the thought; so that from the external form of the clothes one cannot infer the form of the thought they clothe . . . the silent adjustments to understand colloquial language are enormously complicated" (T 4.002).

The *this* of which he speaks in (T 3.343) or the *logic of language* of which he speaks in (T 4.002) is what philosophers today sometimes refer to as "depth grammar." And it is, as we shall eventually see, a basic assumption of the Chomsky/Fodor approach to

50

cognitive science known as "computationalism."

The *Tractatus* Wittgenstein credits Russell with having shown that the apparent logical form of a proposition need not be its real form, and he agrees with Russell that the meanings of words and names are their referents. Frege, as we have already determined, held that all names have sense independent of whether or not they have a referent. Declarative sentences, for him names, have sense or express propositions, and refer to truth-values, the True, or the False. All meaningful sentences, according to Frege, have sense, but some lack reference. Russell and Wittgenstein disagree. They hold that names do not have sense but only reference. But Wittgenstein differs from both Frege and Russell concerning *declarative* sentences. According to Wittgenstein, declarative sentences have *only* sense. They do not refer. But one has to be very careful if one is going to do full justice to Wittgenstein's view of this matter.

At the beginning of the *Tractatus*, Wittgenstein says that the world is the totality of facts, not of things. On his account of the matter, if we can understand the structure of language we can understand reality. The structure of reality is mirrored in language. Although the world is the totality of facts, its substance lies in the objects that comprise facts. The objects are the meanings of the names and words we use to talk about the world. His concept of a name is a technical one, one that he inherits from Russell. According to Russell, all ordinary proper names are disguised descriptions, which, as we have seen, can be eliminated by analysis. Ordinary proper names are different from logically proper names. For Wittgenstein, logically proper names are said to mean or refer to simple objects or particulars, but they do so "only in the nexus of a proposition" (T 3.3). This is how Wittgenstein uses the word 'name.' For Wittgenstein, propositions like "Socrates was the teacher of Plato" are subject to analysis in keeping with Russell's theory of descriptions. Eventually, all such propositions are reducible to what Wittgenstein calls "elementary propositions," which are just concatenations of names for simples. Given that 'a,' 'b,' 'c,' and 'd' are names, and given that the objects a, b, c, and d are concatenated or arranged in the following fashion bcda, the corresponding concatenation of names, 'bcda,' depicts or mirrors reality. The names mean the objects they name. But what about propositional signs or declarative sentences?

Parenthetically, one might very well want to say in opposition to Frege, who we know considered the referents of declarative sentences to be truth-values, that what they refer to are states of affairs. Take, for example, the fact or state of affairs before me at the present moment,

namely, that my favorite coffee mug is on the table in front of me. Call
the mug "Mugomine." Let 'Charles' be the name of the table. About
this state of affairs I can state truly "Mugomine is on Charles." It would
seem to be perfectly correct to say that the statement (use of the
sentence 'Mugomine is on Charles.') in question refers to the particular
state of affairs before me. In summary, there is a sentence composed of
names concatenated in the form A is on B, and not B is on A, that the
sentence in question has a meaning, namely the proposition that
Mugomine is on Charles, and that it has reference to that state of affairs
consisting of Mugomine being on Charles. Had Frege followed this line
of reasoning, rather than legislating that sentences name the objects the
True and the False, no one would ever conclude that unless I were to
reject the principle of substitutivity or distinguish between direct and
indirect reference, my believing that Mugomine is on Charles means
that I believe every true proposition, or that Copernicus believed
every false proposition because he believed that the planetary orbits are
circles. However that may be, Wittgenstein neither thought that
sentences refer to truth-values, nor that they refer to states of affairs.

According to Wittgenstein, as we saw before my parenthetical
remarks, propositional signs or full declarative sentences only have
sense. They do not refer. Accordingly, "only the proposition has sense;
only in the context of a proposition has a name meaning" (T 3.3).[60] He
is not, however, using proposition to mean a thought. A proposition for
him, at the very least an elementary proposition, is the state of affairs or
situation that the sentence concatenates in terms of names. He says,
"What the picture represents is its sense" (T 2.221).[61] According to
Wittgenstein, a "proposition *represents* such and such state of affairs"
(T 4031). "Like a living picture," an elementary proposition "presents
an atomic fact" (T40311).

Unfortunately, when Wittgenstein talks about a proposition, i.e.,
when he uses the expression 'Satz,' he uses it sometimes to mean a
sentence type (as opposed to a sentence token) and sometimes to mean
what other philosophers of the time meant by 'proposition.' And
sometimes he uses it in neither of these ways. Consider the following
inscriptions:

(1) The cat is on the chair.
(2) The cat is on the chair.

Each one of these inscriptions is a sentence token. There are *two* tokens
displayed. But they are both instances of *one* English sentence type,
TY1. Consider now two further inscriptions:

52

(3) Le Chat est sur la chaise.
(4) Upon the chair there is a cat.

(3) and (4) are each tokens of different sentence types, say TY2, and TY3. We now have three sentence types, TY1, TY2, and TY3, two tokens of TY1, and one token each of TY2 and TY3. But there is one thing they all have in common: they express the *same* proposition, or have the same meaning. When he talks about a proposition having a sense as he does in T 3.3, he must surely mean to be talking about a propositional sign or sentence type, because he also says that the sense of a proposition *is* the situation or state of affairs it describes or represents (T 4.031). Unlike Frege, he refused to think of the sense of a sentence as an abstract entity that we all can apprehend. Instead, he regards the sense of a sentence to be a fact or state of affairs. This move, however, seems to have the odd consequence that false propositions represent or describe *negative* facts. Unless, of course, one wants to say that sentence types like 'Bill Clinton is not the present president of the United States,' call it SB, are senseless because they do not describe or represent anything.[62] Wittgenstein would not say this, however. He would say that SB is false. But he also does not want to concede, along with Russell, that there are negative facts.

Wittgenstein's solution to this dilemma *could* be that the sense of the sentence type SB is the situation or state of affairs that *does* obtain, and which renders SB false—presumably, that George W. Bush is the present president of the United States. He does say, "The totality of existing states of affairs also determines which states do not exist" (T. 2.05). However, this interpretation must be tempered by the likelihood that (T 2.05) refers to elementary propositions. Given the fact that for Wittgenstein such sentences as SB are ultimately reducible to elementary ones (T 2.0201), we can for the sake of a meaningful example extend (T 2.05) to include complex propositions like the one conveyed by SB. By doing so, we can resolve the issue regarding negative facts. The sense of SB, that Bill Clinton is not the present president of the United States, is not given any existent status, nor for that matter is any negative proposition.

But as the American philosopher Max Black has pointed out, there are problems with this interpretation that are created by what he says right after (T 2.05): "The existence and non-existence of atomic facts is the reality. (The existence of atomic facts we also call a positive fact, their non-existence a negative fact" (T 2.06). Black attempts to resolve this issue by arguing that Wittgenstein has said, at 2 that a fact is the existence of atomic facts (and here, we notice there is no reference to their non-existence); at 1.1 he said that the world is the totality of facts; taken together, these remarks seem to say that the world consists of nothing but 'positive facts'. That this was Wittgenstein's intention is confirmed by 2.05, with its implication that the sum-total of positive facts (atomic facts) suffices to determine what is not the case.[63]

Black provides an argument to justify his interpretation, which I find convincing, but will not pursue here.[64] If, however, the sense of a positive sentence type is a state of affairs, and the sentence type is a picture of that state of affairs, one very important question remains to be answered: what makes the type a picture of a *specific* state of affairs? In the case of a painting, if it is a true representation of a situation or state of affairs, we can recognize that it is by comparing the picture to the situation. But sentences are more like non-representational paintings. They do not really depict anything.

According to Wittgenstein, "a proposition is a propositional sign in its projective relation to the world" (T 3.12). But what *is* the method of projection? The answer to this question is given in (T 3.11): "The method of projection is the thinking of the sense of the proposition." Now we have an answer to our question. It is *we* who "use the sensibly perceptible sign (sound or written sign, etc) of the proposition as a projection of the possible states of affairs. Here, however, the reference is to sentence tokens rather than sentence types, written signs or sounds are tokens. But this is not surprising, because he is talking about someone using a sentence type with a specific intention. As I read him, what he means to say is something like this: 'The cat is on the chair,' is, whenever I use it to state that a specific cat is on a specific chair, a particular sentence token, and is either a sound or some form of inscription. I can be said to project a possible state of affairs when I do so. The sentence type itself expresses a possible state of affairs, or, what I would refer to as, its standard meaning. My use of it projects an instantiation of the sentence type and assigns reference to its constituent words. So, it is a sentence token that I *use* to depict or describe an actual state of affairs. This suggests to me that what Wittgenstein had in mind is the contextual side of the distinction I previously made between what is meant by some sentence on a particular occasion of use and what it means (contextual versus sentential meaning). What a particular person uses a particular sentence token of a specific sentence type to mean on a particular occasion is an *actual* as opposed to a *possible* statement.

In the passages under consideration, Wittgenstein espouses what can best be described as the *tripartite* theory of meaning, which I described and attributed to the *Tractatus* Wittgenstein in my introduction. According to this theory, symbolic representation is a tripartite arrangement among: (1) a symbol, for example, 'horse', (2) an object of some kind, a horse, and (3) a cognitive process of intending.

Now that we understand that *intention* is an essential ingredient in the method of projection, we are better able to comprehend Wittgenstein's position concerning negative facts. Elizabeth Anscombe explains it by drawing a parallel between pictures and sentences. She points out that "if we 'think the sense of the picture' or of a sentence by correlating its elements with actual objects, we can in fact think in either of *two* ways: namely either as depicting what is the case, or what isn't the case." In the case of a sentence, the correlation is between its words and objects named. About pictures, she claims, "there are two senses which we can 'think' in connection with them." It is, she points out "the very same picture we hold up if we wish to say that *it* holds or that *it* doesn't hold." No other *picture* could be involved: you could not for example make a *picture* of the situation's not existing."[65]

For a picture or proposition to mean, for example, p rather than not p, which for Wittgenstein involves the same picture, a person must intend it one way rather than the other way. We must be careful, however. Remember that we previously entertained the idea that the proposition expressed by 'Bill Clinton is not the present president of the United States' is true because of the truth of the proposition expressed by 'George W. Bush is the present president of the United States.' This would suggest that you *could* picture the situation's not existing, in this case by picturing that Bush is the present president of the United States. But as Anscombe points out, "We must be careful not to confuse *what is not the case* with *what is the case instead of it*; if you tried to make a picture of a situation's *not* existing you would only make a picture of what did exist instead of it."[66]

I want to consider, however, another argument Wittgenstein uses to show that there are no negative facts. In logic, we acknowledge that the denial of the denial of a proposition takes us back to the original proposition. We express this by saying that p and ∼p are logically equivalent. They say the same thing, even though one is an affirmative proposition and the other is a negative one. Wittgenstein says in T 5.44 "And if there was an object called "∼", then "∼∼p" would have to say something other than "p", for the former proposition would treat ∼, the other would not.

The propositions of logic are, for the early Wittgenstein, *tautologies* (an expression that Wittgenstein was the first to use), or so-called "necessary truths." They are propositions expressed by sentences like: 'Nothing is both round and square at the same time,' 'Triangles are three-sided figures,' and 'Brown is a color.' The tradition in philosophy, prior to Wittgenstein, claims that denying a tautology involves contradicting oneself. To say that something is round is to say that it is *not* square, so claiming that something is both round and square amounts to saying that something is both round and not round. Denying that a triangle is three-sided, asserts that a three-sided figure is *not* a three-sided figure. To deny that brown is a color is to say that what is a color is *not* a color. The same traditional account claims that denials of tautologies are contradictions. They are necessarily false, and their denials are necessarily true—tautologies.

According to Wittgenstein, however, tautologies are *limiting* or "degenerate" cases, and the same is true of contradictions. A tautology has the largest possible number of independent truth-conditions in that it has *all* of them. A contradiction has the smallest number of truth-conditions in that it has *none*. All truth-functions can be arranged in a series of propositions with steadily increasing ranges, in such a way that a tautology appears as the limit or the upper bound of the series (T 5.101). Unlike significant propositions, a tautology says nothing (T4.461), has no truth conditions (T 4.461), and is senseless, i.e., it is not a picture of reality (T 4.462). Elsewhere, Wittgenstein compares a tautology to a wheel running idly in a mechanism of cogwheels, and a contradiction to one that has jammed and goes nowhere. Max Black utilizes a maze tracing game to explain Wittgenstein's view of tautologies and contradictions. In a maze tracing game, a player has to trace a pathway through the maze from the beginning point to the end point. An extreme case would be one in which only one path is possible, and a degenerate case would be one in which there is no exit. The former explicates what it is to be a tautology, the latter a contradiction.[67]

When Wittgenstein says that tautologies and contradictions are senseless, he does not mean that they are meaningless, but rather that they do not describe any existing state of affairs. Tautologies do not reflect or depict, as do empirical propositions, a possible mode of connection to objects. They have no dependence upon anything external to them. The same is true of contradictions. Wittgenstein's theory of tautology and contradiction avoids the metaphysical and misleading ideas of the past. Much of the mystery of necessary truths is eliminated.

The most significant task that remains for Wittgenstein to accomplish is the elimination of the *Tractatus* myth that ordinary language has an essence and is governed by fixed rules. This task he achieves in the *Investigations*. There he argues that the essence of language is—*as a matter of fact*—not fixed and eternal. But even more significant is his argument that—*as a matter of logic*—its essence *cannot* be fixed. Language, according to the later Wittgenstein, is organic, not a mechanical contrivance. Its rules are neither rigid nor determinant. I would add that its essence lies in the fact that it allows one always to ignore differences where differences make *no* difference. And perhaps that is reason enough to conclude that it more closely approximates the *ideal* than does any other form of language. I will pursue this matter further in the next chapter.

So far, I have only addressed the issue concerning meaning as referring. One might have gotten the impression from what has been covered thus far that there is no difference between a theory of meaning as reference and a theory of reference. There is, however, a distinction between meaning as reference and meaning as truth-conditions, and I will devote chapter 4 to this topic.

---

[1] Frege (1879)

[2] Frege (1892) p. 85.

[3] The text I am quoting from translates *Sinn* with the word 'sense' and *Bedeutung* with 'nominatum.' Most translators translate 'Sinn' as 'sense,' but some translate it as 'meaning.' 'Bedeutung' is usually translated as 'reference.'

[4] Ibid., n. 2, p. 86.

[5] Ibid., p. 89.

[6] We are actually quoting a translation of his words.

[7] I will follow the custom of referring to this kind of discourse as "oblique discourse."

[8] Ibid., p. 91.

[9] This is a view we will again encounter when we explicate Strawson's views concerning meaning and referring.

[10] Ibid., pp.91-92.

[11] Linsky (1967) p. 25.

[12] Russell (1922) pp. 7-8.

[13] Ibid., p. 8.

[14] Ibid., pp. 8-9.

[15] Russell (1918) pp. 182-183.

[16] Here again Russell seems to be confusing "facts" with the expression of them through language. Descriptions are linguistic entities; facts are what are described.

[17] Russell (1918) p. 191.

[18] Gödel (1944) p. 127.

[19] Russell (1918) pp. 191-192.

[20] Ibid., p. 196.

[21] Ibid., pp. 198-200.

[22] Ibid., pp. 203-215.

[23] Russell (1918) p.260.

[24] Ibid., pp. 260-262.

[25] Ibid., pp. 262-263.

[26] Russell (1910) p. 38-39.

[27] This is in contrast to the "ramified theory of types" that necessitated the introduction of the principle of reducibility, and that gave rise to difficulties which we shall not explore. The reader interested in this issue should start with Reichenbach (1944) pp. 38- 39.

[28] Russell (1918) pp. 264.

[29] Tarski, A. "The concept of Truth in Formalized Languages," in *Logic Semantics and Metamathematics*, pp. 152-278.

[30] Reichenbach, H. (1944) p. 39.

[31] Wittgenstein, L. (1922) *Tractatus Logico Philosophicus* (London: Routledge & Kegan Paul. LTD.) p. 23.

[32] Urmson (1956) p. 7.

[33] Russell (1963) p. 13.

[34] Russell (1905) p. 106 n. 9.

[35] Ibid., p. 107.

[36] Linsky (1967) p. 59.

[37] Russell's statement of the puzzles suffers somewhat by his lack of precision regarding the concepts *sentence, proposition,* and *statement.* In my statement of the puzzles, I endeavor to use the proper word for the entity in question. Our focus here should be upon a sentence, not a proposition or a statement, the former being simply the standard meaning of a given sentence, and the latter being the use of a particular sentence on a particular occasion by a particular speaker. For a discussion of these concepts, see Odell (1984) pp. 221-227.

[38] Russell talks about true propositions, but as Strawson has demonstrated in "On Referring," truth is properly a predicate of statements, not propositions. To be precise, (1) should be read as "Sentence (a), when used with its standard meaning, makes a true statement".

[39] In defense of this notion, one might argue that when we reveal to children that Santa Claus is a mythical personage we are as likely to assert that there is no such thing as Santa Claus as we are to assert that he does not exist.

[40] For Russell, this is to say that they express the same proposition. But to put the matter properly, what should be said is that they are both commonly used to make the same statement.

[41] Russell (1905) p. 108.

[42] Russell (1910) p. 66.

[43] Russell (1905) pp. 110-113.

[44] Russell (1905) p.111.

[45] What he should have said is that if these two sentences were used with their standard meanings to make statements, both statements would have to be false.

[46] For Russell, a logically proper name is used to name what is momentarily present. So, it would be redundant to assert that it exists, and contradictory to deny its existence.

[47] A fact recognized some time ago by L. Linsky (1967) p.14.

[48] Alston (1964) p.2.

[49] Alston (1964) p.2.

[50] Ryle (1949) pp. 16-18.

[51] Linsky (1967) p. 13.

[52] Chisholm (1960) p. 6.

[53] Ibid., p. 13.

[54] Ibid., p. 15.

[55] Meinong (1904) pp. 83-86.

[56] Ibid., p.16. Also see Meinong (1904) p. 86.

[57] Ibid., p.16.

[58] Meinong (1904) p. 82-83.

[59] In modal logic, the former is symbolized as '◊' and 'ﻟ' symbolizes the latter.

[60] According to Wittgenstein, the ideas he expresses in the *Tractatus* follow an order of presentation schema such that the number he assigns to each paragraph indicates its "logical importance." He begins with a passage numbered 1, and ends with 7, so that 4 is more important than 3, and 3.3 is more important than 3.31, but less important than 3.2. Most commentators, however, do not think that he meant this numbering series to be taken literally.

[61] Here and throughout my discussion of Wittgenstein's views I

will abbreviate 'Tractatus' with 'T.'
[62] See Pitcher (1964) pp.44-53.
[63] Black (1964) p.71.
[64] Ibid. p.71.
[65] Anscombe (1959) p. 69.
[66] Ibid., pp. 69-70.
[67] Black (1964) p. 230

2
Meaning as Use

Wittgenstein of the Philosophical Investigations

Wittgenstein eventually realized that his *Tractatus* views were fundamentally mistaken. He recognized his mistake to be that of taking the *essence* of language to be exemplified by *one* among its many *uses*. One use of language was featured at the expense of all the others. Or, to put the point in terms of one of the featured and original concepts of the *Investigations*, one *language-game* was mistakenly assumed to reflect the very essence of language. That language-game is referring. In the *Tractatus* he assumed that the essence of a name is its referent and the essence of a proposition is to describe the world. Here is what Wittgenstein says early on in the *Investigations*:

> But how many kinds of sentence are there? Say assertion, question, and command?—There are *countless* kinds: countless different kinds of use of what we call "symbols", "words", "sentences". And this multiplicity is not something fixed, given once for all; but new types of language, new language-games, as we may say, come into existence, and others become obsolete and get forgotten.[1]

The term 'language-game' is, according to Wittgenstein, "meant to bring into prominence the fact that the *speaking* of language is part of an activity, or of a form of life." He illustrates the multiplicity of language games by examples: giving orders and obeying them; describing objects; making up and telling stories; reporting on events; formulating and testing hypotheses; playing a role in a movie or a play; translating from a given language into another language; praying;

offering greetings; etc.[2] Each of these uses of language, or language games, is governed by distinctive rules.

Wittgenstein compares these various kinds of use that language has with various tools, like hammers, files, saws, planes, and glue pots. All have different uses, and the group cannot be characterized to have an essence, unless, of course, one says something like the various tools in the toolbox are all used to modify something. But as Wittgenstein asks "Would anything be gained by this assimilation of expressions?" Moreover, much important information concerning difference of use would be lost or distorted. Still, as Wittgenstein acknowledges, the critic will not be so easily silenced. She or he may complain that, although Wittgenstein talks about all sorts of language games, he has nowhere said what the *essence* of a language game is, even though this is what Wittgenstein himself pursued in the *Tractatus*. Wittgenstein's reply is that the various language games we play (like the various tools in the carpenter's toolbox) "have no one thing in common which makes us use the same word for all, . . . they are *related* to one another in many different ways." Wittgenstein explains what he means in passage 66, which is one of the most important and influential passages in the *Investigations*:

> Consider for example the proceedings we call "games". I mean board-games, card-games, ball-games, Olympic games, and so on. What is common to them all?—Don't say: "There *must* be something common, or they would not be called 'games' "—but *look and see* whether there is anything common to all.—For if you look at them you will not see something that is common to *all*, but, similarities, relationships, and a whole series of them at that . . . And the result of this examination is: we see a complicated network of similarities overlapping and criss-crossing: sometimes overall similarities, sometimes similarities of detail.[3]

Wittgenstein refers to these similarities in paragraph 67 as "family resemblances." He can "think of no better expression to characterize these similarities . . . for the various resemblances between members of a family: build, features, colour of eyes, gait, temperament, etc. etc. overlap and criss-cross in the same way."[4] No one characteristic or set of characteristics is present in all family members.

An important implication of Wittgenstein's notion of the family resemblance nature of many natural language expressions is that these expressions are not *as a matter of empirical fact* governed by *necessary* and *sufficient* conditions. Instead, such expressions are employed on the basis of over-lapping and criss-crossing sets of characteristics, no one of which, or any set of which, is both necessary and sufficient.

Not only do these passages have important relevance to our discussion of meaning, they also have considerable significance as regards the nature of philosophy. For centuries philosophers have attempted to understand the essence of goodness, knowledge, justice, beauty, etc. But, according to the Wittgenstein of the *Investigations*, this is a futile pursuit, even though he was himself engaged in it in the *Tractatus*. Many of the most important expressions of philosophy, including 'goodness,' 'knowledge,' 'justice,' 'beauty,' etc., are family resemblance expressions. They do not have fixed meanings. So, it is useless to search for them!

This conclusion is not acceptable to many philosophers. They counter Wittgenstein's attack on the purity of philosophical expressions or concepts by arguing that even if Wittgenstein is right as regards the family resemblance nature of such expressions as, 'goodness,' 'knowledge,' 'justice,' 'beauty,' etc., as they are employed in ordinary language, it is the philosopher's responsibility to rectify this situation. They claim, in opposition to Wittgenstein, that the essential task of philosophy is to overcome the shortcoming of ordinary language by fixing the meanings of these expressions.

Wittgenstein is prepared for this attack, however. Consider what he says a few passages later:

> I say "There is a chair." What if I go up to it, meaning to fetch it, and it suddenly disappears from sight?—"So it wasn't a chair, but some kind of illusion."—But in a few moments, we see it again, and are able to touch it and so on.—"So the chair was there after all and its disappearance was some kind of illusion."—But suppose after a time it disappears again—or seems to disappear. What are we to say now? Have you rules ready for such cases—rules saying whether one may use the word "chair" to include this kind of thing.[5]

His point here is quite different from his point concerning the family resemblance nature of many ordinary language expressions. What he wants us to understand now is that it is *not logically possible* to do what he tried so hard to do in the *Tractatus*, namely, to *fix* the meaning of empirical expressions, and to establish that in order for a natural language to accomplish its ends it must ultimately be specifiable in terms of fixed semantic and syntactical rules. He wants us to understand that *no* empirical term's meaning can be fixed, not even mundane expressions like 'chair.' If he is right, then the idea that the philosopher can overcome the deficiencies of ordinary language by specifying conditions both necessary and sufficient for philosophy's principal expressions is fundamentally mistaken.

The Austrian philosopher Friedrich Waismann, who was admittedly influenced by Wittgenstein, wrote an important paper entitled "Verifiability," in which he elaborated on the kind of point Wittgenstein makes with the chair example, and introduced the expression *'open texture'* to refer to Wittgenstein's idea.[6] On the basis of what Wittgenstein and Waismann maintain, a proof can be constructed to show that all empirical terms are open textured, i. e., it is impossible to fix their meanings. I will postpone, however, the production of this proof until I cover Carnap's verificationist theory of meaning, which I will do in Chapter Three.[7]

Instead of *theorizing* about *meaning*, we should, according to Wittgenstein, focus on *use*. He claims that inattention to the details of actual word usage has produced theorizing based on too few examples. And this has led philosophers to formulate pseudo-questions. Their attempts to answer these questions have produced solutions that create further puzzles. He claims that theorizing is *not* the proper role of philosophers, that we should not offer any theories. He claims that we should instead perform only a critical function, which he describes as assembling facts that dispute philosophical theorizing. Consider the following passages from the *Investigations*:

> There must not be anything hypothetical in our considerations . . . problems are solved, not by giving new information, but by arranging what we have always known. (passage 109)

> The work of the philosopher consists in assembling reminders for a particular purpose. (passage 127)

> Where does our investigation get its importance from, since it seems only to destroy everything interesting, that is, all that is great and important? . . . What we are destroying is nothing but houses of cards and we are clearing up the ground of language on which they stand. (passage 118)[8]

Traditional philosophy, according to the later Wittgenstein, is at the core an ill-conceived discipline which can never succeed because the problems it raises, the questions it poses, are pseudo-problems and pseudo-questions. They cannot, he claims, *by their very nature* be solved; they can only be dissolved, and their dissolution depends on recognizing them for what they are. I will say more about this aspect of Wittgenstein's philosophy later in this chapter.

Wittgenstein, who as we determined in the last chapter held a version of the tripartite theory of meaning in the *Tractatus*, eventually discerned that the irresolvable set of issues concerning mental representation (intention) survives *only* because an essential ingredient is left out of the recipe. That ingredient is *cultural* or *social* context. An individual's meaning or intending something by a symbol or word is as much or more an observable and outer process as it is a psychological or neural event. What an expression means can only be fully explained by introducing into its explanation external rules of acting or the *practices* formulated by these rules.

What Wittgenstein wants us to understand is that: (1) human beings as members of society engage in a complex series of actions and practices, one constituent of which is language use; (2) these actions and practices consist in behaving in various ways under various circumstances; and (3) these practices cannot be understood without taking into account the actual circumstances that can or could obtain.

The arguments Wittgenstein utilizes in the *Investigations* to repudiate the tripartite theory of meaning and to promote the importance of context in the determination of linguistic meaning, are scattered throughout much of the *Investigations*. They can, however, be encapsulated, and represented by a couple of analogies.

Using the tripartite model to clarify symbolic representation is like trying to comprehend how a clock tells the correct time by focusing on the clock itself, its internal parts, the face with its numerals and hands. Such an account cannot explain how it is *now* five o'clock in Washington, D.C. but not in San Francisco. It forces one to postulate the existence of some internal *something* other than the gears, batteries etc., which explains that it is somehow, for example, five o'clock—something independent of location and surroundings. One cannot, however, resolve the paradox of the same clock being both right and wrong at one and the same time, right *here* and *now*, unless of course one takes into account the relevance of context. One must make the *here* and *now* part of the solution, rather than part of the problem.[9] Meaning is a function of contextual factors, factors unaccounted for in the tripartite model.

The potency of the force that conventions exert upon us tends to elude us. We assume that the conventional aspects surrounding a specific phenomenon can be set aside and that the phenomenon in question can be understood in itself. But consider what would be the implications of this illusion with respect to monetary value.

Monetary value is in no way attributable to the green-colored, portrait-covered paper we carry in our wallets and purses. To refer to the "greenbacks" we spend, save, invest, and bequeath to our survivors as "currency" is to assign monetary value to them. But that value is obviously not predicated on the *properties* or *characteristics* possessed by these pieces of green paper. Instead, it is a function of *convention*. If one were to talk about currency the way philosophers talk about meaning, by means of a tripartite model, the analog would work out like this: green bits of paper, their value, and a cognitive process of intending these values by those bills. Such a model cannot fail to produce misunderstanding. It would lead to questions like: how can these bills, which would buy so much in 1951, have so little value today? Have our intentions changed so much? The paper is the same! So is the color of the ink!

Obviously, we cannot talk of the monetary value of these green pieces of paper unless we take into account the *context* surrounding their use. The fluctuating market, supply and demand, failing governments, etc., all play an essential role in the determination of monetary value. A parallel observation regarding meaning must be recognized and emphasized if we are to resolve the kinds of problems and paradoxes which philosophers have generated. Meaning is a function of contextual factors, factors unaccounted for in the tripartite model.

As the value of currency is a constantly fluctuating phenomenon, so are the meanings of words, sentences, statements, etc. Currency has no intrinsic value. It has only conventional value. The last person on earth would only think that the money he has in his wallet has value if he fails to appreciate his situation. Treating word, phrase, or sentence meaning as if it were something which could be understood or explained in general, without reference to context of use, and then lamenting that meaning is "inscrutable" or otherwise indeterminate, as some philosophers (notably W.V.O. Quine) have done, leads one to adopt either a cautionary or skeptical attitude regarding our ability to understand one another. And doing so is no more justifiable than trying to establish the "real" or actual value of the dollar without taking into account the daily exchange rate or the current rate of inflation.

According to Wittgenstein, any sentence in a natural language can be said to have a meaning translatable across languages. But to know the meaning of a given sentence is not to grasp some specifiable thing that it always means. Rather, it is to understand that it has numerous correct uses, some of which are incompatible with others. 'That person has on a blue shirt' could not, for example, be used to say something true of me at the moment, but it would be true if used to refer to my wife. To understand the meaning of a sentence is, for Wittgenstein, to understand those conventions that determine its correct uses. Wittgenstein makes this kind of point quite forcefully and succinctly in the following passage:

> Make the following experiment: *say* "It's cold here" and *mean:* It's warm here". Can you do it? And what are you doing as you do it? And is there only one way of doing it?[10]

Wittgenstein's later philosophy has had considerable influence on the direction philosophy has taken. I will begin my examination of that influence by considering the work of P. F. Strawson. I will then examine the work of J. L. Austin and of John Searle. But first, we need to understand that it is one thing to claim that meaning is somehow definable in terms of or *is identical* somehow with use, and it is another thing to claim that meaning is somehow a *function* of use. Wittgenstein's view is the latter one, Austin's and Searle's, the former. Strawson sides with Wittgenstein and criticizes Russell's theory of descriptions for failing to appreciate the importance of use.

Strawson

Strawson claimed in 1950 that Russell's theory of descriptions was still widely accepted among logicians "as giving a correct account of the *use* of such expressions [definite descriptions] in ordinary language."[11] But, according to Strawson, "this theory, so regarded, embodies some fundamental mistakes."[12]

As I pointed out previously, Russell often uses the words 'sentence' and 'proposition' interchangeably. He also sometimes uses them to mark a difference between a symbolic expression and what it expresses, which is what most philosophers, Frege included, consider a proposition to be. According to Strawson, Russell's fundamental mistake is that he fails to distinguish a sentence (or what it means, i.e., a proposition) from the *use* of a sentence, on a particular occasion, by a particular person.[13] It is, according to Strawson, only such uses— statements—which can be said to be either true or false. To put it somewhat differently, the predicates "is true" and "is false" can only be attributed to *statements,* not to sentences or propositions. To illustrate his objection, Strawson focuses on the puzzle concerning the present king of France. He asks us to consider the sentence, 'The present king of France is wise,' and to recognize that:

> if one man uttered it in the reign of Louis XIV and another man uttered it in the reign of Louis XV, it would be natural to say (to assume) that they were respectively talking about different people; and it might be held that the first man, in using the sentence, made a true assertion, while the second man, using the same sentence, made a false assertion. If on the other hand two different men uttered the sentence simultaneously . . . during the reign of Louis IV it would be natural to say (assume) that they were both talking about the same person, and, in that case, in using the sentence, they *must* either both have made a true assertion or both have made a false assertion.[14]

In opposition to Russell, Strawson wants us to understand that *meaning* is a function of sentences like 'The present king of France is wise' and expressions like 'the present king of France,' while *referring and truth or falsity* are functions of the *uses* of such sentences or expressions. He claims that providing the meaning of an expression is providing "*general directions* for its use to refer to or to mention particular objects or persons," and that providing the "meaning of a sentence is to give general *directions* for its use in making true or false assertions." For Strawson, whether or not a sentence or an expression has a meaning is irrelevant to the question of whether "the sentence, *uttered on a particular occasion*, is, on that occasion, being used to make a true-or-false assertion or not, or of whether the expression is, on that occasion, being used to refer to, or mention, anything at all."[15]

Strawson argues that Russell's confusion on these matters led him to mistakenly conclude that the relation that holds between the sentence 'The present king of France is wise,' or the proposition it expresses, and the following sentence, is *entailment*:

> (1) There exists one and only one thing which is at present king of France.

If (1) were *entailed* by 'The present king of France is wise,' call it S, it would have to follow that when (1) is false, S must also be false. According to Strawson, the relation that actually obtains between S and (1) is *presupposition,* which he defines as follows: To say that S presupposes (1) is to say that (1) must be true for S to be either true or false. If (1) is false, then S is to be regarded as neither true nor false.

Strawson's point can best be appreciated if you ask yourself what would be the right response to make if I were to ask you if the leprechaun in your pocket has on a green hat. The proper response would not be either that he did or that he did not, but rather that the question is inappropriate because there is no leprechaun in your pocket. On Strawson's account, it is a mistake to conclude, as did Russell, that both S and not S (where the description 'the present king of France' is accorded a primary occurrence) are false because (1) is false. They are instead, for Strawson, neither true nor false. They are truth-valueless. On Strawson's account some statements are true, some are false, and some are truth-valueless. Remember what Frege said about the sentence about Odysseus. What he said was that since it is quite possible that Odysseus did not exist, the sentence fails to refer to either the True or the False. That is, at least as far as I can tell, pragmatically speaking, to say in a somewhat different way just what Strawson says.

A defender of Russell will most likely argue that Russell, like most logicians, held that all propositions are either true or false, that this is a matter of definition for Russell, and thus that Strawson, who is talking about assertions or statements, is guilty of comparing apples to oranges.[16] In *Referring*, L. Linsky illustrates this defense thus:

> Now, of course, no one refutes Euclidean geometry by pointing out that the triangle on the blackboard has an angle sum of more than 180^0 when measured with the most accurate instruments. Similarly, we must distinguish between the logical calculus, the propositions which are the values of its variables and the utterances, sayings, or statements which people produce in their everyday use of language. Just as geometry remains unrefuted by measurements of physical triangles, so logic is not refuted by the discovery that there are statements which we would not call either true or false, but (say) exaggerated, or vague, or inaccurate. But this is exactly what Strawson does when he criticizes Russellian logic.[17]

Another way of putting this kind of defense of Russell's theory is to insist, as so many contemporary philosophers do, on the distinction between *semantics* and *pragmatics*. Semantics is the study of the truth conditions for sentences, and pragmatics is the study of the actual employment of sentences by particular users in various contexts. Russell can be regarded as a semanticist, Strawson as a pragmaticist. This issue does not end here, however, as not every contemporary philosopher is satisfied with the distinction between semantics and

69

pragmatics, especially in so far as those who live by this distinction tend to look down their formalistic noses at what they regard as the plebeian pursuit of the unkempt distinctions of ordinary language.[18]

I will return to this issue when I discuss the later Wittgenstein's perspective on the controversy surrounding the paradoxical consequences that accrue if one takes either an entailment or a presupposition view concerning the relation between S and (1). I want now to consider some other problems with Strawson's approach, and to point out a distinct advantage of Russell's theory of descriptions over Strawson's presupposition theory.

In his *Introduction to Logical Theory*, Strawson extends his notion of presupposition to the four standard forms of classical or Aristotelian logic: the A form, "All S is P;" The E form, "No S is P;" the I form, "Some S is P;" and the O form, "Some S is not P." The truth of the existence condition is said by him to be a necessary condition "not of truth simply but of the truth or falsity of such statements."[19] According to Strawson's presupposition theory, if one asserts the following E form sentence, what one would be asserting is neither true nor false because the subject term denotes a non-existent object:

(E) No Leprechauns are red-hat wearers.

But according to both Aristotelian and modern logic, this sentence is by conversion said to be logically equivalent to:

(CE) No red-hat wearers are Leprechauns.

Since the presupposition condition is satisfied for (CE), namely, red-hat wearers do exist, it would seem that stating it would be to state what is either true or false. But then how can this be, since (E) and (CE) are logically equivalent statements?

What Strawson does to avoid this kind of objection is to preface all traditional inferences like conversion with the proviso "that the statements concerned *are* either true or false." In other words, when *both* sentences are used to make statements having truth-values, then relations like conversion can be said to yield those consequences asserted by tradition to be validly inferable.

But as Linsky has pointed out, this course of action renders Strawson's view compatible with Russell's. According to Linsky:

Let us assume that S presupposes S' [S stands for a sentence 'The king of France is wise,' and S' stands for 'there is one and only

70

one thing that is king of France.'] What this means is that from the premise that S has a truth-value, it follows that S' is true. But if S is true, it follows that S has a truth-value. Therefore, if S is true, it follows that S' is true. But S is true if, and only if, the king of France is wise, and S' is true if, and only if, one, and only one, person is king of France. Therefore the statement that the king of France is wise entails the statement that one, and only one, person is king of France.[20]

Strawson could attempt to sidestep Linsky's objection, and counter my objection concerning the relation of conversion, by insisting that the presupposition condition must be met for *both* the subject and the predicate term for the relation of conversion to be valid. But how, Linsky would counter, does this condition differ from assuming that the statements concerned are either true or false, which is Russell's position? In other words, if Strawson responds this way, his objection to Russell is no longer significant.

I, on the other hand, will respond by focusing attention on the following sentence:

No Saturn XXX rockets are being designed by NASA to place a manned United States spacecraft on Uranus.

Suppose someone has misinformed members of the press that NASA has in fact designed a rocket for placing a manned United States spacecraft on Uranus. Suppose further that there are *no* Saturn XXX rockets, and in fact *no* rockets of any description are being designed to place such a spacecraft on Uranus. For these reasons, the presupposition condition is not satisfied for either the subject term or the predicate term. Yet, it is clear that the above sentence could be used to assert a true statement. The director of NASA might well use it in the process of a news conference intended to dispel the rumors in question. He might very well say:

Gentlemen and ladies, of the press I wish to make a statement, and I assure you that what I am about to say is true. Saturn XXX rockets are not being designed to land a manned United States spacecraft on Uranus.[21]

What we have is a case where the presupposition condition is not satisfied for either the subject or the predicate term, and we have a paradigm case of what it is to make a statement which would be, under these imagined circumstances, true.

This example would prevent Strawson from avoiding the difficulty which the leprechaun case poses for his theory by requiring that both terms meet the presupposition condition. Also, and more importantly, it reveals that there are cases where the presupposition condition is not satisfied for the subject term, and yet one can succeed in making a true statement or, depending on the circumstances, a false one. In addition, it reveals a distinct advantage of Russell's theory over Strawson's.

Russell's analysis of the NASA official's statement would not only capture what the official wishes to state, but would also captures the fact that it is true, and would avoid the mistaken idea that it is neither true nor false. Russell's analysis would interpret the sentence used by the NASA official to be the *denial* of the following existential proposition:

(E) There exists at least one thing which is both a Saturn XXX rocket and a rocket being planned to land a United States spacecraft on Uranus.

(E) clearly expresses the rumor the official wants to dispel. Its denial on Russell's analysis is:

(not E) Nothing is both a Saturn XXX rocket, and a rocket being planned to land a United States spacecraft on Uranus.

Since (not E) is not about an existent anything, the question of whether or not Strawson's presupposition condition is met is irrelevant. It is about two predicates "is a Saturn XXX rocket," and "is a rocket being planned to land a United States spacecraft on Uranus." What it says is that nothing exists which instantiates both.

Previously I discussed Linsky's use of the analogy between formal logic and geometry in his rebuttal of Strawson's critique of Russell, and I linked this analogy to the distinction between semantics and pragmatics. No account of the controversy between Strawson and Russell would be complete without an explanation of Keith Donnellan's critique of both Russell and Strawson, and especially since it is linked to and has fortified the distinction between semantics and pragmatics.

The American philosopher Keith Donnellan in a paper he published in 1966, "Reference and Definite Descriptions," argues that Russell and Strawson are both mistaken because they overlook the distinction between *referential* and *attributive* uses of descriptive phrases. According to Donnellan:

> A speaker who uses a definite description attributively in an assertion states something about whoever or whatever is the so-and-so. A speaker who uses a definite description referentially in an assertion, on the other hand, uses the description to enable his audience to pick out whom or what he is talking about and states something about that person or thing.[22]

Donnellan illustrates the distinction in question by having the reader consider the sentence 'Smith's murderer is insane.' If someone uses the sentence in question as a comment on the brutality of the murder, he is, according to Donnellan, making an attributive use of the definite description. He contrasts this use of the sentence in question with the kind of case where it is used with the understanding that the audience knows who Smith's murderer is (as they would if they made up the audience in the murder trial of Smith's killer), and the murderer is acting oddly. In such a case as this, we are, according to Donnellan, using the description in question referentially.

An attributive use of a definite description can be said to say something about whomever or whatever is being referred to, and is consistent with Russell's analysis of definite descriptions. When an expression is used referentially, however, it is meant to single someone or some thing out, but may not actually describe that thing. Donnellan criticizes Russell for ignoring the referential use. He criticizes Strawson for: (1) ignoring the attributive use, and (2) having mistakenly held that a referential use of a definite description can only occur if the description is true of the object referred to. He uses an example from Linsky to illustrate his second criticism of Strawson.

Linsky claims that a speaker might *use* the sentence 'Her husband is kind to her' to refer to someone the speaker *took* to be a spinster's husband. He concedes to Strawson that this use of the sentence would be neither true nor false, because it presupposes that the lady has a husband, which she does not. Linsky claims, however, that this example "does refute Strawson's thesis that if the presupposition of existence is not satisfied, the speaker has failed to refer. Here that presupposition is false, but still the speaker has referred to someone, namely, the man mistakenly taken to be her husband. "[23]

Donnellan is not satisfied with Linsky's concession to Strawson that this use of the sentence 'Her husband is kind to her' is neither true nor false. He claims that Linsky's concession would be true only if the definite description is taken *attributively*. But if we consider it as used *referentially*, Donnellan would not agree with Linsky, because "the man the speaker referred to may indeed be kind to the spinster; the speaker may have said something true about that man."[24]

The upshot of Donnellan's distinction is that we should distinguish between the reference of the terms that we use and the speaker's reference, between the semantic content of language and the ways that speakers use/misuse language. Or, in other words, we must distinguish between semantics and pragmatics.

Although the semantics/pragmatics distinction has enjoyed venerable status in contemporary philosophy, most followers of Wittgenstein do not honor or even respect it. In fact, they argue that this distinction is little more than a ploy used by philosophers to shelter their theories from the kind of critique the later Wittgenstein launched against his own, as well as Russell's, earlier endeavors.

Like Russell, the Wittgenstein of the *Tractatus* attempted to solve philosophical problems through the logical analysis of language. The later Wittgenstein regards this approach to be just another misguided effort in a long series of misguided efforts characteristic of traditional philosophy. Wittgenstein argues that philosophers participate in a profession in which constant failure is not only accepted, but also misconstrued. Philosophers justify their enterprise by claiming that its lack of success is simply testimony to the inherent difficulty characteristic of the kind of problems with which it deals. A Rubik's cube presents us with a difficult but solvable problem. Philosophical puzzles likewise frustrate and challenge us. But, unlike the Rubik's cube, any hope that solutions for these puzzles will be forthcoming is, according to Wittgenstein, ill-founded—not because there is *no* hope of discovering solutions to these problems, but rather because there is *only* hope. Philosophers are like people lost in a vast but circular maze from which there is no exit except back through the original entrance. For them, progress is only the illusion of progress.[25]

The ancient Greek philosophers, most conspicuously Plato, sought to understand the essence of things. In contemporary terms, they tried to state the characteristic or set of characteristics that are both necessary and sufficient for the correct application of words to things. The primary reason why some philosophers continue to string along with Plato is that many natural language terms are what I referred to in the introduction as *formal abbreviators*. Consider, for example, natural kind terms like 'gray seal,' 'cormorant,' and 'broccoli.' These terms and those terms we use to refer to sub-species of our own design, for example, 'German Shepherd,' 'Black Angus,' and 'Thoroughbred,' as well as those terms we use to refer to manufactured items, for example, '1968 Mercedes Benz 250,' 'Stradivarius,' and 'Smith and Wesson 38 special,' are all used to refer to classes of things, the members of which exhibit few individual differences. And so are formal abbreviators. Individual members of these various classes are extremely difficult to differentiate from other members of the same class. In the case of manufactured items, color can be a help, but only so long as we are just concerned with differentiating between individuals of different color. Many of us have had the experience of returning to a parking lot and trying to unlock the door of a car which is not our own, but one of the same make, model, year and color. Manufactured items exemplify best the realist's ideal. Plato uses the word 'bed' as one of his examples. Athenian beds must have been boringly similar to one another! Unfortunately, for the platonic or realist's account, not only are many terms *not* formal abbreviators, but those terms of most interest to philosophers, for example, 'knowing,' 'believing,' 'meaning,' 'beauty,' and 'good' are *family abbreviators*, the meanings of which cannot be fixed.

Wittgenstein rejects the idea that natural language deceives us. It is not in need of refinement or replacement by a language like those constructed by Russell and Frege, and ultimately inspired by Plato—a so-called "ideal" language. Instead it is the misuse of natural language by philosophers which creates pseudo-problems, problems which can only be resolved by allowing natural language to work as it is meant to work. The later Wittgenstein provides us with a unique perspective from which to view the kind of philosophical perplexity he and Russell expressed in their earlier joint endeavors. He does not enter into the fray. He does not attempt to provide solutions to philosophical problems. He is not, as some characterize him, a verificationist, a behaviorist, a nominalist, or an "ist" of any sort.

Wittgenstein's later philosophy is meant to be an *exposé* of skepticism, realism, nominalism, idealism, cognitivism, and all the other venerated "isms" of philosophy. Ultimately, the problems which philosophy attempts to solve, the problems which dictate choosing between unsatisfactory alternatives, realism vs. nominalism, phenomenalism vs. the causal theory, skepticism vs. phenomenalism, behaviorism vs. cognitivism, reference theories of meaning vs. use theories of meaning, etc., are for Wittgenstein, conjurer's tricks, brilliant sleights of hand.

Few philosophers are happy with Wittgenstein's view of philosophy, especially those of us who have been, or remain, faithful to Plato and his companions on the historical journey that is traditional philosophy. We cannot believe our ears. This guy must be out of his mind! When it was first revealed that the world was round, no one could accept it. The commonplace response to this announcement was "That's crazy; you're out of your mind; just open your eyes and look; isn't it obviously flat?" Wittgenstein would counter such disbelief by questioning the question. He would ask, "But how would it look if it were round?"

Many philosophers remain unconvinced by Wittgenstein. They claim that the Wittgensteinian perspective has not been proven to be the case, that Wittgenstein does not offer any deductively valid arguments for his conclusions. But he does provide grounds sufficient both to establish the reasonableness of his own perspective and to render suspect the perspectives of the opposition.

Let me now illustrate how I think Wittgenstein would approach the disagreement between Strawson and Russell. Consider again the following sentences:

(a) Some creatures of mythology are centaurs.

(b) Some creatures of mythology are not centaurs.[26]

According to Russell, we understand these sentences and our understanding of them, their propositional content, can be expressed as:

(a') There exists at least one x such that it is both a creature of mythology and a centaur.

(b') There exists at least one x such that it is both a creature of mythology and a non-centaur.

According to Russell's theory, both of these sentences express *false* propositions, because creatures of mythology do not exist. Strawson would agree that there are no creatures of mythology, but his presupposition theory would dictate that neither assertion *is either true or false.*

Common usage is, however, inconsistent with both of these views. Both (a) and (b) are, we want to insist, *true.* This insistence is based upon our common usage of the expressions 'true' and 'false.' Wittgenstein would remind us of this fact concerning common usage. Simply put, what he would say is that we can and do make true and false statements about non-existent objects, and none of us are apt to be confused and think that when we do so we are committed to the existence of such entities. For Wittgenstein, this is a function of how we *use* words and sentences. Semantic rules are abbreviations for complex practices, practices that are *often family resemblant* in nature and are *always open textured*. Failure to understand this fact about natural languages explains why so little progress has been made in philosophy.

The family resemblance nature of many terms (including most, if not all terms of philosophical importance) also explains why Socrates always gets the better of his opponents. He never loses, and the reason he never loses is that he always outfoxes his opponents by maneuvering them in such a way as to force them to assume the onus of explaining precisely what, for example, *justice, knowing, believing, democracy, truth, beauty,* or *goodness,* is. Socrates manipulates his opponents in debate to take the "bull by the horns" and attempt to define the term or terms under discussion. This is the wrong place to be if the presupposition, call it PD, of such discussions assumes, as it did in the era of Socrates, that

> understanding what a term 'T' means is to understand the essence of the thing so designated; or in contemporary parlance to understand what is/are the necessary and sufficient conditions governing the correct application of T.

If Wittgenstein is right, then since Socrates always assumes the position of the one seeking enlightenment by claiming not to know anything, he cannot lose. No matter what his opponent claims to be, the essence of T, Socrates will be able to provide a counterexample to that claim. Witness Socrates in Plato's *Republic*, where the principle question is "What is justice?" Socrates never attempts to say precisely what justice is. Instead he gets his opponents to do the defining. Perhaps Socrates was somehow, at some level, aware that the terms that most interested philosophers were family resemblance terms, terms which could not be defined in terms of necessary and sufficient conditions. Perhaps it was this awareness that motivated him to play the part of the one who knows nothing and seeks enlightenment. Although it is a tantalizing hypothesis, we will never know whether Socrates was sincere or just baiting others. We do know that the others, some of whom were venerated and influential men of Athens, eventually grew tired of being his targets, and brought him up on charges of corrupting the youth of Athens. It led to his conviction and his death by drinking hemlock.

Plato, the author of the *Republic* and other dialogues starring Socrates, was a student of Socrates', and may or may not be putting words in Socrates' mouth when he has Socrates speculate about the essence of various things. I suspect that Plato, having witnessed Socrates defeat various dignitaries, other philosophers, and political figures of Athens, who was inclined to speculation, worked into the dialogues his own ideas regarding the essence of things. What he may himself have contributed was the idea of the *logos*, that heavenly sphere where the eternal *Forms* (the abstract and essential features or characteristics that objects of a specific kind share, and which explain there being objects of that kind) reside, and where, between transmigrations of our souls from one body to another, we reside along side of the Forms. This exposure we take away with us when it is time to inhabit another body. And although we do carry with us faded memories of these Forms or essences, our "incarceration in the flesh" denies us full knowledge of these Forms. This is Plato's explanation for why, given that PD is true, no one can answer the questions Socrates poses. The real explanation, if Wittgenstein is right, is simply that the concepts under investigation are family resemblance concepts.

Linguistic studies and the philosophy of language can make important contributions to our understanding of the very nature of philosophy. From the time of Plato right up to the present day philosophers still seek to specify the meaning of a given word or concept by specifying necessary and sufficient conditions. And they always fail. As soon as one philosopher is satisfied that she has provided the necessary and sufficient conditions for 'knowing,' 'truth,' 'the good,' 'freedom,' 'etc.,' another philosopher comes up with a counterexample, and this leads to a revision in the set of conditions for their use. And so it goes, and has been going for over two thousand years. Formal languages like those proposed by Russell and Frege are simply artificial languages, in the most derogatory sense of the word 'artificial.' Their artificiality is revealed by their failed attempts to solve problems in communication that are not even problems within the context of ordinary language.

Austin and Searle

The Wittgenstein of the *Investigations* offers no theories concerning the nature of meaning or use. In fact, he claims, as we have determined, that the philosopher's work is simply to assemble facts of usage and to disparage the theories that philosophers are prone to postulate. He does, however, open the eyes of philosophers concerning the importance of use and its relation to meaning. He says things that imply that meaning and use are identical. But he also says things that imply that meaning is only determined by use.[27] I am convinced that the best way to read Wittgenstein is to attribute the latter thesis to him. Certainly there are many reasons not to confuse meaning with use, not the least of which is that *many* proper names do not have meaning, though they have various uses.

In an unscripted talk delivered in the Third Programme of the British Broadcasting Corporation, B.B.C., in 1956, the Oxford philosopher J. L. Austin distinguishes between statements, which are true or false, and what he calls *performatives*, which look like statements and are grammatically indistinct from statements, but which "couldn't possibly be true or false." Austin claims that performative utterances are utterances where "one is *doing* something rather than merely *saying* something." One of his examples is the use of 'I do' in the marriage ceremony, where one is "not reporting on a marriage," but is "indulging in it."[28]

In this talk, he acknowledged the importance of the "use of language movement" in philosophy. He cautions us, however, against placing so much importance on the statement-making use of language that we ignore performatives. His performatives are truth-valueless, but are not truth-valueless in the way that Strawson's statements are, because they fail to meet the presupposition requirement. The explanation of the truth-valueless nature of performatives is not due to the fact that their subject terms lack reference. Statements, if Strawson is right, are *sometimes* true, *sometimes* false, and *sometimes* truth-valueless. Austin's performatives are neither true nor false. He offers these examples:

> suppose that I tread on your toe and say 'I apologize.' Or again, suppose that I have the bottle of champagne in my hand and say 'I name this ship the *Queen Elizabeth.*' Or suppose I say 'I bet you sixpence it will rain tomorrow.' In all these cases it would be absurd to regard the thing that I say as a report of the performance of the action. . . . We should say rather that, in saying what I do, I actually perform that action.[29]

When someone makes a statement, it makes perfect sense to enquire, as we so often do, whether or not what was said is true or false. To make such an enquiry about a performative, on the other hand, makes no sense. If someone says he apologizes for some offense, an enquiry about the truth of his apology is senseless, unless of course, the subject of the enquiry means to be enquiring about the *sincerity* of the apology. According to Austin:

although these utterances do not themselves report facts and are not themselves true or false, saying these things does very often *imply* that certain things are true and not false, in some sense at least of that rather woolly word 'imply.' For example, when I say 'I do take this woman to be my lawful wedded wife,' or some other formula in the marriage ceremony, I do imply that I'm not already married, with wife living, sane, undivorced, and the rest of it. But still it is very important to realize that to imply that something or other is true, is not at all the same as saying something which is true itself.[30]

Although performative utterances cannot be true or false, they suffer from "disabilities of their own." He says:

They can fail to come off in special ways, and that is what I want to consider next. The various ways in which a performative utterance may be unsatisfactory we call, for the sake of a name, the infelicities; and an infelicity arises—that is to say, the utterance is unhappy—if certain rules, transparently simple rules, are broken. I will mention some of these rules and then give examples of some infringements.[31]

Austin proceeds to give examples of these disabilities or *infelicities*. One kind of infelicity which he lists results from the inappropriate use of a convention, like trying to christen a boat when one is not the person designated to perform the christening. I cannot succeed in christening your boat by simply breaking a bottle of champagne across its bow while exclaiming, "I christen this boat Boo Bradford." You must give me permission to do so. Another kind of infelicity occurs where no appropriate convention exists. You cannot divorce someone by simply saying 'I divorce you.' Austin also lists insincerity as a form of infelicity. Apologizing, promising, or congratulating requires sincerity. He includes on his list other infelicities as well, and acknowledges both that his list is not complete and that the categories he does list are not mutually exclusive.

After having argued that the distinction between statements and performatives is that statements *can be* either true or false—with respect to the facts they describe—but that performatives are *never* true nor false, but are instead either felicitous or infelicitous, Austin acknowledges that his distinction is not as clear as it might seem to be. Stating is clearly the performing of an act, just as much as is apologizing, and as such, is subject to various infelicities. For example, when someone says something like "I know that what you said was true, but you knew you should not have revealed our position at this point in the negotiation." Revealing too much is an infelicity when one is negotiating. And, on the other hand, the relation of a performative to the facts is not so very different from the relation of a statement to the facts. If I promise to pay you all the money I owe you next Tuesday, when I know full well that I will not have anywhere near enough money on Tuesday to pay off my debt, my promise is certainly one I was in no position to keep, and hence infelicitous. But that seems only to mean that the *facts* are not such as would support such a promise.[32]

Austin attempts to deal with the breakdown of the distinction by distinguishing between what "has been very much studied in the past," namely, what an utterance means, and what may be called the *force* of an utterance. He claims that "What we need besides the old doctrine about meanings is a new doctrine about all. the possible forces of utterances . . ."[33], and although he does not attempt to fulfill this need in the work under consideration, he does make considerable headway in this direction in a later work.

In this later work, a remarkably short and clearly expressed work, Austin pursues the task of providing a new doctrine of all the possible forces of utterances. In doing so, he lays the groundwork for a use or speech act theory of meaning. This work was originally presented in 1955 in *The Williams James Lectures Series* at Harvard University and was edited for publication with the unpretentious title *How To Do Things With Words*.[34] Although he spends a large part of this book explicating further his reasons for collapsing the distinction between the statement and the performative, he ultimately abandons it in favor of, à la Wittgenstein, "more general *families* of related and overlapping speech acts."[35]

According to Austin, there are three major actions which, taken together, comprise a speech act. First, there is what he calls a *locutionary* action, which is uttering various words with both a sense and a reference. This aspect of Austin's theory is tied to what I have referred to throughout the present work as sentential meaning. Second, there is what he dubs an *illocutionary* action or conventional *force*, which has to do with how words are used or contextual meaning. Third, there is what he refers to as perlocutionary actions, which are the non-conventional consequences that are attributable to speech actions. Suppose someone asserts, "I promise to accompany you to the bullfight on Monday." According to Austin, this person has used various words with both a sense and a reference, and the illocution he performs is that of promising—which can only be done if a certain convention exists. A

81

very large variety of perlocutionary actions or consequences are possible. By promising someone to accompany them to a bullfight on Monday you will likely *please* that person, but you might also *annoy* or *make unhappy* a third party who was about to ask you to accompany her to a movie on that same Monday. Pleasing someone, annoying someone, and making someone unhappy are actions that can result because of something you say, and they can be attributed to you.[36]

Illocutions or conventional speech actions are the ones of most interest to speech act theorists. Toward the end of *How to do Things with Words*, Austin attempts to classify these illocutionary actions. And although he is far from satisfied with his classificatory system, he ventures the following five sub-categories: *verdictives, exercitives, commissives, behabitives,* and *expositives. Verdictives* are "typified" by the giving of a verdict. As the word itself implies, they occur in contexts involving juries, judges, umpires, etc. Some of the examples he lists are: estimating, grading, and ranking. Exercitives are "the giving of a decision in favor of or against a certain course of action, or advocacy of it . . . is a decision that something is to be the case, as distinct from a judgment that it is so." His list of exercitives includes: appointing, excommunicating, dismissing, naming, ordering, vetoing, proclaiming, and recommending. Commissives are characterized as having the single purpose of committing the speaker "to a certain course of action." Among his examples are: promising, contracting, guaranteeing, swearing, betting, consenting, and giving one's word. Behabitives are characterized by Austin as being a "very miscellaneous group, and have to do with attitudes and social behavior." His list of behabitives includes: apologizing, thanking, expressing sympathy, criticizing, applauding, and greeting. Expositives are those actions that refer to intellectual and journalistic endeavors. Austin claims that they "are used in acts of exposition, including the expounding of views and the clarifying of usages and of reference." His list of examples includes: affirming, denying, conjecturing, conceding, describing, correcting, and last, but by no means least, stating. The last as we have seen, at the outset of his work on this subject, was contrasted with performatives.[37] Austin summarizes his efforts thus:

> we may say that the verdictive is an exercise of judgment, the exercitive is an assertion of influence or exercising of power, the commissive is an assuming of an obligation or declaring of an intention, the behabitive is the adopting of an attitude, and the expositive is the clarifying of reasons, arguments, and communications.[38]

82

Austin is quite clear about the tenuous nature of his classification system. He allows for the fact that some illocutions fall under more than one category, and that there are cases which do not seem to fall under any of his categories. Unfortunately, Austin died before he was able to develop further the direction of his theory of speech acts. We are not even sure that he would have taken his efforts in that direction. In fact, at the very end of the lectures in question, he provides an example to illustrate the possible applications of his work. The example he provides concerns the word 'good'. He reminds the reader that philosophers have always been interested in this word, and although they have ventured the view that it is used "for expressing approval, for commending, and grading," he is convinced that we will not really understand fully its usage until we "have a complete list of those illocutionary acts of which commending, grading, &c., are isolated specimens—until we know how many such acts there are and what are their relationships and inter-connexions."[39]

Unlike Wittgenstein, Austin does not think that assembling facts about the use of language reveals that all the questions of philosophy are pseudo-questions or that the answers that philosophers provide to these questions are pseudo-answers. As far as Austin is concerned, the careful assembling of the facts of ordinary language use is just an initial step in the process of gaining philosophical truth. In his masterful essay on philosophical method, "A Plea for Excuses," he says:

> In spite of the wide and acute observation of the phenomena of action embodied in ordinary speech, modern scientists have been able, it seems to me, to reveal its inadequacy at numerous points, if only because they have had access to more comprehensive data and have studied them with more catholic and dispassionate interest than the ordinary man, or even the lawyer, has had occasion to do.[40]

Although his untimely death prevented Austin from providing a more comprehensive account of the nature of speech acts, his efforts in this direction have had considerable influence. Today, many philosophers consider speech act theory to be part of pragmatics, as opposed to meaning theory or semantics. This is consistent with what Austin proposed in his distinction between locutionary and illocutionary acts.

One of the most influential contemporary philosophers of language is the American philosopher John Searle. Searle builds a theory of speech acts upon Austin's foundation. His interests are focused upon illocutionary actions, and his leading idea or justification for the study of such actions can be cast in the form of two principles. One is negative or exclusive and the other is positive and inclusive. Together they specify that the *minimal* unit of communication is the illocutionary act:

(SP[1]) The minimal unit of communication is not a symbol, a word, a sentence, or a symbol, word, or sentence token.

(SP[2]) The minimal unit of speech is an illocutionary act, i.e., the uttering of a sentence token under certain conditions.[41]

Most philosophers of language have, according to Searle, mistakenly supposed that the minimal or fundamental component of communication to be a symbol type, word type, sentence type, symbol token, word token, or sentence token. (SP[2]) is the view he wishes to defend. And while he admits that he cannot *prove* that (SP[2]) is true, he does provide what he considers to be good arguments to convince the skeptic. Anyone who takes "a noise or a mark on paper" to be an instance of communication must take it to be something produced by a being with intentions. We cannot simply regard it as a natural phenomenon like "a stone, a waterfall, or a tree." Moreover, when we attempt to interpret, for example, Mayan hieroglyphs, we must regard them to be "produced by beings more or less like ourselves and produced with certain kinds of intentions."[42] In short, we must take them to be speech acts.

Speech acts of the illocutionary variety are, for Searle, rule-governed forms of behavior. Promising, apologizing, etc., parallel "getting a base hit in baseball or moving a knight in chess," in that they can only be explicated in terms of the rules that make them possible. Searle explicates the concept of an illocutionary act in terms of "a set of necessary and sufficient conditions for the performance of a particular kind of illocutionary act." Then, on the basis of these conditions, he attempts to extract "a set of semantic rules for the use of the expression (or syntactic device) which marks the utterance as an illocutionary act of that kind."[43] By these means, he hopes to establish a pattern for analyzing other kinds of illocutions and, eventually in this way, to clarify the general notion of an illocutionary action. Since the concept of a rule figures so importantly in his attempt to understand speech acts, his initial focus is on the concept of a rule.

He points out that although many philosophers of language have tried to clarify the notion of a semantic rule, they have been altogether unsuccessful, and that this lack of success has fostered skepticism regarding the very possibility of successful analysis of the concept of a linguistic rule. Searle does not, however, think that this skepticism is well-founded. He is convinced that the lack of success in this endeavor is due to the fact that philosophers of language have failed to distinguish between different sorts of rules.

According to Searle, we must distinguish between *regulative* rules and *constitutive* rules. The former are rules that "regulate a pre-existing activity, an activity whose existence is logically independent of the existence of the rules." The latter are rules that "constitute (and also regulate) an activity the existence of which is logically dependent upon the rules."[44] Rules of etiquette are of the former kind. They regulate interpersonal relationships, which would and do exist independently of the rules. They are often ignored, especially by the uncultivated. Ignoring them does not render interpersonal relations impossible, though it does have an effect on the quality of those relations. Game rules are constitutive. You cannot score a touchdown, for example, unless the ball is in play. The ball carrier must cross the goal line within bounds, or the receiver must catch the ball within the area set out as the end zone. You cannot play chess unless your moves are all in accordance with the rules defining the way each kind of piece can move.

Searle is inclined to think that the reason so many philosophers of language have failed to offer an adequate account of linguistic rules is because they have taken regulative rules to be the paradigm for what they seek. Searle attempts to rectify the situation by taking his model or paradigm of a linguistic rule to be constitutive. According to Searle:

> The hypothesis that lies behind the present paper is that the semantics of a language can be regarded as a series of systems of constitutive rules and that illocutionary acts are acts performed in accordance with these sets of constitutive rules. One of the aims of this paper is to formulate a set of constitutive rules for a certain kind of speech act.[45]

Searle proceeds by first distinguishing between (1) *propositional content* of an illocutionary act and (2) the *force* of an illocutionary act. Propositional content is what the words that are used mean. The same propositional content can be presented with a variety of conventional forces. One can, for example, use the sentence 'The king of France is wise' in a variety of ways depending upon where emphasis is placed (intonation contour), what transpired previous to one's saying it, and how one uses one's eyes, shoulders, hands, etc., (body language). If one of the members of the king's court whispers "The king of France is wise" (with a note of alarm in his voice) to another member of the court who has underestimated the sagacity as well as the vindictiveness of the king, it is likely meant (conventional force) to be a *warning*. But if instead one courtier says it aloud (with a prideful tone of voice) so that all those present, which includes the king, can hear it, he doubtless means to *praise* the king. The sentence itself has the same proposition content in both cases. The content is what one would be asked to consider if one were asked simply to *entertain* the meaning of the sentence in question.

Although it is highly likely that no one has ever asked anyone to consider the meaning of the sentence, 'There is at the present moment, perched upon the highest point in the Alps, a rotund, purple polka-dotted, emotionally unstable *Tyrannosaurus rex*,' you do understand perfectly what it means, and you recognize that entertaining or considering its meaning is quite different from imagining someone actually using it in conventional fashion to accomplish some specific action. The propositional content of the sentence in question constitutes what I defined previously as a proposition, namely, sentential meaning. What a sentence means is one thing, whereas what someone would mean by it on a particular occasion is quite another.[46]

Searle distinguishes between *propositional indicators* and *indicators of illocutionary force*. Because his focus is on speech acts he doe not bother to say what he means by the former. He illustrates what he means by the latter by those aspects of actual usage which I enumerated in the previous paragraph (intonation contour, body language, etc.) to distinguish one illocutionary use of a given sentence from other illocutionary uses of the same sentence. But he also includes among the indicators of illocutionary force what Austin dubbed "explicit performative" verbs: 'apologize,' 'promise,' 'state,' 'warn,' etc. The conventional force of an utterance involving such verbs is spelled out in the act itself. If I say, "I promise . . ." or "I apologize . . ." etc., I clearly *indicate* what I am doing.[47]

Before he proceeds with his expressed goal of specifying "a set of necessary and sufficient conditions for the performance of a particular kind of illocutionary act" from which he can extract "a set of semantic rules for the use of the expression (or syntactic device) which marks the utterance as an illocutionary act of that kind," he borrows and amends an idea concerning the word 'meaning' from Paul Grice's article

"Meaning."[48] He borrows from Grice the idea that what an agent A means by some expression S is that A intends the utterance of S to produce "some effect in an audience by means of the recognition of this intention."[49] But, as he points out quite convincingly, by an example concerning an American soldier who is captured by the Italian troops, this account must be amended. In his example, the soldier wants the Italians to think that he is a German officer so that he can escape, but he knows only one German sentence: 'Kennst du das land, wo die Zitronen blühen?' (which means "Knowest thou the land where the lemon trees bloom?"). He hopes that the Italians know very little German, and will assume because he speaks German that he must be a German officer. He hopes that they will think that the sentence in question means "I am a German Officer." This example is meant to show both (1) that Grice's account blurs the distinction between perlocutionary and illocutionary effects or consequences and (2) that it fails to make clear the relation between what one means by something one says and what that something actually means. Illocutionary consequences involve conventions and rules; perlocutionary consequences do not. What the American soldier intends to be the consequence of his saying the German sentence is not something that can be accomplished conventionally. It is not a function of what his words mean. Our words mean what they mean and not what we want them to mean.[50]

Searle amends Grice's account by making clear that "one's meaning something when one says something is more than just contingently related to what the sentence means in the language one is speaking."[51] Any account of meaning must take into account the fact that the words in a given language mean what they mean, and that in order for a speaker to perform an illocutionary action, say a promise, the speaker's intention involves his assumption that his words will be taken to mean what they customarily or conventionally mean. Searle makes use of a passage 510 in Wittgenstein's *Investigations* to clarify and fortify his emendation.[52] Wittgenstein says:

> Make the following experiment: say "It's cold in here" and *mean* "It's warm in here". Can you do it?—And what are you doing as you do it? And is there only one way of doing it?

Wittgenstein's point is that you cannot make your words mean something different than they do by intending them differently.

With his emendation to Grice's account in mind, Searle goes on to provide what he alleges are the necessary and sufficient conditions for a specific illocution. The example he chooses is promising, and his approach is like that of Russell. Searle states a number of conditions that are necessary for an act of promising to occur, and when this list is complete, the conjunctive set of necessary conditions is said to be a sufficient condition. And, in reverse, if something is an act of promising, then it will entail this set of conditions.

He hedges his bets right off, however, by pointing out that the set he is about to produce makes him uneasy, and does so primarily because "the notion of a promise, like most notions in ordinary language, does not have absolutely fixed rules." There are, he concedes, "all sorts of odd, deviant, and borderline promises; and counterexamples, more or less bizarre," which can be produced against his set of conditions. For this reason, he claims that his analysis will be restricted to the "center" of the concept of promising, and that he will "ignore fringe, borderline, and partially defective cases."[53]

I am uncomfortable with the idea of a concept's "center." I have no precise understanding of what that would be. As it stands, Searle's talk about a concept's center is in need of clarification. There is, however, a much more serious problem. If promising is, as I suspect it is, a family resemblance concept, then its governing conditions are ones that overlap and criss-cross, and are not ones that form the kind of set Searle proposes. One needs to be careful not to throw the baby out with the bathwater, which may be what Searle does by ignoring what he labels "fringe, borderline, and partially defective cases." Let us have a look at what he proposes to see if that is what he in fact does.

He begins with the analysis of sincere promising, and then modifies the result to account for insincere promising. He poses the problem and then offers his set of conditions, of which there are nine. Here is his analysis of a sincere promise:

> Given that a speaker S utters a sentence T in the presence of a hearer H, then, in the utterance of T, S sincerely (and non-defectively) promises p to H if and only if: [(1) through (9) of Searle's conditions are met].[54]

I do not agree that his set of nine conditions constitutes a set of conditions both necessary and sufficient for a sincere promise. I do not think that any such set can be found. I believe that the concept of promising a family resemblance concept. Moreover, I also disagree with his claim that *each* member of his set of nine is a necessary condition for a sincere promise.

Instead of considering all nine conditions, I will focus on his sixth condition, which is most important to his analysis of sincere promise making, and will argue that it is not a necessary condition for such promising. Here is (6):

(6) S *intends to* do A. The most important distinction between sincere and insincere promises is that in the case of the sincere promise the speaker intends to do the act promised, in the case of the insincere promise he does not intend to do the act. Also in sincere promises the speaker believes it is possible for him to do the act (or to refrain from doing it), but I think the proposition that he intends to do it entails that he thinks it is possible to do (or refrain from doing) it, so I am not stating that as an extra condition. I call this condition the *sincerity condition.*[55]

There are times when one is distracted by events that surround, but are irrelevant to, an act of promising. In such circumstances, one's promise to do something may not incorporate one's full attention. Afterwards, one may make the following observation about one's promise: "I had no idea what I was committing myself to; no one in their right mind would have made such a promise; I know I did promise, and I will honor it, but I certainty had no intention of making such a foolish promise." Or, an individual in similar circumstances of distraction may well promise without believing that it is in his power to do what he distractedly promised. He may later make this claim: "I know I promised to do it, but what I promised is, had I thought about it, something I would have realized was not in my power to do." In my first case, the promise-maker did not have an intention to do what he promised. At the very least he had no clear intention to do it. In my second case, the promise maker did not believe that it was possible for him to do what he promised, and so he could not have an intention. Yet neither case is a case of an *insincere* promise, since neither case involves having a clear intention to do what is promised.

Searle would respond that these are not central cases. They are borderline cases. But this only means, or so it seems to me, that there are cases that Searle's analysis cannot handle. Another way out is to refine Searle's notion of insincere promising by distinguishing between 'not intending to do something' and 'intending not to do something.' Searle defines insincere promising in terms of the former when he should have used the latter. His use of the former is what allows my examples to be raised. They are cases of *non-intending to keep* a promise. They are not cases of *intending not to keep* a promise.

Rather than beat around the bush in an effort to ensnarl a modification suitable for what might appear to prop up the necessity of this condition, why not acknowledge the transient nature of natural language? Why not acknowledge that one's conditions for promising and other speech acts are, at best, sufficient, and not both necessary and sufficient, and by so doing avoid the problems associated with the facts that so many natural language terms are family resemblance and all of them are open textured? Why not stop looking for hard and fast rules to fix the meanings of terms, and recognize, as Wittgenstein does, that the rules of language are constitutive, but only in so far as they are self-correcting. The rules of language are more like "rules of thumb" than they are like game rules. Although the meaning of 'bad' has until recently been antithetical to the meaning of the word 'good,' one of its current senses is synonymous with the common meaning of the word 'good.' We all understand how to add senses to the expressions already in use, and how to introduce new expressions into the language, but this understanding or activity is not governed by rules the way chess is. Communication is an organic, not a mechanistic, endeavor. I will say a lot more about this idea in Chapter Six. I am not through discussing either Searle or Strawson. I will return to their views in Chapter Four, which is devoted to the theory of referring. They are the most prominent defenders of the descriptive, as opposed to the causal, theory of referring. In the next chapter, I will examine a few other theories of meaning, including three, which can be traced to the Wittgenstein of the *Tractatus*.

Endnotes
[1] Wittgenstein, (1958, 3rd ed.) passage 23.
[2] Ibid., passage 23.
[3] Ibid., passage 66.
[4] Ibid., passage 67.
[5] Ibid., passage 80.
[6] Waismann (1951)
[7] See below, p. 94.
[8] See also Wittgenstein's *Investigations*, passages 119, 123-126, 128, 133, 182, 194, 255, 309, and 593.
[9] Ibid., passage 350.
[10] Ibid., passage 510.

[11] It must be acknowledged that G.E. Moore expressed a serious objection to the Russell /Frege idea that existence can only be attributed to propositional functions, in 1936. Moore agreed with Frege and Russell that there are uses of 'exists' where the term in question "does not stand for an attribute of an object or individual." Yet he was unwilling to concede that there are no uses of 'exists' where it does stand for an attribute or property of an object.

According to Moore, Russell is wrong in claiming that the attribution of existence to what is referred to by a proper name is meaningless or without sense. Moore reminds the reader that Russell's principle example of a logically proper name is 'this.' Moore focuses our attention upon the sentence 'This exists.' He argues that in cases where it would be appropriate to say, "This is a tame tiger," it would also be appropriate to point at the object in question and say "This exists," on the grounds that "you can clearly say with truth of any such object, "This might not have existed." Moore cannot understand how it is possible that "This might not have existed" should be true, unless "This does in fact exist" is also true, and therefore that the words 'This exists' are significant." See Moore (1936) pp. 117-120.

[12] Strawson (1950) p. 163.

[13] This is a statement making or asserting use, as contrasted with other conventional uses, for example, warning, promising, postulating, explaining, judging, etc., what Austin refers to as "illocutions." (1962) pp. 98- 163.

[14] Strawson (1950) p. 169.

[15] Ibid., p. 171-172.

[16] Paradoxically, however, Russell maintains in "The Philosophy of Logical Atomism" that propositions are unreal. Sentence types would have then to serve as the bearers of truth and falsity—a view very difficult, if not impossible, to maintain.

[17] Linsky (1967) p. 91.

[18] See Baker and Hacker (1984) for an attack on this distinction.

[19] Strawson (1952) p. 176.

[20] Linsky (1967) p. 94.

[21] What he actually says can be translated into the E form.

[22] Donnellan (1966) p. 316.

[23] Linsky (1963) p. 80.

[24] Donnellan (1966) p. 326-327.

[25] See Wittgenstein (1953) passages 109, 436.

[26] See above p. 48.

[27] See Bede Rundle (1990) and P.M.S. Hacker (1996) pp. 248-249.

[28] J.L. Austin (1956) p. 222.
[29] Ibid., p. 222.
[30] Ibid., p. 224.
[31] Ibid., p. 224.
[32] Ibid., pp. 233-238.
[33] Ibid., p.238.
[34] Austin (1955).
[35] Ibid., p. 149.
[36] Ibid., pp. 94-107.
[37] Ibid., pp. 150-162.
[38] Ibid., p. 162.
[39] Ibid., p. 162.
[40] Austin (1962A) p. 151.
[41] Searle (1965) pp. 253-254.
[42] Ibid., p. 254.
[43] Ibid., p. 254.
[44] Ibid., p. 255.
[45] Ibid., p. 256.
[46] The distinction he employs between an illocutionary act and the propositional content of that act cannot, however, according to Searle, be said to make sense in all cases of illocutionary action. Praising the king's actions may be accomplished simply by exclaiming, "Hurrah."
[47] Searle (1965) p. 258.
[48] Grice (1957)
[49] Searle (1965) p. 259.
[50] Ibid., p. 260.
[51] Ibid., p. 260.
[52] Ibid., p. 260
[53] Ibid., p. 262.
[54] Ibid., pp. 262-266.
[55] Ibid., p. 264.

3
Other Theories of Meaning

A variety of theories of meaning have emerged during the course of philosophy's history, but the majority have appeared within the last hundred or so years. Some are variations on the referring approach; others are variations on the use approach. I am not going to attempt to cover them all. I will instead concentrate on those theories which have had considerable influence or which offer something of importance that can be used to provide a better or more comprehensive theory than any of those currently employed. By far the most influential of these other approaches is the causal approach, an approach that originated in a critique of the theory of referring originally advocated by Frege and Russell and refined by Strawson and Searle, known as the descriptive theory of referring. I will devote the next chapter to the controversy between the causal and the descriptive theories of referring. In this chapter, I will cover three other theories: the *verification theory*, the *truth-conditions theory*, and the *inferential theory*. The seeds of all three are present in Wittgenstein's *Tractatus*. I will consider the verification theory first.

The Verification Theory of Meaning and Essentialism

Although this theory is nowhere stated in the *Tractatus*, it is inescapably embedded in the relation Wittgenstein presumes to obtain between atomic facts or simples and atomic propositions. It owes its full-fledged formulation to a group of philosophers called "logical positivists." The cornerstone of the verification theory of meaning is the verification principle (call it VP), which is sometimes stated as: the meaning of a proposition is its method of verification. The logical positivists were a group of philosophers (often referred to as the *Vienna Circle*) who met from time to time in Vienna at the home of one of the founding members, M Schlick. Other members of importance were: H. Hahn, H. Feigl, O. Neurath, F. Waismann, G. Bergman, and R. Carnap, who is considered by many, myself included, to be the most important member of the group. They relied upon VP, which they attributed to Wittgenstein, to both justify science and discredit traditional metaphysics. Although Wittgenstein never actually asserted VP in the *Tractatus*, two of his students, D.A.T. Gasking and A. C. Jackson, report his saying some years after he wrote the *Tractatus*:

> I used at one time to say that, in order to get clear how a certain sentence is used, it was a good idea to ask oneself the question: "How would one try to verify such an assertion?" . . . But some people have turned this suggestion about asking for the verification into a dogma.[1]

At any rate, the positivists thought that Wittgenstein was committed to the VP, and they did employ it to define *descriptive* or *cognitive* meaning (as opposed to *expressive* meaning).[2] To be cognitively or descriptively meaningful a proposition must be either true or false. A descriptive proposition can be false because it is mistaken, or false because it is a lie. My claim that I have five hundred dollars in my billfold could turn out to be false because I miscounted my money, or it might be false because I lied to make myself seem important. Expressive propositions, on the other hand, refer to one's feelings and are true if the feelings of the speaker are as she or he says they are, and false if not. For a proposition to be descriptive or significant it has to be *in principle* verifiable.

The most articulate and most ingenious defender of the verification theory is the German philosopher Rudolf Carnap. He argues:

> What, now, is *the meaning of a word?* . . . First, the *syntax* of the word must be fixed, i.e., the mode of its occurrence in the simplest sentence form in which it is capable of occurring; we call this sentence form its *elementary sentence*. The elementary sentence form for the word "stone" e.g. is "x is a stone"; in sentences of this form some designation from the category of things occupies the place of "x," e.g., "this diamond," "this apple." Secondly, for an

elementary sentence S containing the word an answer must be given to the following question, which can be formulated in various ways: (1) What sentences is S *deducible* from, and what sentences are deducible from S? (2) Under what conditions is S supposed to be true, and under what conditions false? (3) How is S to be *verified?* (4) What is the *meaning* of S? (1) is the correct formulation; formulation (2) accords with the phraseology of logic, (3) with the phraseology of the theory of knowledge, (4) with that of philosophy (phenomenology). Wittgenstein asserted that (2) expresses what philosophers mean by (4): the meaning of a sentence consists in its truth conditions.[3]

He illustrates his method by producing what he considers to be a successful example, namely, 'arthropod.' He begins by placing the word 'arthropod' in an elementary sentence S. In this way we fix the syntax:

x is an arthropod.

He then determines which sentences S is deducible from, and which sentences are deducible from S, which is to satisfy formulation (1). Such sentences are referred to as *protocol sentences.* The protocol sentences for S are:

a. x is an animal
b. x is jointed-legged
c. x is segmented-bodied.

(2) is satisfied because a, b, and c fix the truth-conditions for S; (3) is satisfied because a, b, and c are the empirical criteria for being an arthropod. One simply observes x to see if it is an animal with jointed legs and a segmented body. The first three are, for Carnap, just different ways of clarifying meaning. Yet, as we shall see, (1), (2), and (3) can be and have been used as the basis for different theories of meaning. (1) is the basis of the *inferential role theory*, which claims that the meaning of a sentence is the set of sentences from which it can be inferred and the set of sentences which can be inferred from it. (2) is the basis for the *truth-conditions* theory of meaning, and (3) is the basis of the *verification* theory. All three are said by Carnap to be different ways of defining meaning, (4). I will focus on the truth-conditions and

the inferential role theories shortly, but for now I will continue to discuss the verification theory.

Carnap attempts to refute traditional metaphysics by arguing that a descriptive term x can only be accepted as meaningful if we know how to verify it, that this condition is not met for most, if not all, metaphysical terms. He offers the following as examples of metaphysical terms whose meanings are not subject to verification: 'God,' 'the Absolute,' 'the Infinite,' 'the being of being,' and 'thing-in-itself.' Statements that contain such words have, according to Carnap, "no sense, assert nothing, are mere pseudo-statements."[4]

The protocol sentences, a, b, and c above, are understood to be *necessary* conditions. That is, if any one of these conditions does not obtain, x is not an arthropod. The conjunctive set is said to be *sufficient*. That is, if a, b, and c are true of x, then x must be an arthropod.

There are two serious problems with Carnap's view: one relies on Wittgenstein's notion of *family resemblance* and one relies on the notion of *open texture*. The first problem is that his *pattern of analysis* assumes that every term is governed by a set of necessary and sufficient conditions. In this case, the analysis cannot apply to family resemblance terms, because they are not governed by sets of necessary and sufficient conditions. As we have seen, they are governed by conditions which overlap and crisscross throughout the sets of things referred to by them.

It has been argued by some philosophers that this defect of natural languages could be easily fixed, and that fixing the meaning of such terms is part of the philosopher's task. It is at this point that the open texture objection becomes relevant. It can be used to show that the meanings of all empirical terms cannot, as a mater of logic, be fixed.

In the last chapter I issued a promissory note to prove the Wittgenstein/Waismann point that, because of the open textured nature of all empirical terms, it is logically impossible to fix their meanings. Here I honor that note. Suppose x at time t^1 satisfies all three conditions for being an arthropod, but at t^2 is no longer jointed-legged, yet at a later time t^3 is again jointed-legged. What are we to conclude? At least three possibilities present themselves: (a) x is not an arthropod; (b) x is a pseudo-arthropod; (c) x is an arthropod at t^1, but is not an arthropod at t^2, although again an arthropod at t^3. These three options are equally plausible. No logical or mathematical proofs can be produced to establish which alternative is the correct one. In such a case, we can only legislate for our own purposes, and legislation cannot establish any objectively or logically correct alternative. It simply introduces what may or may not become widely accepted as a new convention or practice. We are forced to legislate when all else fails. So long as the world remains the way it is, we are not faced with such options, but if the world were to behave quite differently, we would have to legislate our way out of the difficulties produced by this strange "arthropod."

The same argument can be generalized regarding *any* empirical term. One just imagines that one or more of the conditions alleged necessary for the correct use of the term does not obtain at some time t^1, and obtains again at some time subsequent to the t^1. In short, the meaning of empirical expressions or concepts cannot be fixed, and it is a philosophical fancy to think that they can. It follows that Carnap's efforts to establish credibility for logical positivism are seriously misguided. But what about the verification principle itself? Is it defensible?

Unfortunately, VP, which the positivists alleged to provide the basis for eliminating metaphysics, turned out to be the means by which the metaphysicians turned the tide against them. The metaphysicians responded to the positivist's attack by asking about empirical conditions for the truth of VP itself. They claim that it is self-refuting because *no* empirical conditions can be provided to establish its truth. It is therefore as meaningless as any of the pronouncements of metaphysics.

The positivists made a variety of attempts to answer the metaphysician's critique, but none of them were satisfactory. Wittgenstein's answer to the metaphysician's form of objection is given in the last two sections of the *Tractatus*, 6.54 and 7:

> My propositions are elucidatory in this way: he who understands me finally recognizes them as senseless, when he has climbed out through them, over them. (He must so to speak throw away the ladder, after he has climbed up on it.) He must surmount these propositions; then he sees the world rightly. (6.54)

> Whereof one cannot speak, thereof one must be silent. (7)

But what are we to make of this? He seems to be condemning his own method. Does it not follow from what he says here that 6.54 and 7 are themselves senseless? Since by his admission it is impossible to express metaphysical or non-empirical views, it seems to follow that saying so cannot itself be sensibly expressed—to say that we must be silent is itself a violation of sense. Or to put it more forcefully, in the words of Frank Ramsey, a brilliant philosopher and mathematician who was only twenty-seven when he died, "What we can't say, we can't say, and we can't whistle it either."[5] This is not the end of the matter, however.

Although Wittgenstein recognizes that the claims he makes in the *Tractatus* are metaphysical propositions and concedes that they are meaningless, this only means that they are not empirical propositions. They are not about the world. But this does not mean that they are on a par with the kinds of claims that metaphysicians of the past made. Unlike talk about 'The Ultimate,' the propositions of the *Tractatus* are useful. They make it possible for us to discover the limits of language and logic, and at the same time the limits of the world. His conclusion that the outcome of his endeavors is senseless was the result of much effort on his part. Max Black puts it this way: "A negative metaphysics, such as that of the *Tractatus*, has its own rules of procedure: the ladder must be *used* before it can be thrown away."[6]

An altogether different approach is possible regarding the VP, as well as, perhaps, various propositions of the *Tractatus*. If one makes use of the metalanguage/object-language distinction founded upon Russell's "theory of types," one can defend the verification principle.[7]

We can think of VP as applying only to empirical propositions. We can regard it as a *meta-linguistic statement* about empirical propositions. As it was originally stated, it referred to all propositions, and as such included itself within its reference set. But if we state VP to refer only to empirical propositions, and acknowledge that VP is not an empirical proposition, it cannot be criticized for not having empirical truth-conditions. Although this move counters the metaphysician's charge that it is self-defeating, the question remains concerning how one would *justify* or *defend* VP itself. Must we be silent? No, not if one remains faithful to the distinction between object language and metalanguage statements.

One can argue that VP (as a metalinguistic statement) is a *necessary presupposition* for the very existence of a natural language. It is of paramount importance to recognize, however, that it is not any *specific formulation,* not even the metalinguistic formulation, which is necessarily presupposed for the existence of natural language communication. Rather, it is the underlying *practice* of requiring the possibility of confirmation for the acceptance of empirical claims that is necessary for the existence of such languages. To borrow from the language of the *Tractatus*, such underlying principles as VP could be said to be revealed (shown) in the way we act, rather than formulated (said). The function that such practices serve is independent of whether or not they are formulated.

The practice formulated by the verification principle is by no means the only practice that has to be generally adhered to in order for human communication to take place. Those practices formulated by the principle of non-contradiction, NCP, and the identity principle, IP, must also be *adhered* to in order for linguistic communication to be possible—given that human beings are the way they are. If humans were psychic or our brains were "wired" differently, such practices might not be necessary. But we are as we are. Just imagine what it would be like trying to communicate with someone who saw no need for factual confirmation, contradicted himself with great frequency, and never used the same expression to designate the same object. Now imagine a group of such people. They would be unable to take any of the initial steps that language formation requires.

So even though it is impossible to fix the meanings of empirical terms by providing necessary and sufficient conditions, it does not follow that the verification principle itself is without justification. And, although the meaning of a word cannot be defined in terms of its method of verification, it might be the case that the alleged equivalences among (1), (2), (3), and (4) above do not obtain. If not, then it might be possible that even if (3) is false, (1) or (2) may be true. (4) is ruled out because, if it is used in isolation from the other three, it defines meaning in terms of meaning. It is circular. But if, as Carnap claims, Wittgenstein is right in claiming that (2) (which defines the meaning of a word like 'arthropod' in terms of truth conditions) expresses what philosophers mean by (4), then the meaning of a sentence might well consist in its truth-conditions. Let us examine this idea more carefully.

Meaning as Truth Conditions

Wittgenstein does assert in the *Tractatus* what is clearly a version of the truth-conditional theory of meaning for *molecular propositions*—those propositions that are composed of other propositions, i.e., 'This is red and that is white.'[8] He says:

in order to say "p" is true (or false) I must have determined under what conditions I call "p" true, and thereby I determine the sense of the proposition. (*Tractatus*, 4.63)

In the case of 'x is an arthropod,' the truth conditions would be that x is an animal with jointed legs and a segmented body.

It must be understood that Wittgenstein does not offer a truth-conditional account of word meaning, however. As we learned in Chapter one, Wittgenstein claims that *simple objects* provide the meaning of genuine or logically proper names. Logically proper names mean or refer to simple objects or particulars, but they do so "only in the nexus of a proposition" (T 3.3). For Wittgenstein, propositions like "Socrates was the teacher of Plato" are subject to analysis in keeping with Russell's theory of descriptions. Eventually, all such propositions are reducible to what Wittgenstein calls "elementary propositions," which are just concatenations of names for simples. Given that 'a,' 'b,' 'c' and 'd' are names, and given that the objects a, b, c and d are concatenated or arranged in the following fashion, bcda, the corresponding concatenation of names, 'bcda,' depicts or mirrors reality. The names mean the objects they name. The meanings of other expressions are ambiguous, but are translatable into descriptions, which must ultimately be analyzed into logically proper names in order to remove their ambiguity. The elementary or atomic propositions are, for Wittgenstein, true if they mirror reality, and false if they do not. They are directly verifiable. Molecular propositions are truth-functional combinations of propositions that are ultimately simple propositions, the truth or falsity of which depends upon their constituents.

One can, following Carnap's lead, construct a truth-conditions theory of *word* meaning (vocabulary) by inserting the word to be defined into an elementary sentence and determining the truth conditions, both necessary and sufficient, for the elementary sentence, as I did for 'arthropod.' But how are we to deal with the many terms in any given language that are *family resemblance* terms?

As we learned in Chapter Two, it is impossible to provide truth conditions, both necessary and sufficient, for sentences containing family resemblance terms. You cannot say x is a game, for example, if and only if such and such conditions obtain, if, as Wittgenstein has demonstrated, such terms are not governed by sets of necessary and sufficient conditions. Overlapping and crisscrossing conditions govern such terms. And if you try to tinker your way around this, in order to define your way out of the difficulties such terms present, you still have to face the further fact that empirical terms are *open textured*. No matter what conditions you dredge up to bolster your definitions, you cannot, as a matter of logic, fix the meaning of *any* empirical term or word.

A different, more successful, and less obviously flawed truth-conditional approach to meaning is the one that American philosopher Donald Davidson has taken. In order to understand his view we need to look at the Polish-born philosopher Alfred Tarski's efforts to define truth in a formal language. And we will also have to examine carefully the Harvard philosopher W. V. O Quine's thesis concerning the indeterminacy of translation. Both Tarski and Quine have had a significant influence upon Davidson. I will explain Tarski's view now and Quine's when it is appropriate in the course of explaining Davidson's theory.

Tarski's major contribution to truth-conditional semantics was to define truth in terms of *biconditionality*. According to Tarski sentences like 'Snow is white' are true *if and only if* snow is white. The biconditonal operator is to be understood in terms of implication. Implication is represented as 'p implies q' and is logically defined thus: whenever p is true, q is true. If 'p' is 'It is a dog,' and 'q' is 'It is an animal,' p implies q because whenever something is a dog, it follows that it is an animal. That is to say, being a dog is a *sufficient condition* for being an animal. Notice that from the fact that something is an animal it does not follow that it is a dog. Thus, being an animal is not a sufficient condition for being a dog. Cats, rats, and bats are all animals, but none of them are dogs. On the other hand, being an animal *is* a *necessary condition* for being a dog. Something cannot be a dog without being an animal. If it is not an animal, then it is not a dog.

To say that p and q stand in a *biconditional* relation is to say that p is *both* a sufficient and a necessary condition for q, *and* q is both a sufficient and a necessary condition for p. This idea is nicely conveyed in symbolic logic: "p implies q" is formalized as 'p $\rightarrow$ q'; 'p implies q' and 'q implies p' as 'p $\leftrightarrow$ q.' This way of formalizing the difference makes explicit, that unlike implication, biconditionality moves in both directions. Being an unmarried male of a marriageable age is both necessary and sufficient for being a bachelor. 'If p implies q' says that p is a sufficient condition for q, then q implies p must say that q is a sufficient condition for p. If 'q only if p' says that p is a necessary condition for q, then 'p only if q' says that q is a necessary condition for p. Thus, 'p if and only if q' means that that q is both a necessary and a sufficient condition for p, and it also means that p is both a necessary and a sufficient condition for q.

A full understanding of Tarski's truth schema T, which is "'p' if and only if 'p'" involves an understanding of the metalanguage/object language distinction, which I covered on p. 32.[9] Schema T is best understood as a condition for meta-linguistic adequacy. According to John Wallace, T requires that the metalanguage "must have structural descriptive names of, and translations of, all closed sentences of the object language. Convention T requires of a theory of truth that for each *closed* sentence of the object language it have as a logical consequence an instance of the schema."[10] Tarski's conception of truth was meant to be an account of truth suitable for inclusion within a formal language like the first-order predicate calculus. Such a language is equipped with quantifiers, both a universal and an existential quantifier. Universal quantification is captured by the expression 'for every x,' and existential quantification by 'there exists at least one x.' Within the context of formal logic, a closed sentence is a sentence that has no *free* variables; all of its variables are *bound*. Open sentences have free or unbound variables. Whether a variable is bound or not depends upon whether it falls within the scope of a quantifier. If it does, it is bound. Sentences like 'All philosophers are gray-bearded loons' would be translated into first order logic as 'For every x, if x is a philosopher, then x is a gray bearded loon.' Here the variable x is bound in both of it occurrences, by the universal quantifier 'for every x.' The sentence is *closed*. But a sentence like 'All philosophers are gray-bearded loons, but they are tall' is ambiguous and can be formalized either as (a) 'For every x [Px implies Gx] and Tx,' or, as (b) 'For every x [(Px implies Gx) and Tx].' If we formalize it as (a), the scope of the universal quantifier is indicated by the brackets, and so the two occurrences of x that are within the scope of the brackets are bound and the one x that occurs outside the brackets is free. When formalized as (b), the brackets again indicate the scope of the quantifier, and all three occurrences of x are bound. (a) interprets the sentence in question as open; (b) as closed.

In schema T, which says that "'Snow is white' if and only if snow is white," the first occurrence of 'Snow is white' is metalinguistic. We are talking about the sentence 'Snow is white.' The second occurrence of 'snow is white' refers to the way the world is, and is in the *object* language.

Ordinary language is not, however, a formal system. Many of its sentences are *not* closed. This raises lots of questions concerning Tarski's T schema, including a question about its relevance to natural languages. This question is one Donald Davidson answers in the affirmative, by providing a theory of meaning in natural languages in terms of truth conditions founded upon Tarski's T schema.

Davidson's concern is with the *structure* that is common to all languages. He is committed to *holism*: the view that the whole is more important, significant, revealing, etc. than its parts. He does not assume "that parts of sentences have meanings except in the ontologically neutral sense of making a systematic contribution to the meaning of the sentences in which they occur." As far as he is concerned, postulating meanings for the constituent parts of sentences "has netted nothing." He says:

> If sentences depend for their meaning on their structure, and we understand the meaning of each item in the structure only as an abstraction from the totality of sentences in which it features, then we can give the meaning of any sentence (or word) only by giving the meaning of every sentence (and word) in the language. Frege said that only in the context of a sentence does a word have meaning; in the same vein he might have added that only in the context of the language does a sentence (and therefore a word) have meaning.[11]

His holism leads him to modify the commonly held view that a theory of meaning must entail *all* sentences of the form 's means m,' (where 's' stands for a sentence and 'm' for meaning) with "s means that p," and imagine 'p' replaced by a sentence, and not a meaning. What he expects such a theory to do is generate a *matching sentence* to replace 'p' in 's means p,' one that in *some* sense does give the meaning of s. He further proposes that 'p' be restricted to what 's' designates:

> One obvious candidate for a matching sentence is just s itself, if the object language is contained in the metalanguage; otherwise a translation of s in the metalanguage. As a final bold step, let us try treating the position occupied by "p" extensionally: to implement this, sweep away the obscure "means that," provide the sentence that replaces "p" with a proper sentential connective, and supply the description that replaces "s" with its own predicate. The plausible result is:

103

(T) s is T if and only if p[12]

This is, of course, Tarski's T schema. When Davidson says, "let us try treating of the position occupied by 'p' extensionally," what he has in mind by 'p' is the state of affairs that 's' describes. If s is 'Snow is white,' then 'p' will be 'that snow is white." In this way Davidson utilizes Tarski's formal analysis of truth to provide an account of meaning in natural languages.

The fundamental program Davidson's theory promotes bears a strong resemblance to the program in Wittgenstein's *Tractatus*. As Peter Hacker so nicely observes, "the inspiration for Davidson's programme was not the *Tractatus*. But the spirit informing the programme was that of the Tractatus."[13] Hacker elaborates on this idea by pointing out that Davidson, like Wittgenstein, "argued that concealed beneath the forms of ordinary speech lies the complex apparatus of the predicate calculus with identity, enriched in various ways (e.g., by quantification over events) to accommodate all legitimate inferences recognized in normal speech.[14] With this thought in mind, I will continue to explain the details of Davidson's view.

In "Semantics for a Natural Language," Davidson claims that a theory of semantics of a natural language must give the meaning of all meaningful expressions, and that a theory of truth for a language does, "in a minimal but important respect," accomplish this task by an "analysis of their structure." He provides us with three criteria a theory of truth must meet: (1) it must consist of a set of axioms that logically entail the truth conditions for every sentence in the language, (2) it must provide a method for deciding what is the meaning of any arbitrary sentence, and (3) the statements of truth conditions for individual sentences that are entailed by the theory should somehow draw upon the same set of concepts as do the sentences whose truth conditions they state. He then makes use of the object language/metalanguage distinction to show that "theories of the sort Tarski showed how to devise" meet these three conditions.[15]

Davidson uses the terms 'metalanguage' and 'object language' as relative terms.[16] When a language is being used, it is an object language, but when it is being talked about, it is a metalanguage. If you ask me about the color of snow and I tell you that snow is white, I am using language. But if I assert, "'Snow is white' is true if and only if snow is white," I am in the first instance of the string 'Snow is white' talking about and not using 'snow is white.' The sentence whose truth conditions are in question, and which is, in our example, 'Snow is white' has its truth conditions stated in terms of itself. For this reason, it is clear that condition (3) is satisfied by his theory. Since the T schema replaces p by s itself, it clearly makes no use of concepts not contained in s.

The T schema provided by the 'Snow is white' case provides the initial step in a *recursive* definition of truth for a formal language. A recursive definition is an inductive or recursive procedure for defining a term. The initial step provides the paradigm case, and the recursive step that follows is the production of a rule or formula for designating all successive items to which the term applies. It is a form of definition that is indigenous to mathematics. Let us consider a non-mathematical example—the term 'bachelor.' Let the initial step be: 'Tom Jones is a bachelor' if and only if he is an unmarried male of a marriageable age. In this case s is 'Tom Jones is a bachelor,' and p is the proposition that he is an unmarried male of marriageable age. Here 'p' is not a repetition of s but does somehow draw upon the same concepts as s. The concept of bachelorhood is understood in terms of the concept of marriage. The recursive rule or formula would be something like: Bachelors are identical with unmarried males of marriageable age. This rule would determine when the term 'bachelor' is correctly applied.

In this fashion, one could use the T schema to generate a theory of truth for a natural language, which can through its recursive nature explain how we can, on the basis of both a finite vocabulary and a finite set of "stated rules," produce and understand any member of a "potential infinity of sentences." Any conceivable sentence involving 'bachelor' would be understood recursively by way of the rule: Bachelors are identical to unmarried males of a marriageable age. We now have a method for deciding the meaning of any arbitrary sentence, and so criterion (2) is met by Davidson's theory.

Davidson acknowledges that predicating 'is true' of a sentence in a natural language is quite often a relative matter. He recognizes that the predicates 'is true' and 'is false' are not predicates belonging to either sentences or propositions. Whether what is said is true or not depends, he admits, on when it is said, who says it, and even, perhaps, the audience. In other words, it is particular utterances or speech acts (statements) that have truth-values. This concession forces him to revise the T schema to make truth sensitive to context.

He considers another kind of problem natural languages present.

Many things we say are ambiguous, and therefore escape our efforts to cast them in terms of Tarski's formal model. He considers various examples, including a case he labels "ingenious," from Bar-Hillel:

The box was in the pen.

While speakers of English would have little trouble deciphering it, the ambiguity it involves has to do with 'pen.' A pen can be a playpen, or a writing instrument. Bar-Hillel uses this example to argue that a fully automatic machine translation may not be feasible, which, for Davidson, constitutes a threat to a fully formal theory of truth like that of Tarski.[17] Davidson attempts to offset this threat by revising Tarski's T schema to make truth a relation that holds between a sentence, a speaker, and a time, and admits that the acceptability of the revised schema would rest on what one allows into the description of the relevant conditions.

He recognizes that some philosophers and linguists are pessimistic about the possibility of giving a formal theory of truth for a natural language, but thinks their pessimism is premature. He thinks that a theory of truth for a natural language does give the meaning of all sentences within that language, in much the same *spirit* as Wittgenstein's *Tractatus*, and in the *letter* of Carnap's positivistic presentation of Wittgenstein.[18] Davidson asserts:

A theory of truth entails, for each sentence *s*, a statement of the form *"s* is true if and only if *p"* where in the simplest case *"p"* is replaced by *s*. Since the words "is true if and only if" are invariant, we may interpret them if we please as meaning "means that." So construed, a sample might then read "'Socrates is wise' means that Socrates is wise."[19]

It seems clear to me that a theory of meaning for a natural language ought to provide an answer to: "What is the meaning of the word 'W'?", where 'W' is any word in that language. Instances of this kind of question are posed countless times everyday. Anyone reading a book, newspaper, magazine, rail schedule, travel guide, menu, etc., will likely encounter unfamiliar instances of words. When this happens, the question "What is the meaning of the word 'W'?" will follow. Suppose the word in question is 'snow.' And suppose that it is a South Sea Islander who asks the question of you, because she did not understand what you meant when you said that snow would soon be falling in your home in Minnesota. What purpose would be served by your responding with "'Snow is white' if and only if snow is white."? In the arthropod or bachelor cases, the answer provided by the theory would be much more enlightening, because in these cases, instead of substituting s itself for p, we are prepared to substitute for p a sentence that draws upon the same set of concepts as does the sentence 'He is a bachelor.' If asked what the word 'bachelor' means, the response dictated by Davidson's theory would be 'He is an unmarried male of a marriageable age,' which could be *interpreted* as an abbreviation for "'One is a bachelor' if and only if one is a bachelor," which is itself a shortened version of "'One is a bachelor' if and only if one is an unmarried male of marriageable age."

Davidson is, however, concerned about the possibility that his procedure, which ties meaning to Tarski's biconditonal analysis, might "encourage certain errors." He attempts to offset these errors. It must be noted that his efforts to deal with various objections to his truth conditional theory of meaning for a natural language has been an on-going project that he has sustained for a number of years. He acknowledged, in a 1967 essay based upon an essay presented at the Pacific Division of the American Philosophical Association in 1953, that "a staggering list of difficulties and conundrums remain" to be solved. He explains:

> we do not know the logical form of counterfactual or subjunctive sentences, nor of sentences about probabilities and about causal relations; we have no good idea what the logical role of adverbs is, nor the role of attributive adjectives; we have no theory for mass terms like "fire," "water," and "snow," nor for sentences about belief, perception, and intention, nor for verbs of action that imply purpose. And finally, there are all the sentences that seem not to have truth-values at all: the imperatives, optatives, interrogatives, and a host more. A comprehensive theory of meaning for a natural language must cope successfully with each of these problems.[20]

This list in itself is overwhelming. Yet, he considered it to be a list of only "a few" of the difficulties inherent in his theory. He has to his credit attempted solutions to some of these objections in various essays over the years.[21] While I remain unconvinced, I turn now to what I consider to be greater difficulties for Davidson.

When it comes to verifying the truth of his theory, he is convinced it can be tested along the same lines as those described by Quine in chapter two of *Word and Object*. The question of whether or not an alien speaker understands the meaning of some English sentence will be, according to Davidson, tested by determining under what conditions the alien speaker assents to or dissents from a variety of his sentences.[22] Because of Davidson's reliance upon Quine's approach, I will have to explain Quine's approach before I can finish my exposition of Davidson.

In chapter two of *Word and Object*, Quine introduces the concept of the *indeterminacy of translation*. Understanding this concept is tied to understanding his concept of *radical translation*. Radical translation occurs when a linguist attempts to construct a translation manual for a language of a society with which the linguist is totally unfamiliar, and one for which the linguist's background knowledge is inapplicable. In this kind of case there are, according to Quine, no *independent controls* that can determine for the linguist which particular hypothesis, among the various incompatible hypotheses open to him or her, is the appropriate one for mapping the language of the linguist onto that of the society under investigation. According to Jerrold Katz, a follower of Chomsky, the indeterminacy of translation results because the linguist in a radical translation case is like a person lost at sea who has no idea which direction is north, south, east or west. She has no background knowledge of the heavens that can be utilized to determine a course of action. She wants to go towards port, and port is hypothesized to be north of the present destination. But nothing she knows is of any help to her.[23]

According to Quine, although translation from one language to another involves a certain "systematic indeterminacy," we are, however, free to adopt "remedies in the spirit of modern logic" which will resolve the "anomalies and conflicts that are implicit in this apparatus."[24] For Quine, a natural language is simply a set of dispositions to respond to socially observable stimuli, and these stimuli are defined in terms of *surface irritations* (in the case of visual stimuli the surface irritations would be the patterns of chromatic irradiation of the eye). He considers physical objects to be nothing more than postulates, and he claims that we have "no reason to suppose that man's surface irritations even unto eternity admit of any one systemization that is scientifically better or simpler than all possible others." Moreover, he claims "it seems likelier, if only on account of symmetries or dualities, that countless alternative theories would be tied for first place." Any given sentence is for Quine meaningless "except relative to its own theory." They are "meaningless intertheoretically."[25] In short, for Quine our commonsense notion of physical objects as independently existing is simply a hypothesis that we use to explain our experiences. For Quine, it is just one hypothesis among many that are equally acceptable.

Although his pronouncements appear relativistic and inherently skeptical, we need not worry, says Quine, because "we continue to take seriously our own particular aggregate science, our own particular world-theory or loose total fabric of quasi theories, whatever it may be." Furthermore, "we own and use our beliefs of the moment, even in the midst of philosophizing, until by what is vaguely called scientific method we change them here and there for the better."[26] Like Hume, who was the first to argue in this fashion, Quine holds that when doubt due to philosophical reflection arises about the ultimate makeup of the world, habit takes hold and we continue to conduct our lives in keeping with our commonplace views of its nature.

In order to convince us that his philosophical reflections are correct, Quine asks us to imagine a linguist attempting to accomplish a radical translation of a "hitherto untouched people." He goes out for a jaunt with one of these "untouched people," and a rabbit hops across their footpath. The native sings out "Gavagai," and the linguist naturally supplies the translation hypothesis "Rabbit." He then tests his hypothesis by asking 'Gavagai?" in each of various stimulatory situations, and notes whether the subject assents, dissents, or does neither. Quine claims that the general law, which the linguist is assembling instances of, is roughly that the native will assent to or dissent from the question "Gavagai?" under the same set of stimulations we would assent to or dissent from the question "Rabbit?". Quine insists that it is stimulations and not rabbits that prompt the native's assent to "Gavagai?" "Stimulation," he confidently observes, "can remain the same though the rabbit can be supplanted by a counterfeit. . . . In experimentally equating the uses of 'Gavagai' and 'Rabbit,' it is the stimulations that must be made to match, not animals." Quine proceeds by identifying visual stimulations with ocular irradiation, which he claims can be intersubjectively checked to some extent by society and linguists alike, "by making allowances for the speaker's orientation and the relative disposition of objects."[27]

Quine's view is comparable to the view that we could never *really* fill a kettle with fish because the number of possible fish that could be put in the kettle over time is indeterminate. But all that is required to fill the kettle is that there should be present to us, at the time we wish to fill it, a sufficient number of fish to reach its brim. The fact that there are innumerable other possible fillings of it is irrelevant to whether or not it is or can be filled. Perhaps the analogy would be more exact if we were to focus on understanding what it would be to fill a kettle with fish, as opposed to filling a specific kettle with fish. On this analogy, what Quine is saying amounts to saying that although specific kettles can be filled with specific fish, we can never understand what it means to fill a kettle, fine or otherwise, with fish!

A Greek fisherman and I can spend a pleasant afternoon together fishing an island inlet without much misunderstanding, even though we understand few words of each other's language. It would be absurd for me to "hypothesize" that when he and I roll our eyes, smack our lips, and pat our bellies, while pointing in the direction of the fish we have managed to catch, that he is thinking of fish stages and not what consumes my interest—the fish, cleaned, cooked, and placed on the table for my culinary enjoyment.

Quine does concede, however, that there are problems with the view that visual stimulations are momentary static irradiation patterns. He says "too much depends on what immediately precedes and follows a momentary irradiation." Under some circumstances, a "momentary leporiform image" might not prompt assent to the word 'Rabbit' in spite of the fact that this same image would have produced this response when "ensconced in a more favorable sequence." And so we cannot determine concerning an irradiation pattern *itself* whether or not it is "favorable" to 'Rabbit.' According to Quine, we should focus on "evolving irradiation patterns of all durations up to some convenient limit or *modulus*," rather than momentary ones. But how does one kind determine the extent or boundaries of relevant stimulus exposure? The ideal experimental situation, he tells us, is the "one in which the desired ocular exposure concerned is preceded and followed by a blindfold." But he has to concede that although these ocular irradiation patterns are best conceived in their entirety, there are cases like, 'Fine weather,' that are not "keyed to any readily segregated fragments of the scene."[28]

Wittgenstein would most likely object to Quine's view by claiming that Quine's "problems" concerning translation are problems that Quine's approach *creates*. They are not substantive problems. Quine needs to be *reminded* of various facts. It is quite misleading to claim that ocular irradiation patterns are not keyed to any *readily* segregated fragments of the scene. Often they are *totally* irrelevant to one's exclaiming, "Fine weather!" One may be claiming it on the basis of what he or she has heard on the radio, read in an almanac, or from rumors. We sometime assert it sarcastically when the weather is anything but fine. "Fine weather" can be used to perform any one of a number of Austin's *illocutionary* acts. It can be used to warn, inform, greet, etc.

Quine distorts matters further when he claims that "whole scenes" serve better than isolated portions in regard to whether or not one will assent or dissent from "Rabbit." In whole scenes, the subject receives both central and peripheral sensory stimuli. If one perceives the rabbit too peripherally, one will not likely assent to 'Gavagai' or 'Rabbit.' But this is clearly shortsighted. We must not ignore wagering, longing for a sign of life, the hunter's lonely vigil, or a starving person's acutely food-focused consciousness. It is certain that when we are wagering fifty dollars on who sees the rabbit first, peripheral appearances will not be lost on us. And what about the hunter who has waited for hours for his prey to appear? Do you think he will miss even the slightest motion that invades the farthest edge of her visual field?

Eventually, the problems created by Quine's approach force him to acknowledge that *background conditions* do play an important role in speech episodes. He uses the term 'collateral information' to cover these background conditions, and illustrates its importance in translation and understanding by 'Rabbit' with both 'Red' and 'Bachelor.' He claims that the extent of collateral information the subject possesses need not be as great in deciding whether a glimpsed thing is red as it needs to be in deciding whether it is a rabbit. For that reason, words like 'Red' offer the best chance for synonymous translation. But regarding words like 'Bachelor,' he says that meaning is quite susceptible to information not contained in a given sensory context. He insists that the stimulus meaning of 'Bachelor' cannot be equated with its meaning unless the subject in the experiment or situation possesses a great deal of collateral information. How would you ever know that the male waiter you clearly see directly in front of you is a bachelor, unless you already know something further about that person? This leads him to claim that the less collateral information one needs to correctly use a sentence, the greater the plausibility that the stimulus meaning of that sentence is its meaning. He then defines observation sentences as: "occasion sentences whose stimulus meanings vary none under the influence of collateral information," and concludes that the stimulus meanings of such occasion sentences can be said to do full justice to their meanings. He does, however, admit that even the stimulus meaning of 'Red,' his best candidate for reducing meaning to stimulus meaning, can be affected to a small extent by collateral information concerning lighting conditions.[29]

111

Stimulus synonymy does not, Quine cautions, guarantee that two terms are coextensive. Regarding 'Gavagai,' he claims that the linguist has no way of knowing whether the native is using that word to refer to rabbits or to "mere stages or brief temporal segments, of rabbits." It follows, according to Quine, that should the linguist infer from the native's behavior that he is referring to the whole enduring rabbit, as we do, his inference is unjustified. The native might actually be referring to rabbit stages or rabbit parts.[30] Since every case of translation will involve similar indeterminacies, Quine concludes that all translations are indeterminate.[31]

But stimulus conditions do not any more fit the meaning of 'That is red' than they do 'That is a rabbit.' In both cases, background conditions are sometimes more important than at other times. If the episode leading up to the assertion that something is red concerns the evaluation of color harmonies, and includes an agreement on the part of the participants to limit their color assessments to determining whether the primary layer of paint was a red or a blue tone, then the stimulus which elicits the red response may well be one which would not be at all likely to illicit that response under many other even standard conditions. Whether or not something is red is surely not, in opposition to what Quine seems to think, as certain in many contexts, as it is that something is a charging elephant, a skyscraper, or Niagara Falls. Quine's recognition of background conditions is vitiated by his failure to fully appreciate just how extensive their role is in determining what is meant.

The idea that stimulus synonymy needs to exist, ever does exist, or is importantly relevant to successful communication or translation from one language to another is simply mistaken. It is a *given*, not *a theoretical discovery* of importance, that no two speakers ever experience the same phenomenon in *exactly* the same way. Neither do they drive a car or sing a song or play a hand dealt to them in poker in exactly the same way, or even often in a very similar way. Even the same musician plays the same song in different ways at different times.

An account of empirical meaning, and related concepts like communication, synonymy, and translation, in terms of stimulus meaning (involving as it does for Quine the idea that two or more individuals can have a precise *understanding* of one another, use the same terms with the same meaning *only if* they share these meanings, or have the same stimulations) assumes that one can determine the meaning of words, or the stimulations necessary to guarantee sentential synonymy in general, and do so independently of an actual context of use.

112

Now we can return to Davidson. Davidson agrees with Quine that a significant amount of indeterminacy will remain after all the evidence is in, and that there will be a number of theories that will explain the evidence equally well.[32] According to Davidson, in order to translate from an alien's language to the linguist's own language, the linguist must construct a theory of meaning for the speaker of the other language. According to Davidson, what the linguist must do is

> find out, however he can, what sentences the alien holds true in his own tongue (or better, to what degree he holds them true). The linguist then will attempt to construct a characterization of truth-for-the-alien which yields, so far as possible, a mapping of sentences held true (or false) by the alien onto sentences held true (or false) by the linguist. Supposing no perfect fit is found, the residue of sentences held true translated by sentences held false (and vice versa) is the margin for error (foreign or domestic). Charity in interpreting the words and thoughts of others is unavoidable. . . . No single principle of optimum charity emerges; the constraints therefore determine no single theory.[33]

This procedure, adopted and adapted from Quine, provides a test for Davidson's theory. Davidson does not, however, share Quine's wish to reduce language to talk about surface irritations, nor is he willing to accept wholeheartedly the skeptical conclusions that seem to follow from Quine's indeterminacy of translation thesis. Although he recognizes that no single principle of optimum charity exists, he does think it possible for one to *interpret* in charitable fashion what a speaker means, by making the best possible sense of what he or she says in so far as one maximizes the overall truth of the speaker's utterance. To do so is, for Davidson, to take a *holistic* account of all of the speaker's utterances and to assign the maximal amount of truth to the speaker's utterances on the basis of a Tarski kind of truth theory. If the theory implies that some sentence S is true in the speaker's language if and only if snow is white, then that is the meaning of S in the speaker's language.

Davidson thinks that the underlying (logical) grammar of a natural language closely resembles standard quantification logic.[34] On his account, if someone says, "Bachelors are unmarried males of a marriageable age," we interpret this to mean (x) [Bx ↔ Ux], which says that for every x, x is a bachelor, if and only if x is an unmarried male. In principle, recursively speaking, through the finite set of rules for the interpretation of any declarative sentence, we can understand how we are able to interpret any one of the infinite number of sentences that it is possible to formulate within a natural language. This is the heart of holism about linguistic meaning.

The Wittgenstein of the *Investigation's* would, I think, object to both Quine and Davidson on the grounds that they mistakenly attempt to understand meaning as a general phenomenon, when in truth it can only be understood contextually. As there is no general something which can be said to be *the* taste of wine, *the* smell of flowers, or *the* feel of wood—but only this or that taste of wine, this or that smell of flowers, and this or that feel of wood—there is no general explanation of meaning. Grasping your meaning, understanding what you say (as well as most other actions) is something that requires an *action context*. Actions do not occur in vacuums and neither do apprehensions. The fish that fill your kettle on one day will likely be quite distinct in both number and kind from the ones that fill it on another.

But in defense of Davidson, let us not forget that he acknowledged that the predicate "is true" depends on when it is said, who says it, and possibly the audience. He also said that either we must say that it is particular utterances or speech acts, not sentences, that have truth-values, or we must define truth in terms of a relation that holds between a sentence, a speaker, and a time.

But if he really believes this, it seems to me that what follows is not that we need some logical technique, with all that this entails: predicate calculus, Tarski's T schema, recursive definitions, and a principle of charity, to account for the ability to "interpret" what others mean to say. Instead, we need only reflect on how successful we are at deciphering what others mean, including persons from other cultures, and recognize that our success has nothing to do with being able to utilize a truth theory like Davidson's. What possible good would a theory based on the formal principles of logic do me if I were to find myself in a situation where I needed to determine what an alien meant?

Besides, the term "interpretation" loses its distinctive meaning when it is used as Davidson uses it. In cases like the "Gavagai" case, it would mean what it ordinarily means, but in many cases where 'understood' or 'meant' would be appropriate, 'interpret' would be inappropriate. In a case where someone, call him Thomas, says about what Franklin has said, "Franklin meant George Washington when he spoke of the conqueror of Cornwallis," I would never call Thomas's statement an interpretation, even if I were bending over to be *charitable*.

Many words have meanings that are governed by conditions that overlap and crisscross. The meanings of some words are governed by necessary and sufficient conditions. But neither of these two kinds of meaning can be fixed, and the reason for this is that they are, as I previously argued, all *open-textured*.[35] It's not clear how Davidson would treat those words that are governed by overlapping and crisscrossing conditions—family resemblance words. One thing is clear: no theory that employs the 'if and only if' operation is appropriate, in so far as the set of conditions that govern the meanings of family resemblance words cannot be given in terms of necessary and sufficient conditions. Davidson sidesteps this issue holistically by claiming that there are no individual *word* meanings, by which he means no isolatable and individualized entities. But if by meanings one thinks of practices or conventions (rules?), it is difficult to see how one could maintain that there are no word meanings.

Like many other philosophers of language, Davidson is fundamentally mistaken about the nature of natural language. Like the Wittgenstein of the *Tractatus*, Davidson is ingenious, formally proficient, careful, precise, and productive. Unlike the Wittgenstein of the *Investigations*, however, he fails to *fully* appreciate the vast gulf that separates formal or artificial languages from natural languages. Davidson understands that there are many differences between the two, and uses Tarski's schema even though he is aware that Tarski himself did not think it could be extended to natural languages.[36] But he remains captivated by the seductive nature of formal systems. He wants to tinker and tweak natural language until he can fit it into his ever-expanding formalist mold. One can tinker with a formal language just as a master mechanic does with a powerful V8 engine, until it performs just as he wants it to. But one cannot do the same with an *organic* entity. Natural languages are more closely akin to living and breathing, ever-changing biological systems, than they are to mechanical contrivances. Many natural language terms are family resemblance terms. All empirical terms are open-textured. And one can either accept these facts and proceed accordingly or one can ignore them and end up with a patched, clumsy, inarticulate robot that only *looks like* a person.

I am not suggesting, however, that we ignore the importance that truth conditions play in a comprehensive account of meaning. But in order to understand the role of truth conditions in an account of meaning, we must not blur the distinction between sentential and contextual meaning. As we have seen, Davidson explains what a person *means by what he or she says,* by allowing for a *principle of charity* that makes the best possible sense out of what that person says by assigning meaning that maximizes the overall truth of the utterances. In this way he shifts from contextual meaning to sentential meaning. What a person means by something is defined in terms of what an interpreter assigns to that something on the basis of what it would mean if the subject were following the rules of logic, where truth is assigned on the basis of Tarski's T schema. For this reason his analysis does blur the distinction between sentential and contextual meaning, and this is unacceptable.

An adequate account of *sentential* meaning must, as I will explain in the last chapter, incorporate *truth conditions*. But they are not relevant to *contextual* meaning, even though *truth-values* are. One who holds out hope that natural language can be transformed into a game with fixed rules for determining meaning and use must in the end be disappointed. But that does not mean that open-ended and flexible rules cannot be formulated on the basis of actual use, rules that would provide us with all the guidance we need to understand what a sentence means, as opposed to what someone might mean by it on some occasion. I will pursue this theme in Chapter Four.

The Inferential Theory of Meaning

We have as yet, not considered the theory that the meaning of a sentence S, or a proposition P, is given by the sentences or the propositions it entails, and which in turn entail it. This theory, which is sometimes referred to as the *inferential role theory*, has been stated in both propositional and sentential formats. While it is true that sentences in themselves do not have any entailments, what a sentence means does have entailments. If we define propositions, as I prefer to do, and have done throughout the present work, as the standard meanings of sentences, we can say that the second format can be reduced to the first. The sentential format is just an abbreviation of: "the meanings of a sentence S can be established in terms of the meanings of those sentences it entails, and which are entailed by it."

At this point, it should be clear to the reader that this theory, as stated, is subject to the twofold but related deficiency of being unable to do justice to the fact that there are many words in a natural language that are family resemblance words, and that all empirical words are open textured. In order to justify such a theory one would have to *modify* it to accommodate these words. As it stands, it attempts to fix meaning via the biconditional relation of equivalence: if p is the proposition expressed by sentence s, and p' and p'' are the propositions entailed by p, which in turn entail p, then p *if and only if* both p' and p". Rather than modifying an existent theory to take into account the fact that natural languages do not behave like formal languages, I prefer an account that recognizes from the *outset* that natural languages are quite different from formal ones. I will offer such an account in the final chapter.

---

[1] Fann (1967) p. 54.

[2] For an excellent account of the controversy concerning whether or not the positivists were justified in attributing the VP to Wittgenstein, see Hacker (1996) pp-52-53.

[3] Carnap (1930) p. 62.

[4] Ibid., pp. 63-67.

[5] Ramsey, (1931) General Propositions and Causality, *The Foundations of Mathematics* (London: Routledge & Kegan Paul Ltd.), p. 238.

[6] Black (1964) pp. 380-386.

[7] See page 32 above for my explanation of the object language/metalanguage distinction.

[8] See page 29 above for further details regarding molecular propositions.

[9] Tarski (1944) pp. 52-55.

[10] Wallace (1975) p. 50.

[11] Davidson (1967) p. 79.

[12] Ibid., p. 79.

[13] Hacker (1996) p. 269.

[14] Hacker (1996) p. 269.

[15] Davidson (1970) pp. 18–19.

[16] This is a departure from my use of these terms previously. My use is a commonplace use, one Russell used, and defines any metalanguage as a language used to talk about another language, and it does not matter whether the object of your talk (an object language) is in the same or a different language. You could be using a formal or artificial language to talk about an English or French sentence, or an English or French sentence to talk about a sentence in a formal language. But, on this account, a language to talk about the world is not a metalanguage. It is *a first order* object language.

[17] As a matter of fact, it was never meant to be a definition of truth in a natural language.

[18] It allows one to equate any of the four options Carnap lists, and particularly (2) with (4).

[19] Davidson (1970) p.21.

[20] Davidson (1967) p. 89.

[21] He refers to these efforts himself in a footnote added to the 1967 essay. They are Essays 6-10 of Essays on *Actions and Events* (Oxford: Oxford University Press, 1980) and Essays 6-8, and a further discussion in Essays 3, 4, 9, and 10, of *Inquiries into Truth and Interpretation*, D. Davidson (Oxford: The Clarendon Press, 1984).

[22] Davidson (1970) p. 22.

[23] Katz (1988).

[24] Quine (1960) p. ix.

[25] Ibid., pp. 23-24.

[26] Ibid., p.24.

[27] Ibid., pp. 29- 31.

[28] Ibid., pp. 31-32.

[29] Ibid., pp. 40-43.

[30] Ibid., p. 52.

[31] Quine poses a challenge to his own analysis in asking about his translator's indecision concerning whether the native is talking about rabbits, rabbit parts, or rabbit stages. He considers the possibility that any indecision concerning what the native is pointing to might be resolved by a few well-chosen questions and appropriate gestures. But he rejects this idea by claiming: "Nothing not distinguished in stimulus meaning itself is to be distinguished by pointing, unless the pointing is accompanied by questions of identity and diversity." Such questions require, however, according to Quine, knowledge of the native's language that far exceeds anything we know how to explain. Quine (1960) pp. 52-53.

[32] Davidson (1970) p. 22.

[33] Davidson (1967) pp. 82-83.

[34] Davidson and Harmon (1975) p. 5.

[35] See above p. 96.

[36] Davidson (1967) pp. 83-89.

4

Descriptive and Causal
Theories of Referring

We have established that there are, in addition to the reference and use theories of meaning, several other viable candidates, including the verification, the truth conditions and the inferential role theories. Independent of one's choice of theory one must answer the question "How is it that words refer?" Things can be conceived, for example, either as referents or as truth conditions, but independent of one's choice regarding what is ultimately designated, one must answer the question about *how* words manage to designate or refer. Efforts to answer this question are described as *theories of referring*. The prevailing theory for much of the twentieth century was the *descriptive theory*, but that theory has been seriously challenged during the last thirty-five years, and has been knocked off its perch by a newcomer. In the sixties, Keith Donnellan, Saul Kripke, and Hillary Putnam argued that the descriptive theory was seriously inadequate, and proposed "a new theory of referring" to take its place. The new theory they proposed is referred to as the *causal theory of referring*, and sometimes as the *historical theory of referring*.

The Descriptive Theory of Referring
The descriptive theory originated in the works of Frege and Russell, and was later modified by Strawson and Searle. But we must distinguish between the theory often designated as "the Frege/Russell theory" and actual views that Russell and Frege held, to see if there is a single view that can be said to have been jointly held by both Frege and

Russell. The view that is often attributed to them is one that Saul Kripke attributes to them.[1] It is the theory that referring expressions are simply *disguised* or *abbreviated descriptions*. Linguistic terms are said to refer to things by expressing descriptive features or characteristics of the things to which they refer. When I use the *name* 'Aristotle' to refer to the man Aristotle, one who does not know to whom I am referring, cannot understand what I am saying unless I use some description such as 'the ancient Greek philosopher who was the pupil of the philosopher Plato and the teacher of Alexander the Great.' According to this theory, a *general term* like 'lion' is said to abbreviate that set or cluster of characteristics commonly associated with lions. It is because of the properties, characteristics, or *communal* designations which objects have, or are thought of as having, that objects can be referred to. I will refer to this theory as the disguised descriptions theory of referring, abbreviated as DDTR.

Frege's actual theory is, as we learned in Chapter I, that proper names have both a sense and a referent, and that unless we make such a distinction we cannot resolve certain paradoxes and puzzles such as the one about George IV. Russell, on the other hand, refuses to take seriously the idea that proper names have sense. (As we saw in Chapter I, there is a difference between the views he held in "On Denoting" and those he held in "The Papers on Logical Atomism."[2]) At no time did Russell agree with Frege that proper names have sense. His solution to the George IV paradox is quite different from Frege's. He does not have to utilize the notions of customary and indirect senses to avoid this puzzle, as Frege does. He does, however, hold the thesis that what are ordinarily considered to be proper names can be "eliminated" by suitable descriptions.

For Frege, the actual linking, that description which does the work, must somehow be connected to the intentions of the speaker—though in most cases the characteristic or characteristics intended will correspond to a commonly occurring one. According to Frege, one is guilty of *psychologistic* reasoning—confusing propositions, universals, numbers, relations, and meanings with mental states or processes—unless the mode of referring is *commonly* shared with other speakers of the language. Unless we recognize the importance of this distinction and focus upon or define the intentions of speakers in terms of what is commonly understood, logic cannot be objectively founded. Frege exemplifies the distinction by considering the proper name 'Bucephalus.' As he points out, a painter, an equestrian, and a zoologist will imagine or think of Bucephalus differently, though all understand the same sense. The sense of the expression is "the common property of many." It is 'the warhorse of Alexander the Great.' Thus, on Frege's theory, the name 'Bucephalus' abbreviates 'the warhorse of Alexander the Great.'[3]

Neither Frege nor Russell was under the impression that a specific proper name stood in an *identity* relation to a particular description, such that whenever that name appeared in a sentence, and one wished to explain or understand it, one would have to be able to dredge up that description. This is important because, as we shall shortly see, Strawson's version of the descriptive theory turns on this "identity thesis." Before we proceed, it is important to remind ourselves of certain facts concerning the meanings of both general terms and proper names.

We must not confuse having a meaning, in the ordinary sense of 'meaning,' with the possibility of there being some description of what is referred to by a word. *All* general terms have meaning in the ordinary sense of word 'meaning,' and their meanings can generally be found in dictionaries. But this is *not* the case for all proper names. Only *some* proper names have meaning in the ordinary sense of the word 'meaning.'

The nineteenth century British philosopher John Stuart Mill claimed that proper names are meaningless symbols, while general terms, like 'cow' and 'cannon' have meaning. The idea that proper names are meaningless is mistaken, however. Many proper names do have meaning in the sense under consideration. But one must avoid confusing *etymological* meaning with what is commonly referred to as word meaning. The fact that a name like 'Lionel' is etymologically derived from the French diminutive for 'lion' is of little if any importance to the question of whether or not proper names have meanings. I certainly do not mean to imply that Lionel Atwill, the actor who played an inspector in all those thirties horror movies, was somehow of diminutive stature, worth, importance, etc., when I refer to him with his proper name.

Some ordinary proper names do have meaning in other than an etymological sense, and some of these names bear a *descriptive* relation to what they designate. The descriptive relation involved can be: *literal, metaphorical* or *figurative*. Examples of the literal kind are: 'Round Hill, Virginia' and 'the Black Hills.' Round Hill is on a round hill in Virginia, and the Black Hills are black. Other proper names are descriptive of events that do/did occur on/at the place they name: 'Accident, Maryland' and 'Council Bluffs, Iowa.' Some are descriptive of possession or are honorific: 'Georgia,' 'Maryland,' 'Kennedy Airport,' 'Prince Albert, Canada,' and 'Mark Twain High School.'

Examples of metaphorically descriptive names are: 'the Painted Desert' and 'Lake Placid.' Some names are metaphorically descriptive of properties one wishes to bestow upon the bearer of the name. Indian names are examples of this sort, for example, 'Still Water,' and 'Brave Arrow.' Other Indian names are more literally descriptive, but are, nevertheless, figurative: 'Running Wolf,' 'Standing Bear,' and 'Sitting Bull.' Arrows cannot be brave, but bears can stand. The *Registry* of Thoroughbred horses is rich in examples of various kinds: 'Bold Reasoning,' 'What A Winter,' 'Northern Dancer,' 'Swoon's Son,' and 'Seabiscuit.' Plays, operas, movies, and ballets have names rich in descriptive content: 'The Death of a Salesman,' 'The Marriage of Figaro,' 'On the Waterfront,' and 'Swan Lake.'

Henceforth, I will refer to names that have meaning as *descriptive* designators, and I will refer to names like 'Robert Odell' and 'Sarigotha' as *nondescriptive* designators. The latter kind possesses little or no descriptive content. It should be clear at this point that being descriptive of the thing named is not an essential property of the naming relation. If any doubt remains in the reader's mind, just consider how easy it is to name an individual by simply stringing letters together e.g., 'Zzz,' and then using the result to designate an individual. Anyone who chooses to do so could use 'Zzz' to name her cat or dog.

Proper names behave like labels. They identify certain persons, places, and things. Given this, is the main difference between proper names and general terms simply that the former label particulars while the latter label kinds of thing? Not necessarily! There seem to be two major differences between them: (1) proper names can be defined ostensively (by pointing), and general terms cannot; (2) one can consult dictionaries to determine what kinds of things are labeled by general terms, but one cannot do so for proper names. How important is this difference?

To begin with, if I have said something about something that I refer to with the expression 'Sarigotha,' you may be in doubt as regards what I am referring to, and I can point to my dog and tell you that she is Sarigotha. I have introduced you to the referent of the expression in question ostensively. If you have any doubts concerning the truth of my contention, however, you cannot resolve it by looking in a dictionary. If, on the other hand, you do not know what I am referring to when I use the expression 'dog' (suppose that you grew up in a country where there are no dogs, and you have never seen any pictures of dogs), my pointing to my dog may simply mislead you. Suppose my dog is a Pekinese, and I point to it and say "That is a dog." Suppose further that later on you encounter a Mexican Hairless. If my Pekinese is the only example of a dog that you have previously seen, you are not apt to wonder whether or not this thing you are seeing is a dog. You are much more likely to wonder what *kind* of thing it is that you are seeing. A Pekinese and a Mexican Hairless share very few surface characteristics.

Suppose, moreover, that although your country has no dogs, it does have an abundance of wolves, and also suppose that after you have learned that a Mexican Hairless is also a dog, you encounter a German Shepherd. You are, at this point in your education about dogs, apt to take the German Shepherd to be a wolf, particularly if the German Shepherd you encounter is a tall and undernourished specimen. Suppose at this point I use a dog book to introduce you to pictures of all the recognized breeds, as well as their descriptions. There will, even after I have done so, remain lots of crossbreeds or curs that you have not seen either in person, or in pictures, and no descriptions of crossbreeds or curs exist anywhere. But what about the dictionary? Is its entry for the word 'dog' extensive enough to include crossbreeds and curs?

My desk dictionary defines the word 'dog' as "any of a large and varied group of domesticated animals related to the fox, wolf, and jackal." This definition, because of its summarizing nature, does not so obviously fail, as did the conjunctive set of breed depictions and/or descriptions that I mentioned in the last paragraph. Yet its high degree of generality generates problems of its own. It is too general to be of much help to anyone who does not already know what a dog is. It provides a meaning for the word in question, but it does not *enable* one to recognize and identify dogs and distinguish them from all other creatures. Still it serves its purpose, which is to give one a general enough idea of what a dog is to be able to talk about dogs, and to do so with a fair amount of impunity. Knowing all there is to know about dogs is a lifetime pursuit. Knowing what the word 'dog' *means,* in the relevant sense of the word 'means,' *is* simply being able to understand and paraphrase what one finds in a dictionary.

Dictionaries can, nonetheless, be misleading, and so we should not be uncritically reliant upon them. They give the impression that words have meaning in isolation, when in fact the meaning of some words can only be attributed to them when they appear in sentential contexts. The meaning that a word has is a function of the linguistic context in which it appears. Consider the following sentences:

(1) I caught the latest movie at the Bijou.

(2) I caught his meaning.

The word 'caught' has a different meaning in (1) than it has in (2). In (1) it could be paraphrased as 'attended.' In (2) it could be paraphrased as 'understood.' An adequate account of sentential meaning will have to do justice to these facts.

Still, it seems true that proper names can be defined ostensively, and that because of this they do, as Russell thought, have meaning in the sense of reference in isolation from a sentential context. Their referents do exist independent of any sentential context, and can usually be pointed to. Understood in this way, Russell does seem to be right. But general terms are another matter. As I illustrated by the verb 'caught,' most, if not all, verbs do not to have distinctive meanings outside of any sentential context.

Although nouns and noun phrases are not the same as verbs, the following example serves to make the same kind of point regarding nouns:

(1') The bank is the largest building in town.

(2') The bank we climbed was very steep.

The expression 'bank' has a different meaning in (1') than it has in (2'). In (1') it can be paraphrased as 'a commercial institution with the express purpose of safeguarding, changing, and lending money.' In (2') bank can be paraphrased by 'a steep natural incline.' Expressions like 'bank' and 'caught' are what philosophers call *multivocal*. They have more than one sense.[4]

Dictionaries provide lists of possible paraphrases. We sometimes choose, from among them, the one or ones that best enable us to *decipher* sentences about which we are in doubt. The various entries that fall under a given word, what are commonly referred to as the various senses of that word, comprise a set of synonyms. What one ordinarily does when one consults a dictionary is scan that set of senses looking for words, the meanings of which one already possesses, which allow one to make sense out of some sentence containing an unknown word or words. One-word messages and responses are elliptical for complete thoughts, and should be treated accordingly. We do sometimes attribute meaning to isolated words, but when we do so, what we attribute to them is one of their possible paraphrases or senses. When one is doing crossword puzzles, one does this sort of thing. But here the number of squares in the crossword puzzle imposes restrictions. Such activities as doing a crossword puzzle are parasitic on the fundamental or basic linguistic activity of *communicating*.

Although the vast majority of proper names are not found in dictionaries, most dictionaries do, as I pointed out in the introduction, contain some proper names. These are quite distinct from the commonplace entries of the dictionary. They are limited to the names of famous persons, places, and things, persons, places, and things whose identities are important to us. Examples are George Washington, Athens, and Athena.

Frege would not agree with Mill's contention that names do not have sense, nor would he agree with the more limited claim that some proper names do not have sense. As we know, Frege maintained that all proper names (including full declarative sentences, which are for him names) have sense, even though some of them do not have reference. For Frege, what we must focus on when explaining meaning are the *objective* senses of an expression, namely, the descriptions that are commonly attached to objects, as opposed to the varied and numerous sets of possible *personal descriptions* that can or could be intended. Frege is not concerned with the fluctuations or ambiguities that result from variations in the personal and even communal uses of names. He claims that as long as the referent of an expression remains the same, fluctuations in sense can be tolerated. But he claims that they cannot be tolerated in science. For the purposes of science and philosophical discourse, what is needed is an ideal or formal language that specifies one and only one description for each name.[5]

Russell agrees with Frege that we need a formally proper or ideal language for the purposes of science and philosophy, but disagrees as regards the nature of the vocabulary of such a language. Russell considered the language he and Whitehead developed in *Principia Mathematica* to be an ideal language, in need of a vocabulary. Frege would probably have agreed. He had himself devised a formal language quite like that of *Principia*, though in some ways much less elegant. What he would not have agreed with is that this vocabulary need assign only a referent to each word. A proper vocabulary, for Frege, would have to assign *both* a specific sense and a specific referent to all its names. Keeping in mind the views of Russell and Frege, let us turn to the descriptive theories of Strawson and Searle.

Even though Strawson is committed to the importance of word usage, and is critical of referential theorists, he still advocates the descriptive theory of referring. The descriptivist approach cuts across the boundaries of the use versus reference theory controversy. Both reference theorists and use theorists have to answer the question I raised in the opening paragraph of this chapter: "How is it that words refer?" Strawson, like Russell and Frege, answers this question by use of the descriptive theory.

In Strawson's book, *Individuals: An Essay in Descriptive Metaphysics,* written several years after his influential attack on Russell's "On Referring" (covered in detail in Chapter II), he says "one cannot use a name to refer to someone or something unless one knows who or what it is one is referring to by that name." He concludes, "One must, in other words, be prepared to substitute a description for that name."[6] He realizes that this condition in itself is not sufficient. It is not enough that there should be one description that fits the object named. There *must* be some description which applies "uniquely." Such a description he refers to as an *identifying description,*[7] and he says that the uniquely identifying description cannot be what the speaker would describe as 'the one I have in mind.' Strawson then extends his notion of presupposition to explain and justify a descriptivist account of referring expressions as follows:

> Consider the situation in which a reference is made, by name, to Socrates . . . both speaker and hearer, in this situation, satisfy the conditions for successful term-introduction if each knows some distinguishing fact or facts, not necessarily the same ones, about Socrates, facts which each is prepared to cite to indicate whom he now means, or understands, by 'Socrates'. But what is the relation between these facts and the name? Or, to put what is really the same question in another form, what are the conditions *of* my correctly describing them as 'facts about Socrates', where I use, and do not mention, the name? It is in relation to this question that the notion of presupposition is once more relevant. [8]

To answer this question, he enlarges his notion of presupposition (which the reader will remember I both explained and criticized in Chapter II, on pages 69-72) to make it relevant, by speaking of a "presupposition-set," which is that set of propositions that constitute a "complete description" of the referent. A correct use of a singularly referring expression like 'Socrates' depends, says Strawson, upon its being used in such a way that a *reasonable proportion* of the descriptions contained in the presupposition set apply, and that they apply to one and only one individual. But, according to Strawson, "neither the limits of such a set, nor the question of what constitutes a reasonable, or sufficient, proportion of its members will in general be precisely fixed. . ." For Strawson, this situation is not a cause for alarm.

The fact that the presupposition set is not fixed is "not a deficiency" in the set. It is, instead, says Strawson, "a part of the efficiency of proper names."[9]

He also introduces the concept of *reference borrowing*, to explain how one can succeed in referring to someone or something when one does not have an identifying description with which to describe that thing. According to Strawson,

> the identifying description . . . may include a reference to another's reference to that particular. If a putatively identifying description is of this . . . kind, then, indeed, the question, whether it is a genuinely identifying description, turns on the question, whether the reference it refers to is itself a genuinely identifying reference. So one reference may borrow its credentials, as a genuinely identifying reference, from another; and that from another. But this regress is not infinite.[10]

If, for example, a student S learns that Aristotle was a philosopher from professor P, and this is *all* he knows about Aristotle, how could he meet the requirement of the descriptive theorist: that one who uses a proper name *must* be prepared to substitute an identifying description for the proper name of the object referred to? Would we not have to say of S that s(he) did not know whom s(he) was talking about? Not according to Strawson. S can, he claims, use the description 'the person professor P referred to as "Aristotle."'

Strawson's view seems to be that the meaning or sense of a proper name is a uniquely identifying description, which is a member of a *set* of commonly recognized descriptions, true of the referent of that name. If I mean by the name 'Aristotle,' 'the philosopher who invented logic,' and you mean by that name, 'the philosopher who taught both Plato and Alexander the great,' each of us would be using a uniquely identifying description, both of which are members of the presupposition set regarding the name 'Aristotle.' The fact that this set is not fixed or determinate is not a problem for Strawson, but is actually an advantage. Just imagine how difficult communication would be if each of us had to have knowledge of every member of the presupposition set of commonly used descriptions, for every name used in our community. When I talk about Socrates, there are many descriptions I associate with his name, but there are probably other descriptions in common use with which I am not familiar. Many years ago, I remember discussing Socrates with a friend of mine who mentioned that Socrates was married to someone named 'Xantippe.' I was unfamiliar with this fact, which I soon learned was common knowledge, at least among philosophers. I did know who Socrates was even if I was not aware that he was married to Xantippe.

We must note at this juncture that Strawson's focus is quite different from that of both Frege and Russell. Strawson is concerned with providing an account of the way proper names are used in natural languages. Frege and Russell are focused upon the development of formal languages that do not suffer from the lack of specificity inherent in natural languages. Strawson's views concerning natural language usage of proper names mirror to some extent Frege's attempts to construct an ideal language. Both philosophers consider a statement that has as a subject a reference to a non-existent object, as neither true nor false. Frege, however, rejects the idea that natural languages contain descriptions that uniquely identify the referents of proper names. Russell would not agree with Strawson's approach either. As far as he is concerned, there are no genuine proper names in natural languages, only descriptions masquerading as names.

But what if we borrow from Frege the idea that names have sense as well as reference and from Russell the idea that ordinary proper names are just disguised descriptions? We could then construct a view according to which ordinary proper names can be understood as descriptions, disguised or otherwise. Call it a *possible* DDTR (the disguised descriptions theory of referring), or PDDTR. One might try to *mend* PDDTR so as to explain how natural language use is not really as fluctuation prone as Frege deems it to be, nor as hopelessly vague as Russell thought it, because the meaning of proper names can be fixed through the introduction of uniquely identifying descriptions. This is what Strawson attempts to do, and I will refer to his view as SDDTR.

I want now to turn to Searle's version of the descriptive theory. His views are consistent with SDDTR, and he has defended the descriptive theory against some of its most formidable opponents. He refines SDDTR by a procedure for determining membership in the presupposition set, which he refers to as the set of intentional content. He claims that in spite of the fact that there is considerable variation in personal uses of proper names, there is a way to characterize the communal sense of any name which is sufficient for unambiguous discourse. According to Searle, what is understood as the meaning of a proper name is that *set* of *intentional contents* that is comprised of uniquely referring descriptions—a set determined by asking members of the community of language users what they would consider to be "certain essential and established facts" regarding the bearer of a given name.[11] He claims that the answers provided by the community of

128

speakers—the set of uniquely referring descriptive statements—could be used to establish the sense or meaning of a proper name. Searle uses the example 'Aristotle' to illustrate his point. He claims that the "descriptive force" of the sentence 'This is Aristotle' is equivalent to asserting that a sufficient but unspecified number of these uniquely referring descriptive statements are *true* of Aristotle.[12] Searle makes use of Strawson's concept of an identifying description, to claim that whenever a speaker uses a proper name, he must be prepared to substitute an identifying description of the referent, or have credentials borrowed from someone who is prepared to do so.

As I pointed out above, the causal or historical view of referring, associated with the American philosophers Keith Donnellan, Hilary Putnam, and Saul Kripke, was proposed as the best program for overcoming various deficiencies inherent in the descriptivist theory. Searle has attempted to answer some of their objections. I will return to Searle after I have explicated the causal theory and its objections to the descriptive theory.

The Causal or Historical Theory of Referring

The *causal* or *historical* theory, advocated by the American philosophers Keith Donnellan, Saul Kripke, and Hilary Putnam, answers the question concerning how words designate things by claiming that a linguistic expression denotes what it denotes because of its particular causal history. An expression's referent is fixed by an initial act of referring which links the expression to some object or group of objects. An historical or causal chain is said to lead backwards in time to the initial act or acts of referring. Here is how Donnellan characterizes this theory:

> our use of proper names for persons in history (and also those we are not personally acquainted with) is parasitic on uses of the names by other people—in conversation, written records, etc. Insofar as we possess a set of identifying descriptions in these cases they come from things said about the presumed referent by other people. My answer to the question, 'Who was Thales?' would probably derive from what I learned from my teachers or from histories of philosophy. Frequently, as in this example, one's identifying descriptions trace back through many levels of parasitic derivation.[13]

On this account, if I say "Aristotle was an important Greek philosopher," I am referring to someone who was at some specific time in the past given the name 'Aristotle.' I do so by virtue of being in the relevant causal or historical chain of referring. Descriptions may be helpful in clarifying to whom I am referring, but unlike descriptivism, this account does not require that I be prepared to offer a uniquely referring expression, in order, say, to ward off the indictment that I do not know who I am talking about.

In his essay entitled "Identity and Necessity," Kripke carefully explains his distinction between *rigid* and *non-rigid designators*—the foundational platform for the causal or historical theory of referring. Kripke offers as an example of a rigid designator 'the square root of 25.' The example he offers of a non-rigid designator is 'the inventor of bifocals.' His exposition of the difference between them is that while someone else might have invented bifocals, the square root of 25 is, of logical or mathematical necessity, 5. A rigid designator is an expression which necessarily designates a specific object in every possible world. He argues that all proper names are rigid designators, as follows:

> We can say that the inventor of bifocals might have been someone other than the man who *in fact* invented bifocals. We cannot say, though, that the square root of 81 might have been a different number from the number it in fact is, for that number just has to be 9. If we apply this intuitive test to proper names, such as for example 'Richard Nixon', they would seem intuitively to come out to be rigid designators. First, when we talk even about the counterfactual situation in which we suppose Nixon to have done different things, we assume we are still talking about Nixon himself. . . . And it seems that we cannot say "Nixon might have been a different man from the man he in fact was," unless, of course, we mean it metaphorically.[14]

A counterfactual situation is one that is contrary to a known fact. When a short person says, for example, "If I were over seven feet tall, I could have been a professional basketball player," he has described a counterfactual situation. The term 'Nixon' would, according to Kripke, have the same referent whenever it is used to refer to Nixon, and that referent would be the same in *any* possible world, including contrary to fact worlds, such as one in which he was not asked to resign his presidency. For Kripke, our world is the *actual* world. A *possible* world, for him, is an alternative world in which one can imagine various possibilities, including ones not existing in our actual world. His innovative work in modal logic (a logic which explicates the concepts of possibility and necessity) depends upon this distinction. He defines *necessity* as true in all possible worlds, and possibility as true in some possible worlds. An argument against any form of descriptivism can be constructed on the basis of Kripke's distinction between rigid and non-rigid designators, using his distinction between *actual* and *possible* worlds.

According to Kripke, proper names, like 'Benjamin Franklin,' are all rigid designators, and as such, designate the same object in all possible worlds. Most descriptions are non-rigid designators and, as such, do not designate the same object in all possible worlds. The description 'the inventor of bifocals,' while true of Benjamin Franklin in the actual world need not be true of him in all possible worlds. One can imagine a world in which Thomas Jefferson invented bifocals. The exceptions to the rule are those descriptions that logically imply that their referents are what they are and that they could not be anything else in any possible world, e.g., the description 'the square root of 81.'

In short, the logic or grammar of proper names is quite different from the logic or grammar of most descriptions, and so it is a mistake to think that the former can be explicated in terms of the latter. If the distinction between rigid and non-rigid designators is valid, and the view that proper names are rigid designators is true, it would seem to follow that nothing further need be said to refute the commonly held descriptivist views, since their account of proper names relies upon descriptions or sets of descriptions that are non-rigid in nature.

In "Naming and Necessity," Kripke advocates a version of the causal theory to replace the descriptive theory, and he argues that it has distinct advantages over both the original version of the descriptive theory, advocated by Frege and Russell (by which he means DDTR, which we have determined is not precisely the view of either Russell or Frege), and the version (SDDTR) advocated by Strawson and Searle.

Kripke concedes that Frege himself had already seen the problem with DDTR when, as I put it earlier, he acknowledged the existence of the fluctuations or ambiguities inherent in the intentional mélange created by the existence of variations in the personal and communal descriptions in natural languages. The only way to overcome these deficiencies in ordinary language is, for Frege, as we have seen, to construct an ideal or logically perfect language. But according to Kripke, another way out is to argue that ordinary language is not really deficient and to argue along Wittgensteinian lines[15] that what we associate with any proper name is a family of descriptions.[16]

Kripke argues against SDDTR, which maintains both that proper names are abbreviations for clusters or sets of descriptions and that the

131

Descriptive and Causal Theories of Referring

explanation of some cases of referring requires reference borrowing. In the course of pointing out what is wrong with SDDTR, Kripke is led to postulate a "true picture" of referring. He asks us to imagine the following scenario. A child is born, and his parents name him and call him by his name. They talk about him with friends and various other people, who in turn talk about the child. In this way, according to Kripke, the name is spread "from link to link as if by a chain." Kripke uses the example of Richard Feynman to make the point that a speaker on the far end of such a chain may actually refer to Feynman even though it is not remembered from whom he or she first, or ever, heard of him. He points out that his view differs from the SDDTR account in "one important respect." On the SDDTR account, the speaker would have to know from whom he got his reference; otherwise, he could not offer an identifying description, such as 'the man so and so called "Feynman."'[17] On Kripke's account, there is no such requirement.[18]

In a work written after Kripke's critique of descriptivism, Searle answers Kripke's counter-example. I will return to Searle at this point, though I am not through with Kripke. Searle points out that speakers often have in mind much more significant descriptive content than they provide. He refers to this personal aspect as *Intentional content*. He says:

it is the speaker's Intentional content that determines reference. It is not enough to look at just what a speaker says in response to a particular question, one has to look at his total Intentional content, as well as Background capacities associated with a name and at what he would say if informed that different parts of that content were satisfied by different objects.[19]

As regards the Feynman example, Searle's response would be that even if the speaker could not remember from whom he got his reference, he could be viewed as making a secondary kind of reference, as in 'the man called "Richard Feynman" in my linguistic community.' The description in question is determined by what best fits the Intentional content in the mind of the speaker.

But Linsky, in turn, has argued that Searle's emended version of SDDTR is essentially as indefensible as Russell's descriptivism. Both versions "make it a matter of *a priori* truth that our main beliefs about historical figures cannot be false," and both views "are infected with psychologism." That both views are infected with psychologism means, according to Linsky, that both views imply that questions concerning a person's existence cannot be isolated from questions concerning the

132

truth or falsity of our *beliefs* concerning that person. In fact, as Linsky observes, most of our central beliefs about many historical figures might well be false.[20]

How does Kripke's view fare in the light of Linsky's critique of Searle and Russell? Is it superior? Not really. It has serious problems of its own. A case which causes a problem for Kripke, and one that he recognizes would have to be dealt with by a rigorous theory, is how it is possible for children today to refer to Santa Claus without referring to a certain historical saint who was the original referent in the chain leading to our present use of the expression 'Santa Claus.'

While Kripke does not claim to be providing a rigorous theory of referring, which for him would be to provide a set of conditions both necessary and sufficient for properly employing the term 'reference,' he does provide a "rough statement of such a theory," and that statement does include an explanation for the Santa Claus case. According to Kripke:

> A rough statement of a theory might be the following: An initial 'baptism' takes place. Here the object may be named by ostension, or the reference of the name may be fixed by a description. When the name is 'passed from link to link,' the receiver of the name must, I think, intend when he learns it to use it with the same reference as the man from whom he heard it. If I hear the name 'Napoleon,' and decide it would be a nice name for my pet aardvark, I do not satisfy this condition. (Perhaps it is some such failure to keep the reference fixed which accounts for the divergence of present uses of 'Santa Claus' from the alleged original use.)[21]

His theory demands that when one is not present at the baptism of a name, and only learns of its use from another person, one must continue the "chain" by referring to the same individual as the person from whom one learned its use, otherwise, one breaks the chain. After which a new use must be instituted.

But how is this done? How does one manage to *change* the referent of a non-existent thing, and start a new chain or branch? The answer seems clear. It is by the use of a *description*.—by describing the referent in some definite way, as is done today: A jolly fat man in a red suit who lives at the North Pole, makes toys, and delivers them to all the good little children in the world. This would seem to tip the scales back towards descriptivism, since in the absence of a description in cases like the Santa Claus case, we would be unable to answer the question: To whom is one referring when one uses such expressions as 'Santa Claus'?

But before we reach any conclusions regarding what is the better theory of referring, there is another question that needs to be pursued first. We have dealt with how a causal theorist deals with proper names. But, how would a causal theorist explain general terms? Answering this question will help us to get a firmer grasp on the causal theory. For an answer to this question, I will turn to Hillary Putnam, who has provided a causal account of general terms based on Kripke's concept of rigid designation.

In his highly influential work, "The Meaning of Meaning" Hilary Putnam argues that the referents of *natural kind terms*, for example, 'human' and 'water,' are determined by the actual nature of the world. Natural kind terms are terms that refer to entities conceived of as having *modal implications*, which are, as we saw earlier, implications regarding necessity and possibility. If some object x is a member of the natural kind *human*, then x is *necessarily* human. But being a member of the non-natural kind *tall*, on the other hand, is only a *possibility*.

Putnam credits the Chomsky approach to linguistics, about which we will learn more in the next chapter, with its emphasis upon the deep structure of linguistic forms, as having provided an "incomparably more powerful description of the *syntax* of natural languages than we have ever had before." Yet, as far as he is concerned, "the dimension of language associated with the word 'meaning' [*semantics*] is, in spite of the usual spate of heroic if misguided attempts, as much in the dark as it ever was."[22] He goes on to claim that the reason for this unhappy state of affairs is that "the prescientific concept on which *semantics* is based—the prescientific concept of *meaning*—is itself in much worse shape than the prescientific concept of *syntax*."[23] Although Chomsky has enriched our understanding of the syntactic aspects of natural languages, the semantics of natural languages remain uncharted. He claims that although we have used the term 'water' for centuries, we did not really know its meaning until we discovered that water is H_2O. In other words, scientific discoveries about the inner nature of the referents of natural kind terms like 'water' may reveal their *real* meaning. He utilizes what he refers to as a science fiction example to make his point.

He asks us to imagine a Twin Earth, which is described as being just like earth in all respects except one. On Twin Earth what is referred to with the word 'water,' although it tastes like water and has all the other properties we associate with water, is not composed of H_2O. On

Twin Earth, what is referred to with the word 'water' has a different chemical formula, which he abbreviates as XYZ. Putnam asks us to imagine space travelers from Earth visiting Twin Earth. They will no doubt think that when one of the Twin Earthlings uses the word 'water,' he or she means what we mean by the expression in question. But, according to Putnam, as soon as the Earthlings discover that what the Twin Earthlings call water is really XYZ, they will conclude that on Twin Earth the word 'water' means XYZ. And if we reverse the scenario and imagine that the Twin Earthlings visit Earth, they will eventually conclude that on Earth the word 'water' means H_2O. If we agree with this conclusion, we shall have to say that at some prescientific date, Putnam uses 1750, when it was unknown to Earthlings that water was H_2O, and unknown to Twin Earthlings that their water was XYZ, the Earthlings meant something different than the Twin Earthlings. But why would this be true? According to Putnam, these *natural kind terms* are, like proper names, rigid designators.[24] What 'water' means is fixed by its referent. It meant H_2O in 1750 even though we were unaware of it. And 'water' meant XYZ for the Twin Earthlings even though they were unaware of it.

Putnam's Twin Earth hypothesis forms the basis for another criticism of Searle's descriptivism. Putnam says one can suppose that every human on earth has an exact double on Twin Earth, a *Doppelgänger*. We can suppose that both the Earthling and the Twin Earthling, or *Doppelgänger*, speak English, and have identical *Intentional content*. They could both be under the same impression regarding the set of descriptions they intended, including what they assume to be the same uniquely referring description, yet each would refer to a different object when using the word 'water.'[25]

Searle has an interesting way of meeting Putnam's objection. He argues that all our references are indexically tied to our beliefs about *this* world. An indexical is an expression whose reference potential is tied to context, and thus may vary with context. 'I,' 'he,' 'she,' 'it,' 'now,' 'today,' and 'yesterday' are indexicals. I could use the sentence 'he has on a green shirt' today to refer to my brother, and use it tomorrow to refer to a stranger. Its referent in each case is different and is determined in part by the time it was uttered. The fact that an Earthling is different in this way from her *Doppelgänger*, and that her Intentional content is *causally derived* from objects on earth, shows that she is not, and in fact could not, be *referring* to anything on Twin Earth.[26] Her Intentional content cannot be the same as that of her *Doppelganger*. They cannot both be under the same impression as regards the set of descriptions they intend, as they are tied to specific references on their respective Earths. The referents of *all* indexicals would be different for Earthlings and Twin Earthlings.[27]

Peter Hacker has argued very convincingly against this account of meaning, which he refers to as "scientific realism."[28] He believes that its claim that scientific discoveries can reveal the *real* meanings of natural language expressions would, if it were true, "spell ruin" for Wittgenstein's later philosophy.[29] It challenges Wittgenstein's view that the meaning of an expression is given by the rules governing its use. These rules are, according to Hacker, for Wittgenstein neither true nor false, and do not depend upon a correspondence with reality. They are not challenged by scientific discoveries, like the discovery that water is H_2O. Wittgenstein referred to this as the *autonomy of language*.

Hacker offers several arguments against Putnam's scientific realism.[30] First, he argues that since we consider D_2O or heavy water (composed of deuterium and oxygen) to be a kind of water, we need not say about Putnam's Twin Earth liquid, that it is not water. We could just consider it to be another form of water.

Second, he points out that the procedure advocated by Putnam, for defining or introducing natural kind terms, fails to provide an explanation of meaning. As Hacker notes, before the discovery that water is H_2O, no guidance can be given in applying the term by this mode of introducing it. That people in a pre-scientific society were or should have been committed to the idea that future discoveries would or should in any way effect the meaning of the words they found useful is "erroneous." As Hacker so aptly observes "a promissory note on an as yet non-existent bank is no currency."[31]

Hacker's third criticism is tied to the second one. There is, as he observes, a problem concerning whether or not science can ever cash the promissory note. Scientific discoveries can and do diverge from our ordinary meanings of natural kind terms, without cost, because the purposes they serve are "quite different." Making use of J. Dupré's book on the nature of scientific classification,[32] Hacker points out that no purpose would be served by calling garlic a lily even though both are, as science has discovered, members of the family *Liliaceae*.

Hacker's fourth criticism concerns the difficulty in always finding some structural sameness relation that will serve as a paradigm for determining reference. Selecting a paradigm that will pick out, for example, the 290,000 recognized species of beetle is, according to Hacker, anything but obvious. But, as Hacker recognizes, the scientific realist may counter by damning all *pre-scientific* classification. In response to this idea, Hacker again resorts to Dupré's work on scientific classification. He argues that the scientific assignment of organisms to species is "no less purpose-relative, variable, and partly arbitrary than common-or-garden classification."[33]

On the basis of these criticisms, Hacker concludes that the scientific realists have provided no cogent reasons for rejecting Wittgenstein's account of meaning, which says that an expression's meaning is given by explaining the rules governing its use. As Hacker views the matter, the extension of a term is not a constituent of its meaning, although there is a contingent relation between facts and semantic rules. As we learn more about the world, we incorporate this information and *modify* our rules accordingly. There is, according to Hacker, "no action at a distance in grammar." Future scientific discoveries in science cannot determine for us what we really mean in the present by an expression.

In Putnam's defense, it must be noted that he does not deny that society, via practices and rules, is an essential component in the determination of meaning. He in fact claims that:

> we have now seen that the extension of a term is not fixed by a concept that the individual speaker has in his head, and this is true both because extension is, in general, determined *socially*—there is division of linguistic labor as much as of "real" labor—and because extension is, in part, determined *indexically*. The extension of our terms depends upon the actual nature of the particular things that serve as paradigms, and this actual nature is not, in general, fully known to the speaker. Traditional semantic theory leaves out two contributions to the determination of reference—the contribution of society and the contribution of the real world!

Putnam believes that an adequate account of semantics must take into account both the contributions of society and those of science. The difference between Hacker and Putnam seems to boil down to this: the former believes that *all* that is required in an explanation of meaning is the contribution of society, namely, its practices and their formulations as rules, whereas the latter thinks that the contributions of science are at least as important.

It is one thing to claim that the *phenomenal object or stuff* has played a very important role in the history of our use of the expression 'water.' It is quite a different thing to claim that its chemical analysis is part of the meaning of the expression in question. Although the former claim, carefully interpreted, might well be true, the latter claim is extremely dubious. The implication of this claim, which is that we used the expression 'water' for centuries without *really* knowing what it means, is parallel to claiming that I do not really know what I am talking about when I say that my feet are sore, since it is quite likely that science will discover a great deal of additional knowledge about feet in the future. Anything science might conceivably learn about feet would at best only facilitate *change* of meaning concerning the expression 'feet.' Moreover, I doubt very much that the *first dubbing* of the expression 'feet' was in any sense meant to include future knowledge of feet.

In the introduction, I claimed that there is an important distinction to be made between *existence* conditions and *conventional* conditions. The former are those conditions which are the domain of science, and are those *unseen forces* necessary for the very existence of a given or specifiable phenomenon. The latter are those *observable parameters* which society has found good cause to incorporate into its linguistic practices (or its concepts) concerning such phenomena, and which are the domain of philosophy. I am quite willing to accept the view that the chemical composition of water plays a causal role regarding our use of the expression 'water.' If water tasted like quinine, that fact would play a causal role in determining the meaning we would attribute to 'water.'

Did we increase the *content of our concept* of water when we discovered that it was H_2O? I am perfectly willing to concede that such information can, and in fact often does, bring about a change in our linguistic practices. If water were not H_2O, it might not have caused us to conceive of or refer to water as we do. The discovery that water is H_2O certainly has changed both the way we use the expression and *added* to its meaning.

Although the extension of a term can and does have a causal role in relation to the meaning of that term, any initial or pre-scientific causality it has must nevertheless be subsumed under the *phenomenal* or *observable* nature of the extension. Its internal or non-observable nature may be ultimately responsible for its phenomenal nature, but it is its phenomenal nature that was the basis of its original meaning. So, why should we buy the idea that because we did not know that water was H_2O for centuries, we did not know what the word 'water' really means? What reasonable purpose could be served by this bizarre claim? Such views are clever and purposive, but some are only clever. J. L. Austin was terribly clever. But as he so cleverly observed regarding the work of various well-known philosophers of his era "there is nothing so plain boring as the constant repetition of assertions that are not true, and sometimes not even faintly sensible; if we can reduce this a bit, it will be all to the good"[34]

Another issue that concerns me is that although Putnam provides us with an account of one kind of general term, namely, natural kind, we are left in the dark as regards those kinds that fly in the face of the rigid designator analysis. Some of these are: words referring to abstractions, like 'democracy' and 'kindness;' words describing relations, like 'being more informative than' and 'less sophisticated than;' and words referring to actions, like 'apologizing' and 'warning.' I suspect that a large variety of natural language words are not the result of anything like dubbing or naming, but are instead the result of organic processes. Their meanings, uses, and purposes, emerge and continuously transform from one state of readiness to another. They are chameleon-like. This idea or model has much greater generality than the dubbing model the causal theorists advocate. I will address this issue further in the final chapter.

Although I do agree to a large extent with Hacker's understanding of the role that rules play in the determination of meaning for Wittgenstein, it is important to distinguish between a *rule* and a *practice*. A practice is simply a tried and successful way of doing things that has been time-tested to be effective. A rule, for our purposes, is a linguistic formulation of a practice. Practices have a history independent of the rules formulating them. Often philosophers place too much emphasis on rules and ignore the more fundamental role of practices. My view is that linguistic rules are primarily shorthand summaries or abbreviations of very complicated practices.

Linguistic rules are always subject to *modification*. Recall my discussion of the open-textured nature of empirical terms. All such terms are designed to cope with the fact that the world consists of phenomena that exhibit probability, not certainty. In this world the unexpected happens all the time, and we have to be prepared to accommodate the unexpected by modifying our language. Were we to discover a new kind of kind of beetle, one which has some traits that were previously thought to be present only in grasshoppers, we would have to adjust our practices concerning the word 'beetle' to accommodate this newly discovered species.

Linguistic rules are not rigid or fixed the way that game rules are. Communication is not a game. Game rules are *constitutive* rules, they are, as Searle defines them, rules that "constitute (and also regulate) an activity the existence of which is logically dependent upon the rules."[35] One is not allowed to change the rules of a game whenever one wants. If one refuses to abide by the rules of chess, one is no longer playing chess. Efficient and productive communication requires flexibility and the freedom that flexibility produces.[36] Even the most uninformed person manages to talk to the most well-educated. We are organic entities. Our linguistic practices are both flexible and complicated. We are able to act in complex fashion without being inflexible. Machines lack this kind of flexibility. Their success depends upon predictability. What use would we have for machines that were unpredictable? If they were we might well have to contend with them refusing to do what they are expected to do. Like a disillusioned French undergraduate of the sixties, they might refuse to cooperate on the grounds that they are experiencing *ennui*. For these reasons, I am not altogether happy with Wittgenstein's characterization of linguistic actions as *language games*. I much prefer Austin's description of linguistic actions as *illocutions*. I will continue to discuss this topic in the next chapter. Now I want to return to and examine carefully Kripke's concept of rigid designation.

In the quote from Kripke on page 130 above, he explicates what he means by rigid designation with the example 'the square root of 81.' He points out that one cannot say that the square root of 81 might have been a different number from the number it in fact is. It has to be 9. I understand perfectly what it means to say that its *referent* is necessarily the same in all possible worlds, but I recognize this only because I *understand the meaning* of the expression 'the square root of 81.' (On the most recent series of the TV show *Star Trek* the number '7' is used to refer to an extremely well endowed alien female. Here the referent is clearly not the number 7.) Suppose I were to place 'the square root of 49' in the predicate place of a subject/predicate sentence, and place the expression '7' in that same sentence's subject slot. If I were to state it, with its standard meaning intact, would what I state be true or false? I would be forced to say not only that it is true, but that it is necessarily true, or in Kripke's terms, true in every possible world.

However, if I were to place the name 'Richard Nixon' in the subject blank of a subject predicate proposition, and place in the predicate blank *any* predicate other than "the person necessarily referred to with the expression 'Richard Nixon,'" and imagine it being stated with its standard meaning intact, it is possible for it to be either true or false. Its truth or falsity will turn on what predicate is chosen.

The reason for the difference is that the link between 'the square root of 49' and '7' is a conceptual one. If I understand what is meant by the expression '7,' i.e., the whole number between 6 and 8, or 1+1+1+1+1+1+1, and what is meant by 'the square root of 49,' that number which when multiplied by itself yields 49, then I know that the claim that "7 is the square root of 49" is necessarily true. The same kind of thing can be said about 'Richard Nixon' if the predicate is "the person referred to by the name 'Richard Nixon.'" But it *begs the question* as regards whether or not 'Richard Nixon,' or any use of it, would of necessity refer to Richard Nixon. The implication of these observations *seems* to be that Kripke's analysis of the nature of proper names is either circular or simply a form of legislation. In either case it is unconvincing. If circular, it's fallacious. If legislated, one can simply reject it. But this conclusion only follows if we interpret Kripke to hold that rigidity is a property of names. Perhaps this is a mistaken interpretation.

In "Naming and Necessity," Kripke says, "When I say that a designator is rigid, and designates the same thing in all possible worlds, I mean that, as used in *our* language, it stands for that thing, when we talk about counterfactual situations."[37] Counterfactual situations, as the term suggests, are situations that are contrary to the facts, for example, Nixon being an honest politician. But what exactly does the phrase 'as used in our language' mean? It could mean what I previously defined as *sentential* meaning, i.e., what the words themselves mean. But this idea is subject to the objection I raised in the previous paragraph. And besides, Kripke does not believe that names have meaning.[38] What else could 'as used in our language' mean?

Strawson, as we saw in Chapter II, distinguishes between a designator like 'Nixon,' and a particular speaker's *use of it* on a given occasion. Even if we were to grant that Nixon would be Nixon in any possible world, in spite of the fact that his description might be different in worlds other than ours, the question of whether or not a designator has the property of picking out one and only thing in any possible world would seem to depend upon the *use* made of the expression. The name 'Richard Nixon' does in fact serve as a name for many things: persons, including the 37th president of the United States, pets, racehorses, boats, etc. On this account of use, rigid designation is *not* a property of names but is instead, a property of their *use*—it is determined by the *intentions* of the speaker. When I say, for example, "Richard Nixon was the most courageous of all recent U. S. Presidents," the man to whom I refer is necessarily the man to whom I mean to refer, and when you say, for example, "Richard Nixon lives next door to me," the man to whom you refer is necessarily the man to whom you mean to refer. But each of us may be referring to different men. This idea of *use* is tied to what I previously defined as *contextual* meaning, i. e., what the speaker means by an expression.

Given this understanding of use, I might very well be confused and only think that I am referring to the man in charge of the Allied Forces on D-Day. I might be someone who always confuses the two, or someone who has frequent "senior moments," or is dyslexic. Clearly the name 'Richard Nixon' does not always refer to the same man, and equally clearly, in spite of my once having thought so, the man to whom one refers when one uses the expression 'Richard Nixon' is not necessarily the man to whom one thinks one is referring.

But if rigid designation is neither a property of names themselves, nor a property of their actual uses, what is it? A property can be said to belong to every individual comprising a collection of things, or it can be said to belong to the collection. Every member of a football team might perform well, but it does not follow that the team's performance is equally good. So instead of interpreting Kripke to be talking about particular uses that are made of proper names, we should interpret him to mean the collective or type of use that is made of them.

Linsky offers an explication of Kripke's view of general terms and possible worlds which can be used to illustrate the type of use Kripke has in mind. Linsky says:

> Natural kind terms are rigid designators. They denote kinds, the same kinds in all possible worlds. The sense of the kind-term is a concept of the reference of the term. This accounts for our ability to understand the assertions that gold might not have been yellow, tigers might not have had stripes, and so on. We keep our grip on the kind as it moves through metaphysical space from one possible world to another, by means of the kind-name, which rigidly denotes the kind throughout these metaphysical metamorphoses.[39]

What holds for natural kind terms holds for proper names and certain definite descriptions. To move from this world where Nixon was a politician to a possible world where Nixon is not politician, I must keep the reference of the term 'Nixon' constant. This provides a different criterion of rigidity of reference than what I focused on concerning 'the square root of 81' kind of case. The criterion I focused on relied on the meaning of the expression 'the square root of 81,' whereas this criterion covers both *kinds* of case. It claims that the referents of 'Nixon' and 'the square root of 81' *must* be held rigid to move from one metaphysical realm to another and keep a grip on Nixon and the square root of 81.[40] On this interpretation, in order to talk about an entity of any sort, whether it be actual, imagined, particular or general, in terms of its residing in one or another possible worlds one must hold on to the object in question. Rigidity of reference is the tool for keeping a tight grip and is especially useful for the development of modal logic.[41]

I am, however, bothered by this idea of holding reference constant across possible worlds. I can imagine a world in which personal identity is a momentary thing. Just imagine a world in which every object in it is always in a state of changing its properties. In this world, I have to somehow fix reference in order to refer to what is undergoing these changes. But, imagine a world in which every object changes all its properties from one moment to the next. Is it really possible to fix reference in such a world? If not, then here is at least one possible world in which 'Nixon' does not refer to the same thing as it does in our world.[42]

Another potential problem with Kripke's view concerns the role he assigns to ostension. Remember what he said in the quote on page 133 above concerning the initial 'baptism' that assigns reference to a proper name:

> the object may be named by ostension, or the reference of the name may be fixed by a description. When the name is 'passed from link to link,' the receiver of the name must, I think, intend when he learns it to use it with the same reference as the man from whom he heard it.

The problem is one introduced by Wittgenstein in the *Investigations*. Although he uncritically relied on ostensive definition in the *Tractatus* to establish the tie between a name and its referent, when its referent is a simple, in the *Investigations* he claims, "An ostensive definition can be variously interpreted in *every* case."[43] Suppose, asks Wittgenstein, that one points to two nuts and says that that is called 'two.' One who is told this, or has 'two' ostensively defined in this way, is as likely to suppose that 'two' is the name of *this* group of nuts as he is to understand it as a numeral. And, according to Wittgenstein, one might "equally take the name of a person, of which I give an ostensive definition, as that of a color, of a race, or even of a point of the compass."[44]

According to Wittgenstein, one must already be a master of a language game (English, German, French, Swahili, Farsi, etc.) in order to understand and use the expression,'This thing is named "N."' But how would he respond if someone tried to answer his objection by claiming that all that is required to understand what a person means when he uses an ostensive definition is to know or guess what that person is pointing to. All one has to do is to know or guess that he is pointing to the shape, the color, or the number, etc. But, asks Wittgenstein, how does one do that? How does one point to the color as opposed to the shape? Perhaps it will occur to the reader that the way this is done is by concentrating your attention on either the color or the shape. Wittgenstein responds: "But I ask again 'How is that done?'"[45]

Wittgenstein reminds us that we do not always do the same thing when we focus on, for example, the color of something. He then lists a number of ways of focusing upon the color of something, and points out that not one of them, or the conjunction of them all, fully explains what it is to refer to the color and not the shape of a given object. He reminds us that moving a piece in chess does not consist solely in moving a piece in a specific way on the board, or in one's thoughts that occur as one moves the piece. One cannot ignore the "circumstances that we 'call playing a game of chess,' 'solving a chess problem,' and so on."[46] In short, and in other words, one cannot ignore the importance of customs, convention, rules and practices in explaining how definition is possible. And the understanding of customs, conventions, rules and practices involves descriptive vocabulary. An ostensive definition is not possible unless the appropriate circumstances obtain. Unless one knows what it is one wants to name (one's child, one's dog, one's boat, one's etc.), how can one name it? The uses of such descriptions as 'one's x' are *presupposed* in the naming process.

In opposition to the descriptivists, descriptions are not, in the ordinary sense of the word 'meaning', the meanings of names, but they can be, in certain contexts of use, what the speaker *means by* the names he uses. Descriptions are one kind of thing. Referents are another. The former are always linguistic entities. The latter are only sometimes linguistic entities, as for example, when one claims that the expression 'the inventor of bifocals' appears in Kripke's work on the topic of identity and necessity. At any rate, descriptions do not, in contexts where they are what is meant by or what the speaker had in mind, fix reference, if what is meant is that they in any way effect the referents of the names that they explain. What they sometimes do is settle questions regarding who the speaker had in mind or to whom one was referring. In addition, descriptions do not fix meanings in the sense in which dictionaries do, but they do sometimes settle questions regarding what specific speakers mean on specific occasions. Hence they do sometimes fix (determine) *contextual* meaning, i.e., they can be used to decipher what someone meant by something that was said on a particular occasion. I will address this issue more fully in the last chapter.

Various efforts have been made by other philosophers of language to salvage the causal theory,[47] and although some of them are ingenious, they are at best simply stopgaps or *ad hoc* devices sustained by patronage, but vulnerable to counterexamples. If Wittgenstein is right about the family resemblance nature of many if not most general terms and names, and I know of no valid reason for thinking that he is mistaken, there is no value in pursuing them. For this reason, I will not do so.

What are we to take away from this chapter? The descriptive theorists and the causal theorists are both right and both wrong. The mistake they both make is that of looking for an account of referring that explains and justifies our use of proper names and general descriptions which can be stated in terms of necessary and sufficient conditions. It does not take much imagination for one to come up with counterexamples. They are both right in so far as being able to explain a word or expression is *sometimes* simply being able to provide a descriptive paraphrase that removes the misunderstanding, while at *other* times it is simply to point to something which is *the* paradigm (in the case of proper names) or *a* paradigm (in the case of a natural kind term) of what needs to be explained.

What we should be talking about are not necessary and sufficient conditions, but rather *enabling conditions*. By an enabling condition, I mean anything that makes it possible for a speaker to mean something by an expression or to explain to another what an expression means. If a Weimaraner is present when I wish to explain what the term 'Weimaraner' means, there is no need for any description. The presence of the Weimaraner enables me to accomplish my explanation. But if the word in question is 'werewolf,' it is not possible for such a thing to be present, and so I must resort to a description. No historical link could ever be established back to such a referent! My knowledge of what a werewolf is consists in nothing more that my knowledge that a werewolf is a human who, because she or he has been bitten by another werewolf, is transformed into a wolf when the moon is full. The description 'a werewolf is a human who, because she or he has been bitten by another werewolf, is transformed into a wolf when the moon is full,' based as it is on my knowledge of what a werewolf is, *enables* me to understand and explain what the term 'werewolf' means. My having been present at the christening of the navy's newest aircraft carrier, the *Ronald Reagan*, *enables* me to refer to the carrier with the ex-actor's name, and to inform others that the ship is so named. But so would my reading its name boldly painted on its bow.

The one thing that all linguistic symbols have in common is that their usefulness presupposes semantic practices—practices that correlate symbols with their referents. Whether or not a symbol is correctly used is not a question that is answered by determining whether or not the correlated object possesses certain characteristics (even uniquely referring characteristics) or particular causal linkages, but rather by determining whether or not the symbol in question is used in accordance with a given practice.

But why, it may be asked, are practices ignored in favor of other alternatives? It is because the acquired tendencies or dispositions to use the various symbols of one's language are not themselves observable. They have to be inferred, and, for this reason, they are apt to be misconceived or overlooked. We expect there to be something about the objects themselves (their describable characteristics) or their presence (for a linkage to be established) that causes us use the symbols the way we do, and so we overlook the practices we have been trained since childhood to follow. These practices can be formulated as rules. But because these practices are so complicated and multi-faceted their formulations need to be abbreviated.

What we need is an account of meaning that recognizes the importance of practices in the determination of meaning, and which recognizes that many of our linguistic practices are family resemblance in character. All empirical terms are governed by practices that are not and cannot be fixed. They are instead capable of significant change. 'Bad' has come to mean good! I will return to this theme in the last chapter.

---

[1] Kripke (1970)

[2] See above pp. 27, 28, 34, and 39.

[3] Frege (1892) p. 88.

[4] By referring to 'bank' as an expression, I avoid the question as regards whether there are two words 'bank,' or just two different senses of one word. This is an issue I do not wish to discuss here.

[5] Ibid., fn 2, p. 86.

[6] Strawson (1959) p. 181.

[7] Ibid., p. 182, footnote 1.

[8] Ibid., p. 191.

[9] Ibid., pp. 191-192.

[10] Ibid., p. 182, footnote 1.

[11] What Strawson refers to as a "presupposition set."

[12] Searle (1958) p. 159.

[13] Donnellan (1972) p. 373.

[14] Kripke (1971) p.148.

[15] But, as Linsky has pointed out quite correctly, Kripke misrepresents Wittgenstein's view. Wittgenstein's view concerning proper names is, according to Linsky, that they are characteristically used *without any*

fixed meaning; there is neither a unique description nor a cluster of them which fixes the sense of our names. We use these names without a fixed sense." Linsky (1977) p. 93.

[16] Kripke (1970) p. 279.

[17] At this point he actually shifts his example to one concerning the logician Gödel.

[18] Kripke (1970) pp. 287-289.

[19] Searle (1985) p. 341.

[20] Linsky (1977) pp. 100-101.

[21] Ibid., p. 524.

[22] Putnam (1975) p. 215.

[23] Ibid., pp.215-216.

[24] Putnam (1975) pp. 230-232.

[25] This criticism assumes that the meaning of the expression 'water' incorporates the chemical makeup of its referent, which is a highly questionable assumption, and one that Hacker argues against on page 137 below.

[26] Searle (1985) p. 342.

[27] This move will not save Searle's view from Linsky's criticism, however, because all descriptions have to be indexically tied to this earth, and could all be false, and thus none of them nor the whole set of them would be *uniquely* satisfied by their referents.

[28] Although Hacker conjoins, as is commonly done, the views of Putnam and Kripke, he acknowledges in footnote 39, that their account are "rather different," but concentrates on Putnam's account. Hacker (1996) p. 329.

[29] Hacker (1996) p. 251.

[30] Ibid., pp. 252-253.

[31] Ibid., p. 252.

[32] Dupré (1993).

[33] Hacker (1996) pp. 251-253.

[34] Austin (1962) p. 5.

[35] See above p. 85.

[36] For this reason I prefer Austin's description of conventional actions as *illocutions* over Wittgenstein's description of them as *language games*.

[37] Kripke (1970) p. 284.

[38] A view which is inconsistent with the facts concerning both Indian names and the names for Thoroughbred horses, which are descriptive designators. See above p. 5.

[39] Linsky (1977) p. 79.

[40] This interpretation is one I overlooked in an earlier paper when I discussed Kripke's views concerning rigidity of reference. See Odell (1984B) pp. 244-246.

[41] For a lengthy and excellent discussion of the technicalities of modal logic, of natural languages, of Kripke's views on the subject of proper names and general terms, as well as those of Frege, Russell, Strawson, and Searle, see Linsky (1977), especially pp. 42-92.

[42] The concept of individuation could not be instantiated in such a world. In such a world there could not be any individuals. At least one description would have to be true of x for more than a moment in order for anyone to form the concept of x-ness.

[43] Wittgenstein (1953) para. 28.

[44] Ibid., para. 28.

[45] Ibid., para. 33.

[46] Ibid., para. 28-31.

[47] See Donnellan (1972), Devitt and Sterelney (1987)

5

Philosophy, Linguistics, and Cognitive Science

When anyone speaks of linguistics and philosophy or the influence of linguistics upon philosophy at this time in history, she or he invariably means the influence of the M.I.T. linguist, Noam Chomsky. His influence on philosophy of language has been quite significant. His work is the cornerstone for the interdisciplinary subject known as *cognitive science*. Cognitive science incorporates contributions from psychology, neuroscience, linguistics, anthropology, computer science, and philosophy. It is concerned with explaining intelligent behavior in humans, animals, and machines. Today it is primarily concerned with utilizing computer modeling schemata for the simulation and explanation of human cognition.

Chomsky developed a systematic system for the scientific study of natural languages. He accomplished this by utilizing techniques that originated in the philosophical study of formal languages. The literature on the work of Chomsky and his followers is vast, and a comprehensive evaluation of it is well beyond the scope of the present work. I will, however, attempt to state some of the fundamental ideas of the Chomsky program as it concerns philosophy. I will offer a critical assessment of these ideas that is motivated by the work of the later Wittgenstein.

In Chomsky's early work, *Syntactic Structures*, he emphasizes

149

syntax over semantics.[1] Syntax has to do with the ordering or arrangement of words in sentences. The sentence 'Jack's horse tried to throw him' is formulated according to the syntax rules for English. 'To tried him horse Jack's throw' is not. Different languages have different syntax rules. Semantics on the other hand has to do with what words and sentences mean within a given language.

Chomsky poses the question, "On what basis do we actually go about separating grammatical [syntactically well-formed] sequences from ungrammatical [syntactically ill-formed] sequences? He answers this question by denying that grammaticality can be ascertained by examination of any particular set of utterances obtained by the linguist engaged in fieldwork. He also denies that the notion of grammatical can be identified with "meaningful" or "significant," both of which are semantic predicates. He makes his case by having us consider the following sentences:

(1) Colorless green ideas sleep furiously.

(2) Furiously sleep ideas green colorless.

We can see, according to Chomsky, that although (1) and (2) are equally nonsensical, speakers of English recognize that the former is grammatical, while the latter is not. Since semantics will not provide us with an account of grammaticality (it only identifies meaningful and meaningless expressions), he argues that an explanation for such facts as this will require us to *extend* the theory of *syntactic structure* a good deal beyond its familiar limits.[2] The Chomsky of *Syntactic Structures* is content to restrict his attention to the development of a theory of grammaticality based on syntax. He claims that grammar is "best formulated as a self-contained study independent of semantics." But, since the "the notion of 'understanding a sentence' must be partially analyzed in grammatical terms" it follows that "one result of the formal study of grammatical structure is that a syntactic framework is brought to light which can support semantic analysis."[3] Consider the two following sentences:

His dog devoured my potato salad.

His potato salad devoured my dog.

Although one may be inclined to argue that the meaning of a sentence is a function of what the words that compose it mean, reflection upon these two sentences reveals that this idea cannot be generalized. The first and the second sentences displayed above have quite different meanings. The first sentence can be used to describe an empirical state of affairs, but the second one cannot. If it describes anything, what it describes is an empirical impossibility.

Over the years, Chomsky has extended his analysis of these matters to offer an inclusive theory of language that accounts for both syntactic structure and semantics. According to Chomsky, in an essay originally presented at a conference in Madrid in 1986, "talk about the mind is simply talk about the brain at some level of abstraction that we believe to be appropriate for understanding crucial and essential properties of neural systems. . . ."[4] He claims that many of our "many commonly accepted doctrines about language and knowledge" are false and misleading, and that thinking and language use result because of an "innate structure."[5] He concludes this essay by claiming that:

> language and thought are awakened in the mind, and follow a largely predetermined course, much like other biological properties. . . . Our knowledge in these areas, and I believe elsewhere-even in science and mathematics-is not derived by induction. . . . Rather, it grows in the mind, on the basis of our biological nature, triggered by appropriate experience, and in a limited way shaped by experience that settles options left open by the innate structure of mind.[6]

According to Chomsky, natural languages like English, French, Swahili, Sanskrit, etc., are *innate* structures within the brains of their users, and these structures are *universal* in character. Ultimately, all languages have the same underlying structure. Linguists sometimes refer to this structure, or basic design, on which all languages depend, as *universal grammar*. It is responsible for the fact that children can learn the grammar of their respective language. Without some such innate equipment, children could not, according to Chomsky, learn a language. He emphasizes the idea that on the basis of finite information, children are able to process any one of an infinite set of sentences. This fact, that children can after a certain amount of training so process information, can be established in a variety of ways: (1) given that the sentence 'x is a number,' is true for any numerical instantiation of 'x' from which it follows that 'one is a number,' 'two is a number,' 'three is a number,' and hence that for any x, no matter how great x is, x+1 is a number; (2) if S is the sentence 'red is a color word,' then it is true that S, and if SM is the meta-statement that S is true, then

151

SMM, where SMM is the meta-meta-statement that SM, is true, and so on for an infinite number of types or meta–statements. Both ways of proceeding involve *recursive* procedure, the upshot of which is that such information cannot be learned via experience. Why not? The answer is because no one could process an infinite amount of material. Our understanding of the recursive nature of numerals is itself inexplicable empirically. Such understanding depends upon our ability to follow the recursive rule for the formation of subsequent number. This ability is, somehow, situated in the brain. It is part of the software necessary for the brain to perform its functions relating to language.

One of the most important and crucial concepts of Chomsky's approach is the concept of a language of thought that is distinct from any natural language. This language of thought is sometimes referred to as *mentalese*.[7] According to this conception, although this language resembles natural languages, our knowledge of our own particular language is said to be simply translating the language of thought into the particular words and symbols that comprise one's own language. Human infants are said both to possess this language from birth and to be unable to learn a natural language without it.[8]

But how do we manage to get from this mentalese to natural language? According to Chomsky and his followers, including Steven Pinker, our brains are innately equipped with a set of rules, sometimes referred to as a code, called a "generative grammar," that enables us to translate thought combinations into word combinations. It does not, however, operate in a *linear* fashion. Instead, it operates in a descending order best described as a *tree*. The Wittgenstein of the *Tractatus* described facts linearly, as a concatenation of atoms, and the underlying order of all human language as a concatenation of names (logically proper names) for the components of the facts. The fact consisting of abcd, is described as 'abcd.' Language for Wittgenstein, at the simplest level *mirrored* the world. For Chomsky, the underlying order of the sentence is not a linear concatenation of names, but as Pinker puts it, "A sentence is not a chain but a tree. In human grammar, words are grouped into phrases, like twigs joined in a branch."[9] Consider the following example:

The foolish bear stole honey.

The sentence begins with a three-word phrase, which is, according to ordinary grammar, its subject, namely, the noun phrase 'the foolish bear' (abbreviated as 'NP'). In this case, NP is composed of a noun N, preceded by the article 'the,' which generative grammarians refer to as a *determinator* (abbreviated as 'det') and an adjective 'A.' In general, such phrases can have as a determinator such words as 'a,' 'the,' 'this,' 'that,' 'those,' 'these,' etc., and any number of adjectives. In general, an English noun phrases can be captured by the rule.

NP → (det) A* N

In the standard notation of linguistics where an arrow means "consists," and an asterisk means something like "as many as are warranted," this rule can, according to Pinker, be stated as "A noun phrase consists of an optional determiner, followed by any number of adjectives, followed by a noun." And this rule defines an upside-down *tree* branch, which can be displayed as follows:

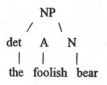

```
        NP
      /    \
  det   A   N
   |    |   |
  the foolish bear
```

The verb phrase or other portion of the sentence in question "stole honey" is subject to the same pattern of analysis:

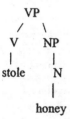

```
        VP
      /   \
    V     NP
    |      |
  stole    N
           |
         honey
```

Pinker then introduces two more rules. The first of which defines an English sentence (S), and the second the predicate of a verb phrase (VP). They both use NP as parts.

S → NP VP (which defines a sentence as a noun phrase followed by a verb phrase).

VP → V NP (which defines a verb phrase as a verb followed by a noun phrase).

We can now combine the analysis of the relevant NP with that of the relevant verb phrase, via the rule for the formation of a sentence, to get:

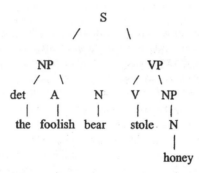

These trees are viewed by the Chomsky linguists as the means for connecting grammatical sentences with their proper meanings, which are "chunks of mentalese." Unlike a chaining devise, or a theory like Wittgenstein's, which links words via the concept of mirroring the world, the phrase structure or tree branching concept mirrors the way ideas are related in the mentalese.

Chomsky's original distinction between *deep* and *surface* grammar has provoked considerable misunderstanding over the years. According to Pinker, deep structure was taken to mean something "hidden, profound and universal." Chomsky's most recent version of his theory involves among other things a refinement of what is meant by this distinction. Deep grammar is now referred to as d-structure. D-structure is defined as simply "a prosaic technical gadget" within the context of the Chomsky theory, which, although quite useful, can be done without. Deep structure, as it is presently understood, refers to the interface between mentalese and phrase structure.[10]

If we think of 'the foolish bear stole honey' as closely paralleling what is the d-structure, and the tree I presented above as a d-structure tree, it can by transformed into various s-structures, for example: 'honey was stolen by the foolish bear,' 'the bear who is foolish stole honey;' 'stealing honey was done by the foolish bear.' And each of these transformations could be arranged according to surface structure trees.

Transformational grammar, for Chomsky and his followers, is the innate equipment children use to process the massive input to which adults subject them. It is a set of phrase structural rules (rules, either innate or theoretical, which define sentences, noun phrases, verb phrases, etc.) which, on the basis of phrase structure trees and transformational rules, transform phrases in the deep structure trees into surface structure trees. Parts of language: noun, noun phrases, verbs, verb phrases, etc., are, according to Pinker's exposition of Chomsky's view, not semantic categories (meanings), but are instead types of tokens that obey certain formal rules, "like a chess piece or poker chip." A noun, for example, on this account, is "a word that does nouny things; it is the kind of word that comes after an article, can have an 's' stuck onto it, and so on."[11]

According to transformational grammarians, all phrases, whether noun phrases, verb phrases, or adjectival phrases, are the same in all languages. In a noun phrase like 'the philosophical poet in the brown overcoat' the noun 'poet' is said to determine the meaning of the whole phrase. The noun 'poet' is said to be the 'core meaning' of the whole phrase, because the phrase refers to a kind of poet, and not a kind of overcoat. The verb 'smokes,' like the noun 'poet' in the noun phrase 'the philosophical poet in the brown overcoat,' determines the meaning of the verb phrase 'smokes camel cigarettes.' The verb phrase is about smoking not about camel cigarettes. These meaning determinants 'poet' and 'smokes' are referred to as *heads*, and in a phrase structure these expressions—nouns, and verbs—are symbolized respectively as 'N' and 'V' with bars over them, as in $\bar{E}$. 'X' with a bar over it is used as a variable standing for any 'head.'[12] All other ingredients or participants in a phrase structure are referred to either as *role-players* (one of the objects or *terms of relation* in a relation) or *modifiers* (a phrase that adds information about a concept). In the sentence 'Handsome Joe gave advice to pretty Jane,' 'Joe,' 'Jane' and 'advice' are all role-players. Russell and other twentieth century logicians referred to them as *arguments*. 'Handsome' and 'pretty' are modifiers. *X-bar theory* is, according to the transformational grammarians, that structure which all phrases are said to have in common in all languages.

X-bar theory is said to simplify things to such an extent that all the phrase and structure rules can be reduced to two super rules, which are, according to Pinker: (1) A phrase consists of an optional subject, followed by an X-bar, followed by a number of modifiers; (2) An X-bar consists of a head word, followed by any number of role-players.[13] In English, the head is generally followed by its role players, but in various other languages, for example Japanese, this order is reversed. We say that the foolish bear stole honey. The Japanese say that the foolish bear honey stole. In English, the order is *head-first* in Japanese it is *head last*. And so the super-rule (2) needs to reflect this fact. It becomes, 'An X-bar is composed of a head X and any number of role–players, in either order.'[14]

According to Chomsky, children are born with an innate knowledge of these super-rules. They need only learn whether their particular language is head-first or head-last. And as Pinker points out:

> if this theory of language learning is true, it would help solve the mystery of how children's grammar explodes into adult like complexity in so short a time. They are not acquiring dozens or hundreds of rules; they are just setting a few mental switches.[15]

One of the most surprising, and for many philosophers, the most objectionable implication of this view is that it excludes from the scientific examination of linguistics *social conventions* or dispositions to behave in conventional fashion. At the very least, the significance of these social parameters are given a greatly diminished role to play. Chomsky says:

> a rather striking feature of the widespread conception of language as a system of abilities, or a habit system of some kind, or a complex of dispositions, is that it has been completely unproductive. It led precisely nowhere. One cannot point to a single result or discovery about language, even of the most trivial kind, that derives from this conception.[16]

This aspect of Chomsky's view is tied to the concept of "core meanings," which are held to be constituents of the innate language of thought or mentalese. This view is unsatisfactory, and the reason that it is unsatisfactory can be grasped through consideration of the following case. Suppose that two detectives are concerned with finding the individual who shot the bank teller during a holdup, and that they are aware of the fact that he was wearing a brown overcoat. Suppose further that the detectives have rounded up all the men in the surrounding neighborhood of the bank who are wearing brown overcoats. Suppose one of the detectives rules out one of these individuals by claiming, "The poet in the brown overcoat was across the street buying cigarettes at the time of the shooting." In these circumstances, it is simply false that the expression 'poet' in the phrase 'the poet in the brown overcoat' in the sentence 'The poet in the brown overcoat was across the street buying cigarettes at the time of the shooting' is "the core meaning of the whole phrase in question," as Chomsky and his followers would have us believe. The purpose or point of the utterance in question, which is clearly context-dependent, is surely at the *core* of the meaning of the phrase or sentence in question, when it is used in the imagined circumstance. Having or not having on a brown overcoat is at the core of what is *meant by* the sentence in question in this particular context. In another context, where one is concerned to identify a poet one had not previously met, who was supposed to meet one at a local bar, the sentence in question clearly signifies or is *primarily meant* to feature the poet. We are disposed to behave in one way rather than another under these differing conditions. Differing circumstances force us to acquire different abilities or dispositions. We learn how to respond (acquire dispositions to behave in various ways) by reacting to our environment. Contextual meaning is at least as important and scientifically relevant as sentential meaning—what the words mean and how they are arranged. To think otherwise is to ignore the distinction I drew earlier between what a sentence means and what someone might mean by it on some particular occasion. Social or speech content cannot be ignored if one wishes to do full justice to the concept of "word meaning."

Moreover, the concept of a " language of thought" or "mentalese," which is distinct from and independent of any natural language, is itself a highly suspect concept. How, for example, can one have the thought "A billion-sided polygon is a greater sided polygon that a billion-sided polygon minus one of its sides" unless one possesses a language? Descartes made use of a similar example to refute the claim of the empiricists that ideas are stored images. One clearly cannot *image* the difference between a billion-sided-polygon and a billion-sided polygon minus one of its sides. But equally suspect is the idea that one could have this idea independent of some kind of *verbal* language. Wittgenstein would ask us to say to ourselves the following string 'A billion-sided polygon is a greater sided polygon that a billion-sided polygon minus one of its sides,' and then he would ask us to think it without saying it to ourselves. He would then ask, "How is that possible?"

But the follower of Chomsky would not be satisfied with this kind of objection. He or she might well point out that although the English speaker would make use of the string 'A billion-sided polygon is a greater sided polygon that a billion-sided polygon minus one of its sides,' a non-English speaker would use a very different string of words to say the same thing, and that this *same thing* is part of the language of thought. My response to this rejoinder is that, although there are different ways to *say* the same thing, there is no way to *think* it without doing so in one of these ways. Just as it does not follow that because there are many different means for driving a nail into a board, for example, hammers, rocks, gun handles, iron bars, etc., there must be something independent from any of these and various other physical means, which is driving a nail. Driving a nail just is a short hand or elliptical expression for one of these ways of proceeding. It is not a *something* distinct from one of these ways of driving a nail. It is an illusory something. It is a nothing! Thinking or having a cognitive thought is likewise not independent from using a given language in a specific way. Mentalese is an illusion.

Chomsky's influence on philosophy has been extensive and ubiquitous. But it is through the work of Jerry Fodor that its impact has been the greatest. Fodor is often credited with being the father of *cognitive science*, which constitutes the mainstream of contemporary philosophy of mind, of language, and of psychology, as well as metaphysics. Fodor is largely responsible for the kind of realism according to which human reasoning is functionally identical to the computational processes of a computer.

As we have seen, Chomsky maintains that the rules of syntax for natural languages are so complex, and potentially so bewildering, that the only way to account for the fact that infants learn language so quickly is to postulate an *innate universal grammar*, a dispositional drive to select from among many possibilities only those forms that infants from all cultures select. This innate or dispositional drive is considered to be the causal mechanism that produces natural languages.

This conception of language acquisition has led Fodor and other cognitive scientists to develop a theory of cognitive or intelligent behavior, which they refer to as *computationalism*. According to the Chomsky/Fodor *computationalistic* account, there are unconscious processes that account for intelligent behavior and these unconscious causes can be translated into *specific* computational processes or programs—processes or programs which are not themselves part of the output. Like computers, we process input following programs. But our programs, unlike those of computers, are innate.

I agree that we are naturally disposed to select efficient and flexible rules. I am not willing to concede, however, that we process information in machine-like fashion. Although the majority of philosophers of language agree with the Chomsky/Fodor program, I am not alone in my skepticism regarding it.[17] Many of us who are skeptical are united in an effort to show that the work of the later Wittgenstein can be regarded as a comprehensive critique of the basic assumptions upon which cognitive science is founded. Wittgenstein would have rejected the Chomsky/Fodor contingent's faith in the efficacy of science to solve certain philosophical problems, problems that he considers to be *pseudo-problems*. In the remainder of this chapter, I will first explicate Fodor's views, and then what I consider to be the essence of Wittgenstein's views regarding language and thought. I will argue that although much that Wittgenstein said in the *Investigations* is inconsistent with the Chomsky/Fodor computationalistic approach, a reconciliation of sorts can be achieved between Wittgenstein and the cognitive scientists.

In Chapter II, we learned that the Wittgenstein of the *Investigations* claims that the irresolvable set of issues concerning mental representation survives *only* because an essential ingredient is left out of the recipe for symbolic meaning, namely, *cultural* or *social* context. We must now see how this is relevant to the issue under consideration. To do this we need to look more closely at Fodor's views.

According to Fodor, natural languages are all learned through a universal, inner and innate language—a full-blown language (which may or may not resemble one's natural language) complete with syntactic and semantic rules.[18] Unless there is an internal system of representation which embodies language in some strict sense of the term, there could not, according to Fodor, be a *science* of cognitive psychology. According to Fodor, there is both sensory input and output in the form of action, and between them, connecting and integrating them, is an internal computational process instantiated in our nervous systems, a process of representation, which is an internal language, complete with semantic rules for representing objects by signs. The mind/brain (the brain and its conscious manifestation) is viewed as a computing machine, processing information via a natural or innate program—an (innate) system of rules for interpreting signs. Human beings are said to embody, although they are not aware of it, a *folk psychology*: a theoretical commitment to the idea that actions are the result of intentions or propositional attitudes; that the latter are the postulated entities of the theory; that there exists between the postulated entities and actions a causal relation; and that the postulated entities are the causes and the actions are the effects.[19] Internal processes or states of the internal language that are associated with a given term, for example, 'believing,' are said to have a dispositional *role* to play with respect to other thoughts, sensations, and behavior.[20] It is in terms of this dispositional or conceptual role that the meaning of a term is explained. On this account of meaning, to say that someone believes that it is raining is to say that that person is in a state of believing with respect to the proposition that it is raining.

A critic of this view might well ask, "But how can this view account for the attribution of a belief like the belief that Aristotle was a better philosopher than Plato, when the person to whom the belief is correctly attributed is focused on a different belief (say, the belief chocolate ice cream is better than vanilla ice cream), or is asleep, or in a coma?" The answer for the cognitive scientist is that there exists at the unconscious level a *dispositional* process or state which, if activated, would produce a further conscious process of believing that Aristotle is a greater philosopher than Plato. The unconscious process of believing that Aristotle is a greater philosopher than Plato, when stimulated by a question concerning who is the better philosopher, would cause the subject to go from the unconscious state to the conscious state of believing that Aristotle is a greater philosopher than Plato.

According to Fodor, learning a language L is possible only if one already possess a language that can be *activated* to learn L. His critics point out, however, that since his account of learning a language L necessitates a previously existing language, Lp, through which L is learned, the existence of L entails the existence of Lp. But the existence of Lp would seem to entail the existence of some prior language Lpp. We seem to be caught in what philosophers call an *infinite regress*, which means that the problem a theory is meant to solve remains as much in need of solution as before, and continues to be one without end. (Lpp would entail the existence of another Lppp, which would entail another, etc. . . .) Fodor responds to this objection by arguing that *the* language presupposed for the learning of languages, call it Lu, has the unique property of being unlearned, it is innate. It functions like a computer program.[21]

How would Wittgenstein respond to this? We know that, according to Wittgenstein, an individual's meaning or intending something by a symbol or word is as much an observable and outer process as it is a psychological or neural event. What an expression means can only be fully explained by introducing into its explanation *external* rules of acting, or *practices*.

Although not everyone would agree with my interpretation of Wittgenstein, I believe that for Wittgenstein language is a set of complex and interrelated practices designed for social communication. Natural languages are social phenomena. As such, they require social interaction. The very idea of an *innate* language involves a

160

contradiction in terms. Words and sentences, the rudiments of languages, are defined in the context of temporal and social episodes. For Wittgenstein, the evolved and presently functioning world view, intrinsically tied to ordinary language and grounded in human capacities, cannot be properly put on a par with other possible world views. The practices in which we engage are ones which result, not simply because of external factors, but from what is possible given the capacities we have. Terms like 'knowledge,' 'justified belief,' 'doubt,' 'uncertainty,' and 'truth,' and the practices associated with them, all have a foundation in and depend upon actual human capacities and evolved as a means for coping with the world in which we find ourselves. Ordinary language is a set of extremely complicated and interrelated practices that enable us to deal effectively with each other and with the world in which we live.

The boat on which we sail—ordinary language—is not, for Wittgenstein, as it is for Frege and Russell, one in need of replacement by an ideal one. Nor is it the kind of vessel imagined by the logical positivist Neurath, one in need of repair by its crew while on course, one that has to be patched and caulked by the efforts of philosophers. Instead, in defense of Wittgenstein, we need to understand that ordinary language is perfectly adequate as it is. It is by its very nature a *self-correcting* vehicle. It contains within itself the mechanisms for ever-finer distinctions and qualifications, as well as mechanisms for the addition and modification of terms and practices. Language is the product of humans. Humans are capable of great diversification and modification. It is not the product of a self-contained and closed system like a machine, and so it cannot be fully understood when it is conceived of as a computational program.

Cognitive scientists respond to this idea of natural language by arguing that the common sense view of the world incorporated into and represented by various natural languages is only one approximation among others, and no more accurate regarding cognitive matters than it is regarding physical ones. They claim that we would not have made any progress in physics if we had remained complacent about the story common sense tells about the physical world. Why should we expect the ordinary language story to be any more reliable concerning cognition than it has been concerning the physical world? Physics takes ordinary language terms like 'force,' 'energy,' 'momentum,' 'solidity,' etc., and modifies their meanings as we discover things about the world, the result of which is progress.

In defense of Wittgenstein, physics does not undermine our common sense categorizations of the physical world. Knife blades, maces, jackhammers, cannon balls, bullets, arrows, etc., are solid and capable of tearing away our flesh. The scientific "fact" that these objects are non-solid entities, composed of objects surrounded by empty space, in no way shows that our ordinary descriptions are false or misleading. What happens at the *microscopic* level is simply what happens at the microscopic level, and not what happens at the *phenomenal* level. What I naturally see as a table is different from what I would see if I looked at it under an electron microscope.

But even if Wittgenstein's account of the way ordinary language works is a true account, the cognitive scientist can agree, and argue that there is still room for a *scientific* account of cognition, which, like physics, attempts to explain phenomena at a microscopic, or non-phenomenal level. Would Wittgenstein be happy with this solution? I think not.

The main reason Wittgenstein would not accept an inner-directed causal account of knowing, believing, thinking, meaning, and various other "psychological" phenomena, is because of his insistence upon the *complexity* and *variable* nature of the *contextual parameters* which such phenomena involve. Whether one "knows that p," "understands that p," "believes that p," or "means p, and not q" cannot be determined solely by the occurrence within the subject of some inner cause, but is instead a function of *inner states* and *most importantly* a function of context. Whether or not one is in pain certainly does depend upon whether or not one has a specifiable kind of feeling. But the same cannot be said of understanding, knowing, thinking, believing, and meaning.

Would Wittgenstein agree that although contextual parameters are necessary ingredients in the makeup of such things as believing, knowing, meaning, etc., certain *specifiable* inner states might *also* be necessary conditions for the existence of these actions? Again, the answer is no. He argues that there is no single *specifiable* conscious activity, process, or state of an organism, entity, or whatever, which must occur in order for one to be properly said to be engaging in any of these actions. According to Wittgenstein, any number of different inner processes, actions, sensations, etc., *could* occur when one is said to understand something, no one of which *must* occur.[22]

The cognitive scientist of the Fodor/Chomsky camp commonly counters this sort of objection by eliciting the *Freudian* premise that inner causes need not be conscious entities. This is tantamount to claiming that unconscious causes can be translated into *specific* computational processes or programs, which are not themselves part of the output. Wittgenstein's reaction to this suggestion would be, I think, to concede that *something* must occur in the brain at the unconscious level in order for one to be said to act in any way whatever. But he would hasten to point out that many actions couldn't be fully understood without reference to social practices or conventions. He would also insist that that the causal conditions for an action of a given kind need not always be of the same kind. I will say more about this last point shortly.

As I pointed out above, Wittgenstein never explicitly denies, nor need he deny, the possibility that in each and every case of understanding, and other so-called "psychological processes," there is at the *unconscious* level a computational process, or some other unconscious process or activity of the brain, non-computational[23] in nature, the elimination of which would make it impossible for there to be any understanding, believing, knowing, etc. Consistent with this observation, one could argue that such processes as those postulated by the Chomsky/Fodor computationalists, while not sufficient conditions for the existence of understanding, because they ignore the importance of social practice, *could* turn out to be somehow *necessary*. Inspired by this possibility, one could argue for a distinction between *existence* conditions and *conventional* conditions. The former are those conditions which are the domain of science, and which are those *unseen forces* necessary for the very existence of a given or specifiable phenomenon. The latter are those *observable parameters* which society has found good cause to incorporate into its linguistic practices (or its concepts) concerning such phenomena, and which are the domain of philosophy.

Given that the distinction between existence and conventional conditions is valid, one might be able reconcile Wittgenstein's views and those of the cognitive scientists. In defense of Wittgenstein's approach, one could argue that it does not depreciate or undermine our commonplace understanding of cognitive processes such as understanding, knowing, wishing, hoping, believing, and meaning, etc., which are in large part social phenomena, either by reducing these phenomena to theoretical entities or by requiring them to complete the analysis of these processes. At the same time, one could concede that the cognitive science approach could prove to be quite helpful. Did we not increase the content of our concept of water when we discovered that it was H_2O? The eventual confirmation of these unconscious processes or causes could enrich our concept of the conscious processes involved in our concept of understanding.[24] Such discoveries might well bring about a change in the practices surrounding our use of the words 'understanding,' 'knowing,' 'wishing,' 'hoping,' 'believing,' 'meaning,' etc.

Although this line of thought seems quite promising, there is a serious problem with it that will prove fatal unless it can be overcome. In order for an action to be *properly characterized* as an apology, the relevant practice must exist. But what *causes* one to perform such an act might well be an internalized replica of a computational process. Suppose that some person realizes, at some level, that someone she has offended is capable of doing her great harm and that a public apology might very well appease the offended person. Suppose, because of this, she apologizes. In this kind of case, fear seems to be the significant causal factor in the equation. But fear is certainly not the only motivation for apologizing. Apologies are *multi-motivated* phenomena, in that the motivation for a given apology on one occasion may well be different from what motivates it on another occasion. So it seems that the causal conditions (motives) for an action of a given type need not always be *tokens* of the same *type*, as Wittgenstein has argued throughout the *Investigations*.

Would the computationalistic explanation have to posit different underlying or unconscious processes for each possible motive, and does this rule out the possibility of a uniform or unvarying explanation of psychological phenomena of the sort championed by the cognitive scientists in question? The answer to this question is that everything turns on how the computational processes responsible for actions of a given type are to be construed. If it can be established that these computational processes are, like *modus ponens*, purely formal operations that can be instantiated by tokens of different types, Wittgenstein's objections can be surmounted. *Modus ponens* says that if p implies q, and p is true, then q is true. One instantiation of *modus ponens* would be: It is a dog implies that it is an animal; it is a dog; therefore, it is an animal. A different instantiation would be: It is an iris implies that it is a flower; it is an iris; hence, it is a flower. An apology could, on this account, be said to result from a specific computational process which is instantiated by such diverse phenomena as fear, guilt, desire for gain or profit, sympathy, exasperation. A problem remains, however, since fear, guilt, desire, profit, sympathy and exasperation can also cause one person to lie to another person, as well as a variety of other actions. The fear that causes one to apologize would have to be instantiated differently than the fear that causes lying. Otherwise, we would not be able to account for the difference between apologizing and lying. I do not know how to resolve this problem. But, unless I am mistaken, this is an issue that needs to be addressed by the cognitive scientists.

Having established that a difference exists between a causal account and a conventional account of various kinds of actions, including using words and sentences to express meaning, I will devote the next and last chapter of this book to conventional meaning.

---

[1] Chomsky (1957)
[2] Chomsky (1957) pp. 14-15.
[3] Ibid., pp. 106-108.
[4] Chomsky (1986) p. 510.
[5] Ibid., p. 526.
[6] Ibid., p. 526
[7] Chomsky's work is not easy to digest. He offers little in the way of exposition. For this reason one needs to consult secondary sources. The best secondary source is, in my opinion, Steven Pinker's book, *The Language of Instinct*. And while I will make use of this work in my presentation of Chomsky's theory, I have neither the expertise nor the space to delineate the full particulars and implications of the theory. The reader interested in pursuing the matter further would do well to consult Pinker's book.
[8] Pinker (1994) pp. 72-73.
[9] Ibid., p. 91.
[10] Ibid., pp. 113-117.
[11] Ibid., p. 98.
[12] Ibid., p. 99.
[13] Ibid., p.103.
[14] Ibid., p.104.
[15] Ibid., p.105.
[16] Chomsky (1986) p. 516.
[17] P. Hacker, G. P. Baker, B. Rundle in England, as well as J. Canfield in Canada, and J. Searle at Berkeley are critical of the Chomsky/Fodor approach, and their criticisms are often inspired by Wittgenstein's later philosophy.
[18] His version of the language of thought or mentalese.
[19] Fodor (1988) pp. 135-154.
[20] Other philosophers have modified Fodor's view to include the idea of rigid designation, in an effort to do away with notions like Frege's "sense," and to account for or replace any need for traditional semantic distinctions. Although these efforts are interesting, I believe that this approach is not as productive as one that distinguishes between causal and conventional accounts, and

simply treats them as consistent with one another. See below pp. 155-157.

[21] His argument greatly resembles Aristotle's introduction of an *unmoved mover* to avoid an infinite regress as regards the movement inherent in the universe.

[22] Wittgenstein (1953) para. 148-178; pp. 58e-72e.

[23] Not all cognitive scientists are computationalists. *Connectionism*, or *neural network* modeling, proposes that we abandon the computer symbol manipulation model in favor of a set of neuron-like entities that are connected to one another via their tendrils, and by these connections excite or stimulate each other to produce cognitive events like knowing, believing, etc.

[24] By 'unconscious process' or 'cause' I do not mean to include mentalese since I believe, as I argued on pp. 157-158, that it is a bogus concept.

6

The Cipher or Paraphrastic Account of Conventional Meaning

Having distinguished between a conventional account of meaning and a causal account, and having argued for a reconciliation between them that puts a premium on the former, I will now attempt to provide a defensible form of the conventional variety. As we determined in Chapter 2, Austin recognizes the distinction between sentential meaning and contextual meaning. He does so by differentiating between a *locutionary* action, which consists in uttering various words with both a *sense* and a *reference*, and an *illocutionary* action or conventional *force*, which has to do with how words are used. If we separate the action component of the locutionary action from the meaning component, what remains corresponds to sentential meaning. Contextual meaning primarily consists of illocutionary actions. Austin does not pursue the topic of sentential meaning. He instead shelves it and concentrates on contextual meaning. In this chapter, I will take sentential meaning off the shelf and offer a comprehensive account of it. I will extend this account to explain contextual meaning

A question that has worried many of the philosophers we have studied is whether or not an explication of sense or meaning can be based entirely upon linguistic structure and truth. Bertrand Russell thinks it possible to do so. Frege does not think that it can be done. He argues that we must distinguish the meaning or sense of an expression

167

from its reference. P. F. Strawson makes use of a kindred distinction in his critique of Russell. He argues that meaning is a function of the sentence or expression, and that referring, and truth and falsity, are functions of the *use* of sentences and expressions. Donald Davidson argues that a theory of truth for a natural language provides the meanings of all meaningful expressions on the basis of their structure. He claims that a theory of truth for a natural language has to take into account the fact that many sentences have truth-values that vary as a function of context. He also claims that we can "accommodate" this aspect of natural language by legislating either that it is *speech acts* that have truth-values, rather than sentences, or by treating truth as a triadic relation which obtains among a sentence, a speaker, and a time. The difference between Strawson and Davidson can be illustrated in terms of the distinction between sentential and contextual meaning. Strawson recognizes and utilizes the distinction. Davidson, as I pointed out previously, blurs the distinction.[1] My account maintains this distinction, and explores a *paraphrastic* or *cipher* account of both kinds of meaning

A paraphrastic definition is a definition in terms of words other than the word being defined. A dictionary is, in addition to being a flexible and ever-changing record of conventional word meaning, a collection of *paraphrases* that can be used to unlock or *decipher* impasses in conversation or reading. The subset of paraphrases that are relevant to removing the kinks or snags in conversation can be described as *ciphers*. Ciphers can be used to decode or unlock the puzzle that presents itself when one encounters a word one doesn't know.[2]

The majority of the entries found in dictionaries are word meanings. Words can be thought of as symbols that represent or stand for something else. Included in the large and open class of things that words can stand for are: kinds of existent things, such as horses, atoms, words, thoughts, nations, planets, persons, etc.; properties that things can have, such as redness, height, width, temperature, intelligence, goodness, etc.; kinds of non-existent things, such as fairies, vampires, witches, flying cows, etc.; abstractions, such as democracy, justice, idealism, etc.; actions, such as running, sailing, thinking, feeling, etc.

Among the various symbols that make up a language, some have restricted usage. They are not used to refer to classes or kinds of thing, but to individual things. Philosophers of language refer to these kinds of symbols as *singularly referring expressions*. This class includes: *proper names*, which are names for particular existing and non-existing persons, places, or things, such as, 'Jake Lamotta,' 'Dick Tracy,' 'Athens,' 'Metropolis,' 'The Washington Monument,' and 'Excalibur;'

The Cipher or Paraphrastic Account of Conventional Meaning

personal pronouns, such as 'I,' 'she,' 'it,' 'me,' and 'he;' *demonstratives,* such as 'this' and 'that;' and *definite descriptions,* such as, 'the present president of the United States,' 'the first major league baseball player to hit sixty homeruns in a single season,' and 'the winged horse of Greek mythology.' Personal pronouns and demonstratives are words. Definite descriptions are composed of words. But names are not words.

Although proper names are not words, some of them are found in dictionaries. Those proper names that are included in dictionaries are names of famous persons, places, and things, whose identities are culturally, historically, geographically, etc. significant—George Washington, Athens, and Athena. For the most part, when we look up a proper name in a dictionary, we are trying to find out *who* or *what* someone or something is. If I consult a dictionary, I can find out quite quickly, for example, that William F. Cody was a legendary plainsman, army scout, pony express rider, buffalo hunter, and showman, who is commonly referred to as "Buffalo Bill." Someone attending a lecture given by a noted historian of the west who praises William F. Cody may not know that Cody is Buffalo Bill. When he gets home, he consults his dictionary and finds out that Cody is Buffalo Bill. The mystery is solved. The *cipher* or key for him is the name 'Buffalo Bill.' But if our subject had not known who Buffalo Bill was, and our lecturer had referred to Cody not as Cody, but as Buffalo Bill, our subject would also have been in the dark regarding who was meant. The cipher needed for this person is more extensive. He needs to be told, "'Buffalo Bill' was an expression commonly used to refer to a man named William F. Cody, who was a legendary plainsman, army scout, pony express rider, showman, and prodigious hunter of buffalo."

At least two very important points are illustrated in this example about Buffalo Bill:

(1) We would be less apt to draw misleading conclusions regarding the purpose of dictionary usage, if we think of the dictionary as containing conversational ciphers—keys for unlocking kinks in our understanding of what someone has said;

(2) What is a cipher for one person can be, for another person, what needs to be deciphered.

Let us continue our discussion of dictionaries by examining these two questions: "What is the meaning of the word 'dog'?" and "What is the meaning of the word 'democracy'?" These are common everyday

169

The Cipher or Paraphrastic Account of Conventional Meaning

sorts of questions. One might very well answer the first one by pointing to a dog or to a picture of one. We do, of course, sometimes find pictures set into the dictionary entry, but these are not *part* of the meaning of the word. They are simply heuristic devises for identifying the object in question. Such devises are not, however, possible for many words. With a word like 'Pekinese' a picture is possible, and the picture does help one to understand what sort of object this word refers to. But what about the second kind of case? The meaning of a word like 'democracy' cannot be pointed to or depicted. It follows from this that the word 'meaning' can only have a *univocal* (one) sense if it means something other than what is provided by ostensive definitions.

Paraphrasity is a viable candidate for this role. Every word in a natural language can, if it is found within a sentence of that language, be paraphrased or put into other words, and the kind of paraphrase that is sought is a cipher, i.e., a paraphrase that eliminates kinks in the flow of conversation, reading, writing, and translating.

To the untutored ear it sounds odd to talk about meaning in terms of paraphrases or ciphers. We prefer familiar vocabulary. But it is sometimes necessary to illuminate our common usage by wrapping it in unfamiliar trappings. This is what I am doing when I refer to meanings or senses as ciphers or paraphrases. But there is more to it than this. When we talk about actually communicating about the *world*, and not about linguistic entities themselves (words, symbols, names, personal pronouns, demonstratives, or definite descriptions), we can see how when we ask for the meaning of words and other symbols, what we seek is a cipher to put us back on track. The use of the word 'cipher' sheds light on the subject of meaning.

One might object to my procedure by claiming that definition through other words is in principle *circular*, since what is the *definiens* (the word or phrase that needs to be deciphered) on one occasion will become the *definiendum* (the words or paraphrase that does the deciphering) on another. I would agree with such critics, but point out that this objection is really inappropriate. What we generally do when we define some word or phrase is render the *unfamiliar* in terms of the *familiar*. What is familiar to one person will be unfamiliar to another and so there is really no danger of circularity for cases of actual or living definition. That there is no final definition is no more relevant to whether or not we can succeed in defining one word by other words than is, to utilize an analogy from Wittgenstein, the fact that we can always build another house at the end of the road relevant to whether or not there is *in fact* a last house on the road.[3]

In what follows I will provide an account of both the sentential and

The Cipher or Paraphrastic Account of Conventional Meaning

contextual aspects of conventional meaning which is founded upon the notion of paraphrasity. My sentential account is meant to be an analysis of the meaning component of Austin's locutionary action. My account of contextual meaning is intended to be compatible with Austin's account of illocutionary actions.

Sentential Meaning

The account of sentential meaning I want to promote assumes, along with those of many linguists today, that an account of meaning cannot be based solely on linguistic structure and truth. The analysis of difference of sense that I will provide in this section is based on work that I co-authored with Jerry Kress.[4] It is tied to what a word means in a given sentence (sentential meaning) and not to what it *might* mean when used by a particular person on some particular occasion. I will be using a 'paraphrastic criterion' to accomplish this task. The question whether or not a paraphrase is an *acceptable* one will be said to depend in part, but only in part, upon whether or not the paraphrase is truth-preserving. For this reason, the concept of truth, and more specifically that of *truth-conditions*, plays a fundamental role in my account.

The concept of *oddity* plays an equally important role. One can imagine a sentence which in all probability has never been stated:

The Pink Mountain greeted the playful purple Tyrannosaurus rex.

In spite of the fact that no one has ever made a statement with this sentence, we can ask about its meaning. If asked to explain what it means, we might well respond with something like this:

The word 'the' picks out one individual as opposed to more than one (or as Bertrand Russell would have it, it means *one and only one*). 'Pink' is the word for a color derived from red by adding white to it. A 'mountain' is a large landmass that projects conspicuously above its surroundings. Greeting someone is a ceremonial welcoming of one person to another or others. 'Purple' is the name of a color derived by combining red with blue. A 'Tyrannosaurus rex' is a gigantic dinosaur, with small forelegs.

Now consider the following sentences:

(1) Lauren Bacall greeted Humphrey Bogart

(2) The Pink Panther was greeted by Sam Spade.

171

(3) The prime minister of Greece during the nineteen-eighties may not have been red, but he sure was pink.

(4) The workman fell off the bank.

With the exception of the second of these sentences, I have heard them all used. But we do not have to imagine a context of usage before we can determine (a) what they mean, (b) if some of the words in one of them mean the same as they do in others, (c) if a word in one of them means something different than it does in another, and (d) if some of the words in them are ambiguous. The 'greeted' of (1) means *welcomed*, and it has the same meaning in (2). But the 'pink' in (2) does not mean what it does in (3). The last sentence is ambiguous because the word 'bank' is ambiguous. It is one thing to make these observations; it is quite another to establish that they are true. To accomplish this latter task we need criteria for difference of sense or meaning (*multivocality*), sameness of sense or meaning (*synonymy*), and *ambiguity*.

Multivocality, Synonymy, and Ambiguity

Multivocality, or difference of sense, can be distinguished from ambiguity thus:

An expression *e* is *multivocal* in a language L if and only if *e* has a different sense in some sentence S^1 than it has in another S^2.

An expression *e* is *semantically ambiguous* in language L if and only if there are some sentences S^1, S^2, . . . in L which contain *e*, and within which *e* may be used in more than one sense, and the meaning (and truth conditions) of S^1 S^2, . . . varies depending upon the sense attributed to *e*.

These explanations clearly reveal a connection between multivocality and ambiguity. They both admit of explanation in terms of the notion of *a sense*.

They also reveal some interesting differences. First, ambiguity is, apparently, a much more complex notion than multivocality. To be ambiguous, an expression must be multivocal, and there must be, in addition, more than one interpretation (meaning) for at least some of the individual sentences in which it appears. Second, it is evident that there is a kind of multivocality which does not involve ambiguity. An expression may be used in one sense in a sentence S^1 and in another sense in a sentence S^2, without being ambiguous in either, as is illustrated by the following sentences:

    (a) I had a rare steak for the first time last night.

    (b) Blue diamonds are rare.

The expression 'rare' in (a) means "lightly cooked." In (b) it means "hard to find." In neither is 'rare' ambiguous. Since multivocality and ambiguity are distinct, there may be some expressions which are multivocal in a certain language but not ambiguous in that language. And it is even possible for there to be a language which contains multivocal expressions but no ambiguous expressions. Moreover, ambiguity is a defect from the point of view of those interested in clear and precise communication of fact or belief, whereas multivocality cannot be so regarded.

    In a language containing multivocality, how is one to know whether an expression as it appears in one sentence possesses a sense different from that which it has in another sentence? Since the examples to be discussed are from English, we must not allow ambiguity to muddy the waters. For this reason, I shall do as Kress and I did in our essay, and provide a third person paraphrase for all of my examples, which is found within parentheses. Consider the following used to exemplify this procedure:

    My sow Lucy likes her litter (Lucy, the sow of the speaker, is fond of her brood).

    Since the criterion for multivocality will make use of the concepts of *truth-conditions* and *oddity*, I will have to explain how I will be using them. I will begin with the concept of *oddity*. The kinds of oddity that simply involve unusual ways of expressing oneself, or descriptions of unusual events, are of no concern to me. I am concerned with syntactic and semantic oddity. The first of the following sentences is syntactically odd, and the second, Chomsky's famous example, illustrates various kinds of semantic oddness:

    (1) She most assuredly me stared at.

(2) Colorless green ideas sleep furiously.

Sentence (1) is not syntactically well-formed. If it were rearranged in accordance with the rules of syntax as 'She most assuredly stared at me,' it would be perfectly acceptable. Chomsky's example (2) is syntactically well-formed, but is, nevertheless, odd in several respects. Ideas and green things belong to totally distinct categories and so do ideas and sleeping things. It is logically impossible for colorless things to be green. And sleeping is not the sort of thing that can be done furiously. For these reasons, it is semantically uninterpretable. Some strings of English words are odd, either syntactically or semantically, while others are syntactically well-formed and semantically interpretable along familiar lines.

Different non-odd sentences ordinarily have different truth-conditions. We commonly verify the claim that a sentence S^1 has different truth-conditions than does another sentence S^2, by citing an actual situation, or by giving a consistent description of an imagined situation, in which S^1 is true and S^2 false, or vice versa. Accomplished speakers of a natural language can successfully determine which sentences are true of, which false of, and which are neither true nor false of actual or imagined situations.

Since the criterion for multivocality that Kress and I introduced made essential use of the notion of truth-conditions, we had to offer these two caveats: (1) The criterion is not applicable to expressions within truth-value-less sentences, since such sentences have no truth-conditions; and (2) the criterion is not applicable to expressions within sentences which express logical truths, or self contradictions, because in those cases it makes no sense to talk about differing truth-conditions. Logical truths are always true, and contradictions are always false. Consider the following version of a criterion for multivocality:

> An expression *e* has a different sense in one sentence than it has in another sentence if: there is a word or phrase which is a metaphrase of it in one of these sentences, but is not a metaphrase of it in the other, and neither sentence is odd.

A *metaphrase* is simply a paraphrase (or substitution instance) of the original expression which neither changes the truth-value of the original sentence nor produces a sentence which is odd. An acceptable metaphrase must be both *truth-preserving* and *non-nonsense producing*.

The Cipher or Paraphrastic Account of Conventional Meaning

This criterion can be tested by comparing its results with our common linguistic convictions or their institutionalized counterparts, namely, dictionaries. As test cases, consider the following sentences containing the word 'litter':

(1) The accident victim was carried out on a *litter* (stretcher).

(2) *Litter* was strewn all over the floor (trash).

(3) The sow's *litter* squealed all evening (brood).

(4) Wild orchids flourish in the forest *litter* (ground cover).

(5) We made a bed of *litter* for the sow to sleep on (straw).

Since it seems that none of the metaphrases contained in the parentheses are metaphrases of one another, we can conclude that 'litter' has a different sense in each of the above examples.[5] It is possible for one who seeks an answer to the question concerning the meaning of 'litter,' in order to understand one of the above sentences, say (2), not to know what the metaphrase I supplied means. In this case, a cipher for him would have to be a different metaphrase. Any one of the following metaphrases might do the job: refuse, waste, or rubbish.

There are certain implications of the metaphrastic approach that need to be clarified. The criterion for multivocality cannot be expected to mark every difference of sense. Its success is dependent on the richness of the language to which it is applied. In order to get a final answer regarding a specific case of difference of sense, both uses of the expression must have metaphrases, and both must have *different* metaphrases. A possible source of difficulty for the criterion lies in the fact that in order to distinguish, by means of it, the sense possessed by a certain expression e in one context from the sense it possesses in another context, we *must* find metaphrases for e in each context which are never metaphrases of each other.

It may be conceded that where this can be done we do indeed have a proof of the multivocality of e. But the difficulty lies in the possibility that perhaps such metaphrases are not *producible* for certain expressions, or for certain expressions within certain contexts. If no metaphrases are producible for e in some sentential context, then our criterion does not sanction the conclusion that e in that sentential

175

context has a different sense from *e* in another context, no matter how different they may seem intuitively. Moreover, even where metaphrases are producible, a similar difficulty presents itself. Suppose the metaphrases to be found for two intuitively quite different-sensed occurrences of *e* are not distinctive enough that they are never metaphrases of each other. We would again not be able to conclude on the basis of our criterion that *e* has different senses in these two contexts.

For this reason, the Kress/Odell criterion for multivocality has to be understood as a *sufficient* condition of multivocality, rather than as a condition that is both necessary and sufficient.[6] Hence, one need not claim, and we do not claim, that no single case of multivocality can be found where our criterion fails to yield the conclusion of multivocality. However, we do claim that for almost all expressions in almost all the sentences in which they appear, sufficiently distinctive metaphrases can be found.[7]

Having formulated and exemplified the Kress/Odell criterion for multivocality, I can now formulate a criterion of synonymy rather easily, because of an intimate connection between synonymy and metaphrasity. There are, however, two kinds of synonymy, namely, *monotypical* and *multitypical* synonymy:

> An expression e in one sentence is *monotypically synonymous* with *e* in another sentence if (1) there is a word or phrase f which is a metaphrase of e in both sentences; (2) there is no word or phrase g which is a metaphrase of e in one of these sentences, but not in the other; and (3) neither sentence is odd.

> An expression *e* in one sentence is *multitypically synonymous* with an expression *f* in another sentence if (1) there is a word or phrase g which is a metaphrase of e in one sentence, and of f in the other; (2) there is no word or phrase h which is a metaphrase of e in one sentence, but not of f in the other; and (3) neither sentence is odd.[8]

The way these criteria work can be illustrated by use of the following sentences:

> (A) He is *extremely mad at* me.
> (B) I am *extremely mad at* that silly impressionist painter.
> (C) Erin is *furious with* me.

The 'extremely mad at' of (A) is monotypically synonymous with the

The Cipher or Paraphrastic Account of Conventional Meaning

'extremely mad at' of (B), and it is multitypically synonymous with the 'furious with' of (C). Remember the type /token distinction I explicated and used previously? Monotypical synonymy concerns two tokens of the same type. Multitypical synonymy concerns two tokens of different types. Notice that (A) and (B) both involve the same expression 'extremely mad at me.' Sentence (A) contains one token of the type 'extremely mad at me,' and (B) contains a different token of the same type 'extremely mad at me.' But those tokens in (A) and (B) are a different type than the 'is furious with me' of (C). Both types have the same meaning, or are synonymous.

The synonymy criterion should also be regarded as simply a sufficient condition, and not as both a necessary and a sufficient condition. As was the case for multivocality, it is possible that two uses of an expression are synonymous, but there is no common metaphrase available for the establishment of synonymy. The language under scrutiny may not be rich enough to have more than one way of expressing that sense, and so there is no metaphrase available for either expression. Or the language may be rich enough, but those attempting to establish synonymy for two token expressions may simply lack either sufficient imagination or knowledge to find the needed metaphrases.

The most complicated of the three parameters of sentential meaning is *ambiguity*. It is the hardest one to define. The sentential ambiguity of an expression is a function of the sentential context in which it occurs. *Contextual* ambiguity, on the other hand, is the result of many parameters including body language, intonation contour, what was said before and after a given utterance, as well as the *background* of the utterance (which includes how well the auditor knows the speaker, how sophisticated the auditor is, whether he is being spoken to in his own language, and how much he knows regarding the topic of conversation). Contextual ambiguity is virtually impossible to formally define. It is the result of a variety of factors, none of which, nor even any subset of which, are *always* present. I will discuss these later in the present chapter.

Sentential ambiguity exists because words occur in sentences that do not provide sufficient cues to make their meanings precise. Ambiguous expressions are expressions whose meanings are incomplete. A word or an expression can be said to be ambiguous when there are at least two different things it could mean, and there is nothing about the sentence in which it is found which favors one of these meanings over the other. Consider the sentence:

177

The Cipher or Paraphrastic Account of Conventional Meaning

(A) In his youth he fell off a bank and broke his arm.

It could mean either (B) or (C):

(B) In his youth he fell off a *mound of earth adjacent to and surrounding a river* and broke his arm.

(C) In his youth he fell off a *monetary institution* and broke his arm.

We establish that (A) is ambiguous by offering two different paraphrases for the word 'bank,' which are italicized in (B) and (C). If those paraphrases meet the conditions we require for a metaphase, we ought to be able to formulate a criterion for ambiguity that is in keeping with those we have created for multivocality and synonymy. These considerations suggest the following criterion for *ambiguity*:

> An expression e is *ambiguous* in a given sentence if (1) there are two words or phrases f and g and (a) replacing e by f in that sentence results in a sentence with a meaning that is different from the sentence that would result if you replace e by g; (2) there are no sentences in which either f or g is a metaphrase of the other; and (3) none of the sentences involved are odd.

In the case of (A), e is 'bank,' f is 'a mound of earth adjacent to and surrounding a river,' and g is 'monetary institution.' (B) and (C) are not odd. And there are no sentences in which 'a mound of earth adjacent to and surrounding a river,' and 'monetary institution' metaphase each other. Their meanings are too different. Unfortunately, this criterion is unsatisfactory.

The problem with this criterion (call it CA) is that an acceptable criterion of ambiguity *must* incorporate some kind of *semantic link* between e and both f and g. Otherwise, we could substitute 'tricycle' and 'horse' for e in (A), and claim that we have ambiguity in (A) since there are no sentences in which 'tricycle' and 'horse' are metaphases of each other, and the resulting sentences would not be odd..

(D) In his youth he fell off a *tricycle* and broke his arm.

(E) In his youth he fell off a *horse* and broke his arm.
In order to establish the necessary semantic link between our

178

paraphrases, the criterion must be modified in a complicated fashion that involves both modification of the concept of a metaphrase and the addition of further steps in the criterion itself. If the reader is interested in the details of these modifications, she or he should see my article "Paraphrastic Criteria for Synonymy and Ambiguity."[9]

We must not overlook the fact that a sentence can be ambiguous because more than one word is ambiguous. In such cases the test for ambiguity would have to be applied to each of the suspect words and the result would have to be positive. Otherwise the criterion would be inadequate. The effectiveness of any criterion for ambiguity should be judged in terms of how well its results fit our linguistic intuitions. As far as I can determine, by testing it against numerous cases, my criterion for ambiguity does justice to these intuitions. There are, however, some cases that are apt to be perceived as posing a serious problem for my criterion.

In the spirit of Bertrand Russell, one could claim that 'In his youth he fell off a bank and broke his arm' is not only ambiguous because the words 'bank' is ambiguous, but also because the pronoun 'he' is ambiguous. Somewhere in his papers on logical atomism, Russell claimed that the pronoun 'I' is among the most ambiguous words in the English language. Russell is wrong. With the exception of proper names, about which I will say something shortly, singularly referring expressions (names, definite descriptions, pronouns, and demonstratives like 'this' and 'that') are rarely, if ever, *sententially* ambiguous. The meanings of most singularly referring expressions are clear even when their referents are indeterminate. The meaning (sense) of the expression 'I' is always something approximate to 'the speaker.' Its *referents* are as numerous as the number of English speakers. The question "To whom do you refer?" is like the question "What did you mean by that?" Such questions can only be resolved by examining the utterance's full *context*, including the speaker, the way he or she said it, what was said just prior to the utterance, what was done or said after the utterance, etc. The meaning of 'he' is approximately *the subject of the speaker's discourse*, and like 'I', its referents are numerous (though less numerous, since it only refers to males), and can only be known contextually.

Proper names are more bothersome. Since there are numerous people with the names like 'John Brown,' 'Jane Clark,' 'Joseph Smith,' etc., who have lived and are presently living, someone might maintain that the following sentence is ambiguous, because it could be about the famous abolitionist or it could be about my colleague John Brown who has visited Harper's Ferry.

John Brown went to Harper's Ferry.

Proper names do not all have meanings, and so it is odd to say that they are ambiguous. One approach would be to claim that they should be treated as indexicals are treated. In this case, their referents would be relegated to the *time and place* of context of usage. In this way, any ambiguity they have could be said to be *contextual*. Referring with proper names is something we *do* with language, and whatever ambiguities surround our *use* of them is a function of the context in which they occur.

One could instead claim that all names, even ones like 'zzzk' have sentential meaning in so far as whenever any occurs as a subject in a sentential context, as in 'zzzk is an interesting fellow,' it contributes to the meaning of the sentence. The sentence in question could then be said to mean that some person named 'zzzk' is an interesting fellow. This paraphrase is not what we ordinarily think of for the meaning of the sentence in question, but it is, I maintain, the sort of thing that does occur to us when we encounter sentences with unfamiliar names as their subjects. We could say that such sentences *suggest* such readings as the one above, or we could say that such sentences express minimal cognitive content, content which they share with all sentences involving names. Ultimately, it doesn't matter so much how we say it, so long as we recognize that although proper names are not ordinarily said to have meaning, we can quite legitimately say that they do have for us *cognitive content*, not identifiable with their referents, and that this content is closely related to what the symbol means rather than what someone means by it. In short, this aspect of meaning is *sentential* rather than *contextual*.

But if we take this approach, and consider proper names to have sentential meanings, we will have to answer certain questions. Are the sentential meanings of proper names, in any sense, either multivocal, ambiguous, or monotypically synonymous with other tokens of the same type? Are they multitypically synonymous with other expression types? The idea that they have minimal cognitive content does not

The Cipher or Paraphrastic Account of Conventional Meaning

imply that they have distinct meanings. A name like 'zzzk' fits the definition of Russell's "incomplete symbols." They have no meaning in isolation, but their minimal cognitive content contributes to our understanding of the sentences in which they occur. In general, only words have distinctive sense, and names are not words, though some are composed of words, and are descriptive of their referents. Since most of them do not have *distinctive* sense or meaning, it would not make any sense to ask about most of them, if they are used in different senses in different sentences. The minimal cognitive content they contribute to the meaning of sentences in which they occur is the *same* for all proper names. For that reason, most proper names cannot be said to be ambiguous, nor can they be said to be either monotypically or multitypically synonymous.

A full account of the role of language in communication or discourse must explain or account for the contextual as well as the sentential dimensions of meaning.[10] I will now discuss contextual meaning.

Contextual Meaning

All meaning ultimately depends upon usage. Practice precedes rules or definitions. Just consider the meaning or connotation that 'bad' had until sometime after 1970. It had a distinctively negative connotation. The following are among its senses before and after the seventies: inferior, evil, wicked, sinful, unpleasant, rotten and spoiled. Today, it also means what was previously thought of as its antithesis. It now sometimes means good. The recent use of the word 'bad' has led to changes in its meaning.

Language is an organic, always changing and adapting entity. Sentential meaning is extrapolation based upon the current state of usage. A pre-seventies analysis of difference of sense for the word 'bad' would not have revealed a paraphrase of it that captured a positive attitude. A sentential analysis which *simply* looks at sentences and asks about the meaning of expressions within them cannot help but be misleading about the nature of language and about such notions as synonymy, multivocality, and ambiguity. Because our practices and the rules which formulate them (definitions) are always changing, sentential meaning is in a constant state of flux. And this fact explains why an account of the conditions governing multivocality, synonymy, and ambiguity must be limited to *sufficient* conditions.

The idea that sentential meaning is fundamental, and prior to contextual meaning is a holdover from Plato's conception of the *Logos*. Plato had it backwards when he argued that reality consists of the

181

The Cipher or Paraphrastic Account of Conventional Meaning

eternal Ideas or Forms—the world of thought—while the world of changing ideas and objects—the world of sensation—is unreal. The truth is that the latter is reality, and the former nothing but a mirage created by our desire to freeze the ever-changing, ever-adapting reality so that we can, at least momentarily, comprehend fully our surroundings and ourselves. Words and sentences are contemplated in the abstract, and as such can appear to have fixed meaning. But this is a mirage. Words continue to serve ordinary everyday purposes, and so their meanings become modified and adapted and preempt the efforts of the philosopher in his or her quest for formal clarity.

There are few limits on what someone might mean by something on a specific occasion. Remember the bartender case from earlier? The customer means "Bring me another drink!" when he says "Why not?" There is, however, even in these cases, a sense in which it is appropriate to call what the speaker means a *paraphrase*. If you don't understand what was meant by the "Why not?" of the bartender case, it would be quite natural for me to use 'Bring me another drink' as an explanation of what the customer meant, which is nothing more than saying in other words what the customer said. And this is paraphrasing.

A metaphrase is a word or phrase which is substituted for another word or phrase in a *sentence*. Paraphrasing of the sort exemplified by the example in the previous paragraph is paraphrastic within *an existing context*. When we metaphrase a word or phrase in a sentence, we supply a meaning for the word or phrase in question and hence one for the sentence. In the bartender kind of case, what we have is the substitution of one sentential element for another in the *context of utterance*—call it "contextual paraphrasing." What will paraphrase a given sentence in one set of circumstances may be totally inappropriate as a paraphrase of it in a different set of circumstances. If you tell me that you are not going to the movies with me, and I ask you "Why not?" your answering my question with, "Yes, give me another drink" would be inexplicable.

The parallel between a sentential paraphrase and a contextual paraphrase is, however, far from exact. Some of the conditions governing metaphrasing one expression for another in a sentential context couldn't possibly hold for *contextual paraphrasing*. Paraphrasing in a sentential context or sentence incorporates the notion of syntactic structure—a notion inextricably wedded to sentences and word sequences. But sentence and word sequences are, in fact, inexplicable with respect to speech episodes. Although there are loose parallels existing between the concept of a linguistic structure and the structure of a speech context, in so far as they both involve the notion

The Cipher or Paraphrastic Account of Conventional Meaning

of a *structure,* there is an inherent indeterminacy about the structure of speech contexts which cannot be analyzed the way that sentential structure can. The structure of sentences has been extensively analyzed by contemporary linguists. Nothing even close to this has been done concerning the contextual structure. Nor do I think it is even possible to do so. But one can, as I have done elsewhere, enumerate various parameters of context which determine what is meant by an expression in a specific context.[11]

When sentences are used in everyday contexts, their meanings are determined by a large number of *contextual factors.* It would be presumptuous of me to pretend, or talk as if, the list of contextual factors I am about to propose is exhaustive, or even that it is exhaustive of all the *significant* aspects affecting meaningful discourse. Nevertheless, I offer the following list:[12]

(1) Communication through a natural language is, in large part, a function of context. *Where* and *when* something is said largely determines what was *meant by* what was said (*Context principle*).

(2) What is *meant by* what we say is also a function of *how* we say it. Where or upon what word or words we place an emphasis (intonation contour), as well as how we move various parts of our bodies (body language), will frequently affect what we mean.(*Emphasis Principle*).

(3) What is *meant by* what we say is also a function of the relationship we have to one another, how much knowledge the various participants in a given speech episode share, whether or not the participants have had previous conversations on the topic under consideration, what has taken place earlier in the given speech episode, etc. (*Background Principle*).

(4) The range of things (speech acts) a given sentence can be used to accomplish is limitless (*Multiple Speech Acts Principle*).

(5) What a sentence *means* (a proposition) is often quite different from what we mean by it, which is sometimes a statement, sometimes a warning, sometimes a request, and sometimes something else (*Intentionality Principle*).

(6) What a given string of words means is not a function of the formal characteristics those strings possess, e.g., "Why not?" can

The Cipher or Paraphrastic Account of Conventional Meaning

be used to make a request, even though its *form* is that of a question (*Non-Functionality Principle*).

(7) The meaning of a speech act is often intentionally creative and non-standard. We use language in inventive and innovative ways to amuse, clarify, convince, annoy, insult, etc. Punning, poetry, word play, and superlative prose all depend on our ability to use language with a certain impunity (*Creativity Principle*).

(8) Since many general empirical terms of a natural language are family resemblance terms, it follows that in order to get at their meaning one must be able to specify the set of overlapping and criss-crossing characteristics which determine the similarities and differences relevant to the question of whether or not some imagined or existing case falls under the term in question (*Family Resemblance Principle*).

(9) Even if we legislate sets of necessary and sufficient conditions to govern what they mean, we can't be sure that our legislations will preclude the existence of contexts where we will be uncertain what our words mean; we can always imagine cases where we wouldn't know whether or not a given word applied. The empirical words of natural language are open-textured (*Open-Texture Principle*).

(10) The meaning expressed by any given word in a natural language is inextricably tied to the meanings expressed by nearly every other word in the language. While the words themselves are *discrete,* the meanings they involve, or are tied to, are *continuous* with other meanings (*Continuity Principle*).

(11) A very large number of speech acts that can be implemented in a natural language involve expressing one's emotions. A natural language incorporates the distinction between a genuine and a non-genuine expression of an emotion. Expressing concern and expressing genuine concern are recognizably different (*Sincerity Principle*).[13]

Most of these principles have been explained in other sections of the present work, but nothing has been said about (7) and very little has been said about (10). I will now say more about them.

One of the more remarkable and noteworthy features of a natural

The Cipher or Paraphrastic Account of Conventional Meaning

language is that it allows its users to be enormously creative and original in their use of it. Where would poets, novelists, comics, writers, etc., be if natural language was not as flexible as it is? What makes one writer more interesting and captivating than another is partly an ability to use language in innovative and unique ways. When Sir Walter Raleigh asks, in poetry, for his "scallop-shell of Quiet," and his "Staff of Faith," we feel the sentiments he expresses. And who among us does not enjoy an occasional pun or a bit of clever graffiti? Just consider these gems: "Smoking causes cancer, but it cures ham" and "I would rather have a bottle in front of me than a frontal lobotomy."

When I focused upon the work of Donald Davidson in chapter 3, I noted that he was committed to *holism* about language. Holism is the view that the whole is more important, significant, revealing, etc., than its parts. Principle (10) makes a point that is holistic in nature. Any word always involves other words, which, in turn, involve still others. No word in a natural language can be understood in isolation from *all* other words, and ultimately from *most* other words. A word in a natural language is like a piece from a jigsaw puzzle. The role of any individual piece can be grasped only in the context of the complete puzzle. Without the rest of the pieces, a given piece is meaningless because it has no function. But couldn't it be given a function? One could, of course, drill a hole through it, run a string through the hole and use it as a necklace. But then it is no longer functioning as it was *meant* to function. Strictly speaking, it is no longer a jigsaw puzzle piece, even though one might recognize it as such and so describe it. A word in a natural language, like a piece from a jigsaw puzzle, loses its function and its meaning when it is separated from all other words (pieces) which comprise the language (puzzle).

The observant reader may have noticed that in chapter headings prior to the present one, I referred to *theories* of meaning, but that in the present one I referred to an *account* of conventional meaning. My reason for doing this is that I agree with Wittgenstein's view that the philosopher's task *is* to assemble reminders, including factual reminders. An account of a phenomenon presents the facts surrounding it. The task of the philosopher, according to the later Wittgenstein, is to remind us of the way language *actually* works, and to thereby prevent philosophers of language from straying too far from the truth. We do not need a *theory* of conventional meaning, but we do need an *account* of the way that language works. We need to recognize that both kinds of conventional meaning, contextual meaning and sentential meaning, are as unruly and as hard to contain as a cat who realizes that her owner is about to bathe her. Meaning is founded upon organic, transforming,

185

The Cipher or Paraphrastic Account of Conventional Meaning

self-correcting linguistic practices, defined by open-ended and family resemblance rules—far more closely akin to "rules of thumb" than to "rules of logic" or "game rules." The principal virtue of natural languages is that they *allow us to ignore differences where differences make no difference.* One's response to another's question concerning what one was doing on a recent business trip to Atlanta, "I was buying a trainload of furniture," will likely be sufficient, unless, of course, the questioner is one's business partner. The partner may want specifics concerning number and kinds of furniture purchased. Most others would be put off by such details concerning differences in kind of furniture, texture of fabrics, etc. Such differences make no difference. Natural languages enable us to be as specific as we need to be for some people, while at the same time allowing us the freedom to accommodate the interests of the less-interested.

In the last chapter, I argued that such processes as those postulated by the Chomsky/Fodor computationalists, while not sufficient conditions for the existence of understanding, because they ignore the importance of social practice, *could* turn out to be somehow *necessary.* Inspired by this possibility, I distinguished between *existence* conditions and *conventional* conditions: the former are those conditions that are the domain of science, and that are those *unseen forces* necessary for the very existence of a given or specifiable phenomenon; the latter are those *observable parameters* that society has found good cause to incorporate into its linguistic practices (or its concepts) concerning such phenomena and that are the domain of philosophy.

The philosopher's task is to provide a detailed account of linguistic conventions. The task of the cognitive scientist is different. Her task, like that of any scientist, is to provide an explanation of hidden mechanisms that make communication possible. Such explanations *are* theories because they employ hypothetical and theoretical entities to account for communication. Conventional *accounts* of meaning and causal *theories* of meaning can exist simultaneously. They complement one another and provide us with a comprehensive understanding of language use that neither provides in isolation.

---

[1] See above pp. 115-116.

[2] The first phase in the development of this cipher theory of meaning was a paper on difference of meaning or *mutivocality* for *sentential* meaning (Kress and Odell 1982). Later I (a) elaborated upon and extended the scope of this theory to include *synonymy* and *ambiguity* (Odell 1984a); (b) explicated important principles concerning natural languages (Odell 1984b); and (c) further explicated the theory and

extended it to provide a paraphrastic account of *contextual* meaning (Odell 1984c). James Platt, who wrote his PhD under my direction, developed an account of *translation* from one language to another that is derived from and consistent with my paraphrastic or cipher theory of meaning. Anyone interested in the problem of translation should consult this excellent work. Platt (1991).

[3] Wittgenstein (1953) passage 29, p. 14.

[4] Kress and Odell (1982).

[5] Unfortunately, the criterion for mutivocality used here has problems that can only be solved by a complicated revamping of it. The concept of "metaphrase" has to be modified to avoid certain counterexamples. If the reader is interested in discovering what those counterexamples are, and how the criterion can be revamped to solve them, see Kress and Odell (1982), pp. 187-192.

[6] If C is a sufficient condition for X, then it is not possible for C to be the case and for X not to be the case. If something is a dog then it is an animal. If C is a necessary condition for X, then if C is not the case, X is not the case. If there are no nimbus clouds, it cannot rain.

[7] I will not here attempt to prove this second claim, as it would involve a lengthy discussion of examples. It was, however, for this reason that Kress and I provided an extended discussion of examples in Kress and Odell (1982) pp. 182-196.

[8] These simplified criteria must also be revamped in keeping with the revamping of the criterion for multivocality I mentioned in endnote 5 above. See Odell (1984C) for the revamped criteria, p. 119.

[9] Odell (1984C) pp. 118, 121-124.

[10] For an excellent secondary source regarding the paraphrastic or cipher approach, see J. Platt (1991) pp. 128-217.

[11] See Odell (1984A) pp. 137-139 and Odell (1987) pp. 36-38.

[12] The list that follows is a revision of my (1984A) list.

[13] For an application of my parameters to information processing, see J. Sowa (1984) pp. 341-344.

BIBLIOGRAPHY

Allwood, J., L. Anderson, Ö. Dahl. (1979) *Logic in Linguistics.*
Cambridge: Cambridge University Press.

Alston, W. (1964) The Philosophy of Language (Englewood Cliffs,
NJ: Prentice-Hall)

Austin, J. L. (1956) "Performative Utterances" reprinted with minor
verbal corrections in J. L. Austin (1961) *Philosophical Papers*,
ed. J. O. Urmson and G. J. Warnock (Oxford: Oxford
University Press).
(1962) *How to do Things with Words*, (Cambridge
MA: Harvard University Press).

Ayer, A. J. (1936) *Language Truth and Logic*, 2nd edition (New York:
Dover Publications).
(1972) *Bertrand Russell*, Modern Masters, ed. Frank Kermode
(New York: The Viking Press).

Baker, C. P. and P. M. S. Hacker, (1984) *Language, Sense & Nonsense*
(Oxford: Basil Blackwell).

Black, Max, (1964) *A Companion to Wittgenstein's Tractatus.* (Ithaca,
NY: Cornell University Press).

Carnap, R. (1930) "The Elimination of Metaphysics Through
Logical Analysis of Language" reprinted in *Logical
Positivism*, ed. A. J. Ayer (New York: The Free Press, 1959).

Chisholm. R. (1960) "Editor's Introduction" to *Realism and the
Background of Phenomenology* (New York: The Free Press,
Collier-Macmillan Limited).

Chomsky, N. (1986) "Language and Problems of Knowledge" in *The
Philosophy of Language*, 2nd Edition, ed by A. P. Martinich
(New York: Oxford University Press, 1990).

Churchland, P. (1984) *Matter and Consciousness* (Cambridge, MA:
Harvard University Press).

Davidson, D. (1967) "Truth and Meaning" reprinted in *Perspectives in
the Philosophy of Language: A Concise Anthology*, ed. R. J.
Stainton (Ontario: Broadview Press, 2000).
(1970) "Semantics for Natural Languages" reprinted in

Bibliography

The Logic of Grammar, ed. D. Davidson and G. Harmon (Encino, CA: Dickenson Publishing Company, 1975).

Davidson, D. and G. Harmon (1975) "Introduction" to *The Logic of Grammar*, ed. D. Davidson and G. Harmon (Encino, CA: Dickenson Publishing Company).

Devitt, M. and K. Sterelney (1987) *Language and Reality* (Oxford: Oxford University Press).

Donnellan, K. (1966) "Reference and Definite Descriptions" reprinted in *Perspectives in the Philosophy of Language: A Concise Anthology*, ed. R. J. Stainton (Ontario: Broadview Press, 2000).

— (1972) "Proper names and Identifying Descriptions" in *Semantics of Natural Language*, ed. D. Davidson and G. Harmon (Dordrecht, Holland: D. Reidel Publishing Co.)

Dupré, J. (1993) *The Disorder of Things-Metaphysical Foundations of the Disunity of Science* (Cambridge MA: Harvard University Press).

Fann, K.T. (1967) *Wittgenstein: The Man and His Philosophy*. (New York: Dell Publishing Co., Inc.)

Fodor, J. (1975) *The Language of Thought*. (New York: Thomas Y. Crowell).

— (1988) *Psychosemantics* (Cambridge, MA: The MIT Press).

Frege, G. (1879) *Begriffsschrift*, translated by Peter Geach, in *Translations from the Philosophical Writings of Gottlob Frege*, ed. Peter Geach and Max Black (Oxford: Basil Blackwell, 1960).

— (1892) "Sense and Reference" in *Readings in Philosophical Analysis*, ed. H.Feigl and W. Sellars, (New York: Appleton-Century-Crofts, 1949)

Godel, K. (1944) "Russell's Mathematical Logic" in *The Philosophy of Bertrand Russell, The Library of Living Philosophers,* ed. Paul Arthur Schilpp (New York: Tudor Publishing Company).

Grice, H. P. (1957) "Meaning" reprinted in *Perspectives in the Philosophy of Language: A concise Anthology*, edited by R. J. Stainton (Ontario: Broadview Press Ltd., 2000).

— (1967) "Logic and Conversation," reprinted in *the Logic of Grammar*, ed. Donald Davidson and Gilbert Harman (Encino and Belmont, CA: Dickenson Publishing Company, 1975) pp. 64-75.

— (1961) "The Causal Theory of Perception" *Proceedings of the Aristotelian Society, Supplementary Volume* (XXXV).

Hacker, P. M. S. (1996) *Wittgenstein's Place in Twentieth Century*

Analytic Philosophy (Oxford: Blackwell Publishers).

Katz, J. (1988) "The Refutation of Indeterminacy" *Journal of Philosophy*, May, 1988.

Kress, J. and S. J. Odell "A Paraphrastic Criterion for Difference of Sense" *Theoretical Linguistics*, Vol. 9, No. 2/3.

Kneale, W. and M. (1962) *The Development of Logic* (Oxford: The Clarendon Press).

Kripke, S (1971) "Identity and Necessity" in *Identity and Individuation*, ed. M. K. Munitz (New York: New York University Press).
   (1970) "Naming and Necessity" reprinted in The Philosophy of Language, ed. A. P. Martinich (Oxford: Oxford University Press, 1980).

Kolak, D. (1998) *Wittgenstein's Tractatus* (Mountain View CA: Mayfield Publishing Company).

Linsky, L. (1963) "Reference and Referents" in *Philosophy and Ordinary Language*, ed. Charles Caton (Urbana: University of Illinois Press).
   (1967) *Referring* (New York: Humanities Press).
   (1977) *Names and Descriptions* (Chicago and London: The University of Chicago Press).

Meinong, A. (1904) "The Theory of Objects," reprinted in *Realism and the Background of Phenomenology* ed. R. Chisholm (New York: The Free Press, Collier-Macmillan Limited, 1960).

Moore, G. E. (1936) "Is Existence a Predicate?" reprinted in *Philosophical Papers* (London: George Allen & Unwin LTD, 1959).
   (1952) *The Philosophy of G. E. Moore, The Library of Living Philosophers*, ed. Paul Arthur Schlipp (New York: Tudor Publishing Company).

Odell, S. J. (1984A) "On the Possibility of Natural Language Processing," *Theoretical Linguistics*, Vol. II, No. 1/2.
   (1984B) "A Paraphrastic Theory of Meaning," *Theoretical Linguistics*, Vol. 11, No. 3.
   (1984C) "Paraphrastic Criteria for Synonymy and Ambiguity" *Theoretical Linguistics*, Vol. II, No. 1/2.
   (1987) "The Powers of Language: A philosophical Analysis" in *The Powers of Language*, ed. Leah Kedar (Norwood, NJ: Ablex Publishing Corp.)
   (2000) *On Russell* (Belmont, CA: Wadsworth).
   (2001) "Practice Consequentialism: A New Twist on an Old Theory" in *Utilitas*, Vol. 13, Number 1.
   (2003) *On Consequentialist Ethics* (Belmont, CA:

Wadsworth)

Odell, S. J. and J. F. Zartman (1982) "A Defensible Formulation of the Verification Principle," *Metaphilosophy*, Vol. 13, No. 1.

Pinker, S. (1994) *The Language Instinct: How the Mind Creates Language*, reprinted in (2000) as a First Perennial Classics edition (New York: HarperCollins Publishers)

Platt, J. (1991) *Saving the Meaning: The Cipher Theory of Synonymy and the Problem of Cross-Cultural Translation*, PhD Dissertation, under the direction of S. Jack Odell, The University of Maryland, College Park, MD.

Putnam, H. (1975) "The Meaning of 'meaning'" reprinted in Putnam's Mind, Language (Cambridge: Cambridge University Press).

Quine, W. V. O. (1960) *Word and Object* (Cambridge MA: The MIT Press).

Ramsey, Frank. (1931) *General Propositions and Causality, The Foundations of Mathematics*. (London: Routledge & Kegan Paul Ltd.)

Reichenbach, H. (1944) "Bertrand Russell's Logic" Schlipp (1944).

Rundle, B. (1990) *Wittgenstein and Contemporary Philosophy of Language* (Oxford: Blackwell).

Russell, B. (1903) *The Principles of Mathematics* (London: Allen & Unwin).

(1905) "On Denoting" reprinted in *Readings in Philosophical Analysis*, ed. H. Feigl and Wilfrid Sellars (New York: Appleton-Century-Crofts, 1949).

(1908) "Mathematical Logic as Based on the Theory of Types" *American Journal of Mathematics*, XXX, pp. 222-262, reprinted in *Logic and Knowledge*, pp. 59-102.

(1910) *Principia Mathematica to *56* (Cambridge, England: Cambridge University Press, 1964).

(1912) *The Problems of Philosophy* (New York: A Galaxy Book, Oxford University Press, 1959).

(1918A) *Mysticism and Logic*, selections reprinted in *Selected Papers of Bertrand Russell* (New York: Random House, The Modern Library, 1927).

(1918) "The Philosophy of Logical Atomism" reprinted in *Logic and Knowledge*, ed. by Robert C. Marsh (London: George Allen & Unwin, 1956).

(1929) *Our Knowledge of the External World*, 2nd Edition (New York: Mentor Book, The New American Library, (1960). Delivered as Lowell Lectures in 1914.

(1940) *An Inquiry into Meaning and Truth* (Baltimore, MD:

Pelican Book, 1961).

Ryle, G. (1949) *The Concept of Mind*, (New York: Barnes and Noble, Second Printing, 1960).

Schlick, M. (1936) "Meaning and Verification" reprinted in *Readings in Philosophical Analysis*, ed. H. Feigl and W. Sellars (New York; Appleton-Century-Crofts, 1949).

Schlipp, P. A. (1944) *The Philosophy of Bertrand Russell* New York: Harper Torchbooks, The Academy Library, Harper & Row).

Searle, J. R. (1958) "Proper Names" *Mind*, n.s. 67, pp. 166-173, reprinted in *Philosophy and Ordinary Language*, ed. C. Caton (Champaign, Illinois: University of Illinois Press).
(1965) "What is a Speech Act?" reprinted in *Perspectives in the Philosophy of Language: A concise Anthology*, edited by R. J. Stainton (Ontario: Broadview Press Ltd., 2000).
(1985) "Proper names and Intentionality" in *The Philosophy of Language*, ed. A. P. Martinich (New York: Oxford University Press).

Sowa, J. (1984) *Conceptual Structures: Information Processing in Mind and Machine* (Reading, MA: Addison-Wesley Publishing Company).

Strawson, P. F. (1950) "On Referring" reprinted in *Philosophy and Ordinary Language*, ed. Charles E. Caton (Urbana, IL: The University of Illinois Press, 1963).
(1952) *Introduction to Logical Theory* (London: Methuen & Co.).

Strawson, P. F. (1959) Individuals: An Essay in Descriptive Metaphysics (London: Methuen & CO LTD).

Tarski, A. (1944) "The Semantic Conception of Truth" reprinted in Readings in Philosophical Analysis, edited by H. Feigl, and W. Sellars (New York: Appleton-Century-Crofts, 1949).

Urmson, J. O. (1956) *Philosophical Analysis: It's Development Between the Two Wars* (Oxford: The Clarendon Press).

Waismann, F. (1951) in *Logic and Language* (First Series), ed. A. Flew (Oxford: Basil Blackwell).

Wallace, J. (1975) "Nonstandard Theories of Truth" in *The Logic of Grammar*, ed. D. Davidson and G. Harmon (Encino, CA: Dickenson Publishing Company).

Wittgenstein, L. (1922) *Tractatus Logico Philosophicus* (London: Routledge & Kegan Paul. LTD.).
(1953) *Philosophical Investigations*, trans. G. E. M. Anscombe, 3rd edition (New York: Macmillan Publishing Co.,. 1981).

Index